Migration, Ethnicity, and Mental Health

Routledge Studies in Cultural History

Contents

Tables and Charts

TABLES

CHARTS

Acknowledgements

This collection stems from 'International Perspectives on Migration, Ethnicity, and Mental Health', an international symposium held at the University of Otago in April 2010. We are grateful to all our contributors and the audience for their enthusiasm, interest, and enlightening discussions during this event and for their patience as we brought the edited volume to fruition. We would like especially to thank the Royal Society of New Zealand Marsden Fund for funding our project 'Migration, ethnicity and insanity in New Zealand and Australia, 1860–1910' (08-UOO-167 SOC). For the provision of symposium funding we are grateful to the Royal Society of New Zealand and the Centre for Irish and Scottish Studies and the Department of History and Art History at the University of Otago. The event was held at the Hocken Collections, and we are very grateful to the staff there for their assistance, especially Sharon Dell and Anne Jackman.

Angela McCarthy and Catharine Coleborne

1 Introduction

Mental Health, Migration, and Ethnicity

Angela McCarthy and Catharine Coleborne

Until fairly recently, international scholars working in the field of the histories of mental health have privileged national episodes and sites in the histories of institutions and institutional confinement, particularly through the eighteenth- and nineteenth-century eras, with some work focused on the twentieth century.[1] 'Mental health' has been defined largely through institutional confinement because of the large number of accessible archival materials relating to the nineteenth century, with historians focused on studies of single institutions, often plotting demographic patterns of confinement for hospitals, as well as assessing their place in the wider contexts of mental health policy and changes over time. Several volumes of collected essays examine national contexts for mental health, including studies of Canada, Australia, Wales, and Britain more widely.[2] Another wave of edited volumes locates the study of institutional confinement as a global phenomenon, with studies of international perspectives on the worldwide trends for mental health hospitalisation, studies of European approaches to psychiatric treatment inside institutions, a volume which considers the way psychiatry was bound up with practices of 'empire', and most recently, a volume which situates the study of institutional mental health inside the approaches of transnational and comparative histories of psychiatry.[3]

Yet despite the new and developing attention to looking *across* sites at similar and divergent practices and at shared knowledges of mental health, the subject of migration has received far less specific attention than these other strands of inquiry outlined above. There have been exceptions, specifically those contributed by American historians and studies. Richard W. Fox, for instance, used a sample of 1,229 case histories in his book *So Far Disordered in Mind: Insanity in California, 1870–1930* (1979) to identify, inter alia, the social backgrounds and behaviour of the insane. His methodology and analysis are therefore important to us, particularly his stress on age as a factor in explaining the over-representation of the foreign-born among the insane.[4] In this sense he reiterates Benjamin Malzberg's identification of age as an important component when examining asylum admissions.[5] Gerald N. Grob, meanwhile, made some of the most important critical interventions in the American literature between the 1960s and 1980s. His work in *Mental Illness and American Society, 1875–1940* (1983) explores issues of hostility and fear towards new immigrants and minority ethnic groups in the period he investigated. In an earlier work, *The State and the Mentally Ill* (1966) which focused on a Massachusetts hospital, incorporation of foreign-born inmates, including the Irish, formed part of his analysis of patient populations.[6] Yet inside existing studies of Britain, and the white settler colonies we include—Canada, Australia, New Zealand, and Fiji, as well as numerous studies of India—immigrants themselves mostly appear in the discussion as subject to colonial economies, or as 'at risk' populations because they allegedly lacked familial networks and were often among the very poor. The social and geographical origins of patients at specific institutions also receive some attention, as does their ethnicity, an important aspect of this volume, as we discuss below.

We argue, then, building on the range of ways that the histories of mental health has been represented, that migration ought to be considered as a particular focus of a new generation of inquiries into mental health and institutional confinement. Here, we place special emphasis on a few themes emerging from recent collaborative research, including the relationship between mental health and migration itself; the analytical category of ethnicity inside institutional populations, including questions surrounding ethnicity and institutional confinement; and the significance of the migration of intellectual ideas and trends in psychiatry, as well as personnel. Overall, we elaborate on the ways that contributors to this volume tackle these various themes, as well as others, using a variety of tested and new approaches to the analysis of their sources.

In this way we contribute more broadly to the field of migration studies, in which many analyses focus on successful migrants and their contributions to new societies, or emphasise the discrimination and prejudice migrants encountered. More recent investigations draw on concepts such as transnationalism and networking to highlight the ties between the homeland and the respective diasporas.[7] A further key aspect of the extant historiography is a focus on individual migrant groups, with explicit comparative investigation rarely undertaken.[8] Several works encompass diverse 'types' of migrants including settlers, entrepreneurs, soldiers, women, juveniles, and appropriate to this volume, medical personnel. Such individuals were among a vast outpouring of around 60 million people leaving central and western Europe for overseas shores during an era of mass migration between 1815 and 1930. Among the largest flows were 11.4 million from Britain, 9.9 million from Italy, 7.3 million from Ireland, and 5.0 million from Austria-Hungary.[9] In addition, beyond a focus on human mobility, the migration of ideas is also increasingly examined by historians.[10]

But what do we know about those who struggled with their relocation abroad? Previous investigations of the relationship between migration and mental health predominantly appear in the work of epidemiologists, transcultural psychiatrists, and social scientists, but with a particular focus on the twentieth century. Malzberg, for instance, examined first admissions to mental hospitals in New York State. He found that although the rates of foreign-born admissions varied according to how long they had been in the country (with the most recent arrivals more likely to be institutionalised), high rates of first admissions among the foreign born compared to native born were skewed by scholars by failing to account for age discrepancies.[11] Transcultural psychiatrists Roland Littlewood and Maurice Lipsedge are sceptical about the stresses generated immediately after migration, claiming that strains may be greatest some years after relocation when 'new life in the adopted country has fallen short of expectations'.[12] In this volume, Angela McCarthy considers this issue among a sample of New Zealand's foreign-born patients in Dunedin's public asylums, and similarly finds that migrants were more likely to be admitted several years after settlement.

McCarthy therefore makes an important contribution, for studies of nineteenth-century migration and mental health are somewhat fleeting. From a Canadian perspective, David Wright and colleagues suggest that migration is often downplayed as a factor in asylum committals, despite migrants being suspected of mental illness because of their strange appearance, habits, lack of language skills, and lack of kin resources.[13] The applicability of these findings to diverse ethnic groups in distinct locations remains to be seen, recent research having demonstrated the movement of Irish migrants, especially, in robust networks of family and friends.[14] Other studies of migration typically focus on internal movement, particularly from rural to urban areas. Andrew Scull and John Walton, for instance, perceive a link between long-distance migration and committal.[15] Still other scholars refute any correlation between long-distance migration and admission to the asylum.[16] More recently, Joseph Melling and Bill Forsythe, in their study of the Devon Asylum, suggest that more settled individuals were increasingly likely to be admitted to asylums than recent migrants or migrants with sustained mobility.[17] In this volume, Jacqueline Leckie points to those indigenous Fijians classified as insane who had been 'wanderers' outside their villages and become destitute, not only in a material sense but also in a social sense.[18] Akihito Suzuki also engages with this theme in his study of psychiatric hospitals in Japan. In particular, he focuses on the urban-rural 'loop', encompassing young migrants sent back to cities where they became disabled and unable to work and support themselves, before returning again to the households of their parents or relatives in native countryside villages. In this way, he incorporates the striking differences between institutional provision in urban areas and the care provided in rural households.

Yet as McCarthy indicates in this volume, the migration process does not necessarily result in asylum admission, for not all migrants were institutionalised. Nevertheless, examination of case book records and official asylum and immigration documents reveals an acknowledgement by patients, their family and friends, and medical authorities that anxieties relating to the migration process could result in institutionalisation. McCarthy's work also draws attention to areas of analysis little studied among migration and madness including the role of the voyage and migration pathways. The voyage also appears in Leckie's study of Indian indentured migrants bound for Fiji in the later nineteenth century. There, she argues, migrants of all backgrounds were displaced due to physical dislocation and 'profound shifts in their cultural worlds', resulting in institutional confinement, repatriation, or suicide.

Movement from overseas destinations to new countries is not, however, the only process of migration that scholars of mental health have explored. The subjects of return migration and repatriation are also noteworthy. Littlewood and Lipsedge queried whether mentally ill migrants were encouraged to voluntarily return home 'in the belief that the illness is caused by the stresses of migration and that the patient will recover back in his original country'.[19] Return migration remains under-examined in this volume and in migration studies as a whole,[20] although Leckie points to the repatriation of the insane from Fiji, and McCarthy highlights briefly the critical role of family and friends as instrumental in the relocation of patients from New Zealand.

While some migrants experienced mental health issues in their new homelands, other migrants were employed as psychiatric staff to care for patients.[21] These psychiatric workers were among a range of medical personnel migrating globally to provide general health care. A particular contingent of workers, 200 'suitable girls' assisted from Britain in 1946, is the focus of Kate Prebble and Gabrielle Fortune's chapter. Situating their analysis within a framework that incorporates immigration policy, the professionalization of nursing, and domesticity, Prebble and Fortune contend that unqualified women with no previous history of employment in the psychiatric sector were best suited to psychiatric work.

Male superintendents in the nineteenth century feature in Elspeth Knewstubb's analysis of Ashburn Hall, New Zealand's only private lunatic asylum. As Knewstubb argues, these men were products of their time both culturally and intellectually, with a range of cultural, social, educational, and employment attitudes and influences at play in their diagnoses, treatment, and general comments about patients. In this sense, Knewstubb's work focuses on the migration of ideas, arguing that rather than an assumed movement of ideas from England to New Zealand, a range of international influences were present, particularly French and Scottish. The doctors' intellectual influences are further nuanced by the mobility of ideas in medical circles through publications and correspondence between practitioners. In this way Knewstubb adds to the work on the circulation of medical theory, as evident in Crowther and Dupree's exploration of the global dissemination of Joseph Lister's theories and insights about antiseptics.[22]

The mobility of ideas is also covered by Maree Dawson in her study of diagnoses made at the Auckland Asylum in New Zealand. Drawing on case books, medical journals, text books, and government reports, she considers whether there was an Empire-wide conception of identifying congenital idiocy and how these ideas were disseminated through the 'organs' of the profession. Dawson's study points to the diagnosis of congenital idiocy which legitimised fears of racial degeneracy and the inherited nature of mental disease across the British Empire, particularly in 'white settler' colonies. As Dawson indicates, however, differences in localised social concerns are reflected in diverse ideas about congenital idiocy and various ways of treating the condition, in a medical sense. But concerns about a 'degenerate residuum' were part of wider discussions of national efficiency which permeated the British Empire.

ETHNICITY AND MENTAL HEALTH

Indeed, the concept of 'race' or biological difference rather than 'ethnicity' has featured more readily in studies of asylums to date. This has emerged from a focus on colonial medicine and psychiatry in the past decade of studies of institutional confinement.[23] Sloan Mahone and Megan Vaughan argue that settler colonies, in particular, developed complex systems and discourses of racial difference.[24] Harriet Deacon indicates that Robben Island was established in 1846 as the earliest separate institution for the insane at the Cape, and that racist ideology and socio-economic and political conditions outside the asylum influenced racial segregation within the asylum's walls.[25] Meanwhile, in India, Waltraud Ernst highlights the existence of separate asylums for Europeans and Indians (and lower class Eurasians). She also points to further ethnic differences including asylum labour where work was seen as detrimental to Europeans but not to other patients, as well as the language applied to European patients being less derogatory than other patients.[26] Ernst fails, however, to differentiate the ethnic distinctions of India's European population. In her contribution to this volume and in her prior work on the St. Giles Asylum in Fiji, Leckie similarly elides the diverse ethnic backgrounds of European patients. She does, however, reveal various distinctions between Europeans and other ethnic groups including separate wards and superior conditions for European patients. As with Ernst, she also indicates work divides with Indo Fijians termed 'malingering' if they refused to work, whereas truculent European workers were considered of 'unsound mind'.[27] Beyond these approaches, Leckie identifies behaviours considered inappropriate among Indians, including women not customarily clothed and displays of dirty habits.[28]

Other histories of colonial psychiatry in settler colonies consider race and ethnicity by including studies of indigenous patients, rather than focusing on the vast influx of foreign-born newcomers in the nineteenth century. Robert Menzies and Ted Palys provide a rich account of Aboriginal patients in British Columbia from 1879 to 1950, arguing that mental health institutions formed a 'complex' in which indigenous peoples became caught and confined, and in the process, defined as recipients of state care in the racialising discourses of the period.[29] Following them, in her study of Māori patients in the Auckland Asylum, Lorelle Barry locates all Māori patients institutionalised to 1900, showing how they too were subject to colonial discourses about racial difference.[30]

Some scholars, however, examine specific ethnic groups, and the Irish are striking in this regard, primarily because of their high rates of committal at home and abroad. In her contribution to this volume, Elizabeth Malcolm examines Ireland and its diaspora, surveying a wide range of explanations spanning the nineteenth and twentieth centuries to account for the disproportionate institutionalisation of the Irish. Although no definitive answer emerges, she states that the ethnicity of the Irish generated stereotyping and discrimination that may have contributed to their marginalisation. Whether, as Littlewood and Lipsedge contend, 'each ethnic group seems to have its own characteristic pattern of difficulties', such as high rates of alcoholism among the Irish (and Scots) compared with other ethnicities, is uncertain.[31] Further sustained comparative study may, however, clarify this uncertainty. Indeed, David Wright and Tom Themeles examine committals to Canadian mental hospitals in the mid to late nineteenth century and while acknowledging an Irish and Scottish over-representation, they argue that this declines over time and also differs from asylum admissions in the homelands.

By contrast with studies of patient populations, most studies of ethnicity and ethnic identities in relation to institutional confinement rarely engage with the practices or relationships of ethnicity. This is in stark contrast to the wider migration literature on ethnicity which incorporates the existence and continuity of visible signs of ethnic affiliation;[32] formal associations, networks, and communities;[33] and cultural essences. Such approaches also incorporate 'outsider' perceptions of ethnic groups as well as self-identification.[34] Within studies of madness, however, some exceptions exist including Leonard Smith's investigation of Jewish patients in the mid-Victorian asylum where 'the most direct religious or cultural dilemma they faced was in relation to food'.[35] McCarthy, meanwhile, identifies the significance of ties to place of origin, language and accent, and cross-cultural relations.[36] She likewise argues for the importance of comparing ethnicities, revealing that in a New Zealand context, at least, most ethnic groups except the English-born received some discussion of their ethnic identities.[37] In her contribution to this volume, Catharine Coleborne draws on the patient case notes of the Yarra Bend Hospital for the Insane in Victoria, Australia, from 1873 to 1910, to argue that medical and social perceptions of ethnicity generated new questions about colonial identity, susceptibility to mental disease, and racial hybridity. Building on McCarthy's work about ethnicity, Coleborne suggests that reinterpreting the archival productions around insanity, through case books and clinical notes about patients, historians might find meanings about ethnicity and identity that were being produced at a high point of anxiety about immigration and population in the colonial setting.

THIS COLLECTION

This volume, then, blends themes that have individually but not collectively received attention. It examines the difficulties that migrants underwent in adjustment abroad through a focus on migrants and mobile peoples, issues of ethnicity and ethnic differences, and the impact of migration on the mental health of refugees. By incorporating a study of the experiences of current refugee groups along with studies of nineteenth-century 'stressful migration', the volume enables readers to consider patterns of similarities and difference over time. It also extends the migration paradigm beyond patients to incorporate the international exchange of medical ideas and institutional practices, and the recruitment of a medical workforce. The volume's global focus also reflects the variety of destinations to which migrants, medical personnel, and ideas gravitated in the nineteenth and twentieth centuries. We suggest that this volume provides a set of rich findings which will also be available to other researchers in the global setting, and even pave the way for more international studies of migration, ethnicity, and insanity.

Certain gaps still exist. A sole focus on the United States is absent in this volume, but discussion of the Irish experience there appears in Malcolm's comparative examination of the Irish and mental health. Future research in the field should examine the experience in the United States which differed from many colonies with its longer history of settlement, greater degree of urbanisation, and more highly developed mental health care. In addition, we are conscious that many studies utilising patient records from asylums end around the turn of the century due to privacy restrictions imposed by legislation shaping the governance of state and national archives. Whether archival access in the future enables further contributions to the issues raised in this volume, or generates new areas of enquiry, remains to be seen. Acknowledging that ethnicity incorporates the multigenerational descent group, we are also conscious that the main focus of this volume is on the foreign-born generation of migrants. Whether the children of mixed parentage in many colonies were discriminated against and experienced increased admission to asylums as Eurasians did in India is as yet unknown. Alternatively, it may be that India's practice of repatriating insane Europeans explains this increase among those of mixed descent.[38]

In adopting a focus on migration and ethnicity, we are aware not to make exaggerated claims about these issues in connection with mental health. Similar concerns arose with a focus on women and mental health which overlooked the similar experiences men had in psychiatric care. Indeed, gender (and class) identities, or representations of these, have been singled out by historians of the asylum for a number of reasons including the influence of Marxist histories and feminist histories from the 1970s and 1980s.[39] Crucially, patients were among those rescued by historians of medicine as part of this shift from the study of doctors to patients with asylum case books recording partial biographies of people otherwise hidden from history.[40] Similarly, the families of the insane have received new attention which to some extent obscures the nature of institutional power and the regime of the institution itself, as scholars have been quick to point out.[41] Nonetheless, all of these areas have opened the door to exciting ways of reading the vast archival sources in the field of the histories of psychiatry.

SOURCES AND METHODS

As numerous scholars indicate, the use of asylum case books has enriched studies of the asylum.[42] Many contributors to this volume analyse asylum case books and admission registers in both a qualitative and quantitative fashion. Wright and Themeles, for instance, draw on a database compiled from the admission registers of more than 12,000 patients admitted to four Canadian mental hospitals to show elevated rates of Irish admissions. McCarthy, meanwhile, makes quantitative and qualitative use of the case books compiled by medical officials at the Dunedin and Seacliff asylums in New Zealand, supplemented by case books from Scotland. These are used in conjunction with official immigration records and asylum reports. In tracing the earlier admissions of migrants and their family members, McCarthy points to the importance of considering prior experience as well as migration and settlement as factors for committal.

A reinterpretation of patient case records to locate different forms of the representation of ethnicity is advocated by Catharine Coleborne in her chapter. If patients, or 'those deemed to be "foreigners" in the world of reason', were also literally from elsewhere, their ethnicity compounded feelings of dislocation.[43] Extracts from patient case notes from the Yarra Bend Hospital for the Insane between 1873 and 1910 infuse Coleborne's reflections on understanding the institutional production of colonial identities, covering such themes as birthplace and origins, bodies and behaviours, sound, language, gestures and expressions. Drawing also on annual reports from the Immigrants Aid Society, Coleborne discusses those transferred to Yarra Bend from the Immigrants' Home in Melbourne. Colonial society was being shaped through understandings of class, gender, and ethnicity, and institutions like Yarra Bend helped to produce these categories in their records.

Patient records also feature in Leckie's study of colonial Fiji with a particular focus on *Girmitiyas* (Indian indentured workers). Like McCarthy she follows the *Girmitiyas*' journey to Fiji, as well as disembarkment and indenture to explore the link between migration, mental illness, and suicide. Akihito Suzuki, in his study of rural and urban systems of care in

Japan, similarly draws on case notes to examine in detail four individual experiences which reveal a mixed economy of psychiatric care encompassing urban and rural areas, and formal and informal care. Suzuki also examines in detail legislative requirements to reveal the development in Japan of two very distinct patterns of psychiatric care in urban and rural areas. The Confinement Act of 1900 in particular resulted in the creation of nine psychiatric hospitals between 1899 and 1910 (two had existed prior to the act).

Comparing case notes with other sources is a feature of Dawson's examination of medical ideas at the Auckland Asylum. She uses key medical journals such as the *British Medical Journal* and the *New Zealand Medical Journal*, as well as the migration of medical personnel, to examine the flow of medical ideas about degeneracy and heredity from Britain to Auckland. By comparing the content of these medical journals with the case notes of patients at Auckland, Dawson shows that degeneration and 'family and vice' were commonly cited both in medical journals and case notes at Auckland.

The interaction between case notes and other sources continues with Knewstubb's exploration of medical doctors at Ashburn Hall in Dunedin. Taking a biographical approach, Knewstubb examines the ways in which medical education, travel, asylum employment, journal reading, and international networks all contributed to doctors' medical knowledge. She moves beyond these influences, though, to also consider the ways in which bourgeois cultural standards shaped doctors' judgements of patients with a particular focus on gender, ethnic, and religious differences apparent from case notes.

If most studies of nineteenth-century mental health rely on archival and documentary sources such as patient records, the exploration of such issues from the mid-twentieth century benefit from oral interviews. A somewhat under-utilised tool in histories of mental health, this is an approach showcased in Prebble and Fortune's study of British women who were recruited to New Zealand to work in mental hospitals after World War II. Interestingly, their interviews reveal a convergence with the examination of official documents and contemporary correspondence. Prebble and Fortune also situate their analysis within two main discourses: the professionalisation of psychiatric nursing, and the ideology of domesticity.

Interviews with refugee migrants experiencing mental health issues feature in Lynne Briggs's exploration of refugee settlement in New Zealand. All told, 100 interviews were conducted to explore the concept of 'demoralisation'. Briggs reveals that women were more likely than men to be depressed and feel hopeless and demoralised. Incorporating two case studies with female refugees, Briggs highlights the importance of incorporating pre-migration, migration, and post-migration experiences. Her contribution also highlights the policy implications of such research for providing clinical care to refugees.

An overarching synthetic approach drawing on statistics and second-ary literature characterises Malcolm's survey of Irish institutionalisation, demonstrating their over-representation in asylums, both as a percentage among the foreign-born as well as among the total population. Although future work needs to adjust such statistics for age and gender variations, it is likely that the Irish-born will still be over-represented among asylum admissions as they were in Malzberg's study of New York State mental hospitals in the mid-twentieth century.[44] Malcolm advances beyond statistics, however, to reflect on the multitude of explanations put forward to explain Irish asylum admissions offered by lunacy inspectors in Ireland, historians, anthropologists, sociologists, and psychiatrists.

SIMILARITIES AND DIFFERENCES

Finally, read as a whole, this volume addresses questions of comparisons—across both time and place—and of contrasts between the various geographical and cultural sites of mental health treatment under examination. We began this introduction by asserting that most studies of mental health focus on institutional sites and records, and with some exceptions, this book is no different. However, the differences between institutional settings also remind us of psychiatry's own global histories, as well as the limits of its mobility. For example, modes of institutional care in Japan and those in the colonial settings here, including Fiji, Australia, New Zealand, and Ontario (Canada) differed in critical ways. Institutional care was privileged over familial care, despite attempts in colonial settings to modify this emphasis over time.[45]

The discussion of psychiatry's mobility as a discourse is raised in several chapters. Malcolm ranges over the Irish diasporic communities which extended to the United States, Australia, and beyond. Wright and Thelmes also challenge the tendency to focus on single sites through their analysis of four institutional sites in Ontario, deepening knowledge about the Irish and Scottish as populations supposedly more subject to institutional controls. McCarthy similarly finds evidence of a global history of insanity in her contribution to the discussion about how migration scholars might use asylums and patterns of mental illness over time to examine the wider world of migrations and the experiences of immigrants. In a different vein, Knewstubb and Dawson both explore the discourses of doctors and their own mobility through medical biographies and travelling ideas; the use of medical journals to investigate the global discourse of psychiatry is important to emerging studies which move between sites of institutions and medical personnel. Likewise, Prebble and Fortune show how in the twentieth century, personnel and ideas in this field of psychiatric practice kept travelling, part of global migration work patterns and trends which extended from old worlds to new.

In addition, this volume contributes to the important new emphasis on a transnational and transcultural discussion about the effects of migration on mental breakdown. Although we have not set out to explicitly answer the question of whether migrants find themselves under more stress than the locally born, chapters in this collection examine this problem from a variety of perspectives. In particular, separate chapters show that the dislocating experiences of migration left migrants vulnerable to the stresses and strains of a major life change. In the nineteenth century this could mean long distances and family separations, whereas in the twentieth century, it is now well documented that violent and forced transitions from one's place of origin, as shown by Briggs's chapter, can result in an increased tendency to mental illness or intervention from mental health professionals. Some in the nineteenth century were also subject to forced migrations, and the effects of these are poignantly examined by Leckie's chapter about the colonial Pacific site of Fiji. Ethnicity and racial differences have compounded these problems for migrants, across both periods, as several authors also demonstrate.

Internal migration, one result of increasingly urbanised societies, also generated new institutional modes of care and influenced legislative changes in mental health, as Suzuki's chapter shows. In addition, we might look at new ways of investigating the institutionalisation of mobile peoples in colonial societies by thinking about a wider network of institutions in the colonies. For instance, Coleborne's chapter examines the role played by welfare institutions such as the Immigrants' Homes in colonial Victoria, Australia, and the populations of immigrants who became vulnerable to the challenges of colonial life following their arrival in the colonies. The ways that mental hospitals interacted with other social institutions remain to be fully examined and tell historians more about the perils of mobility in the colonial world. Leckie's chapter also concentrates on the notion of vulnerable mobile peoples in the Pacific, with a focus on Fiji as a 'hub' for indentured migrants, displaced peoples, and the 'lost souls' of the colonial period. It was in Fiji, under British imperial control, that the full impact of the inevitable disruption of imperialism could be felt. Not only did immigrants—both forced and free—fall victim to mental instability here, but the very spectre of institutionalisation as a European form of managing 'madness' also migrated into this colonial space.

By interrogating the way that ethnicity was also a shaping category inside mental health institutions we have questioned the very presence of immigrants and internal social differences and their effects on institutional cultures. 'Norms' of ethnicity established in a range of colonial settings, for instance, as Knewstubb and Coleborne both suggest, contributed to new expressions of institutional treatment, even in subtle ways, and hinted at deeper fears about colonial demographic patterns. This focus also reveals greater consideration of the diverse ethnic identities of 'European' patients, often subsumed in the past under that broad overarching label.

Although the diverse approaches and foci of chapters in this volume preclude overarching conclusions about patient populations, several contributions reveal the elevated rate of Irish admissions and contrasts between male and female admissions. Readers are encouraged to reflect on these similarities and differences, not only across geographic region, but over time.

NOTES

1. See, for example, A. Digby, *Madness, Morality and Medicine: A Study of the York Retreat, 1796–1914* (Cambridge: Cambridge University Press, 1985); E. Dwyer, *Homes for the Mad: Life Inside Two Nineteenth-Century Asylums* (New Brunswick, NJ: Rutgers University Press, 1987); E. Malcolm, *Swift's Hospital: A History of St Patrick's, Dublin* (Dublin: Gill and Macmillan, 1988).
2. See, for instance, J. E. Moran and D. Wright (eds.), *Mental Health and Canadian Society: Historical Perspectives* (Montreal and Kingston, London and Ithaca: McGill-Queens University Press, 2006); C. Coleborne and D. MacKinnon (eds.), *'Madness' in Australia: Histories, Heritage and the Asylum* (St. Lucia: University of Queensland Press, 2003); P. Michael, *Care and Treatment of the Mentally Ill in North Wales, 1800–2000* (Cardiff: University of Wales Press, 2003); J. Andrews and A. Digby (eds.), *Sex and Seclusion, Class and Custody: Perspectives on Gender and Class in the History of British and Irish Psychiatry* (Amsterdam: Rodopi, 2004).
3. See, for instance, R. Porter and D. Wright (eds.), *The Confinement of the Insane: International Perspectives* (Cambridge: Cambridge University Press, 2003); M. Gijswijt-Hofstra, H. Oosterhuis, J. Vijelaar, and H. Freeman (eds.), *Psychiatric Cultures Compared: Psychiatry and Mental Health Care in the Twentieth Century* (Amsterdam: Amsterdam University Press, 2005); S. Mahoe and M. Vaughan (eds.), *Psychiatry and Empire* (Basingstoke: Palgrave Macmillan, 2007); W. Ernst and T. Mueller (eds.), *Transnational Psychiatries: Social and Cultural Histories of Psychiatry in Comparative Perspective, c. 1800–2000* (Newcastle-upon-Tyne: Cambridge Scholars, 2010).
4. R. Fox, *So Far Disordered in Mind: Insanity in California, 1870–1930* (Berkeley: University of California Press, 1978).
5. B. Malzberg, 'Are immigrants psychologically disturbed?', in S. C. Plog and R. B. Edgerton (eds.), *Changing Perspectives in Mental Illness* (New York: Holt, Rinehart and Winston, 1969), pp. 395–421.
6. G. N. Grob, *Mental Illness and American Society, 1875–1940* (Princeton, NJ: Princeton University Press, 1983); and *The State and the Mentally Ill: A History of Worcester State Hospital in Massachusetts, 1830–1920* (Chapel Hill: University of North Carolina Press, 1966). See also G. N Grob, 'Class, ethnicity and race in American mental hospitals, 1830–75', *Journal of the History of Medicine and Allied Sciences*, 28 (1973), pp. 207–29.
7. N. G. Schiller, L. Basch, and C. Blanc-Szanton, 'Transnationalism: A new analytic framework for understanding migration', in N. G. Schiller, L. Basch, and C. Blanc-Szanton (eds.), *Towards a Transnational Perspective on Migration: Race, Class, Ethnicity, and Nationalism Reconsidered. Annals of the New York Academy of Sciences, 645* (New York: New York Academy of Sciences, 1992), pp. 1–24.
8. Exceptions include A. McCarthy, *Scottishness and Irishness in New Zealand Since 1840* (Manchester: Manchester University Press, 2011, Studies in

Imperialism series); and *Personal Narratives of Irish and Scottish Migration, 1921–65: 'For Spirit and Adventure'* (Manchester: Manchester University Press, 2007).

9. D. Baines, *Emigration from Europe, 1815–1930* (Basingstoke: Macmillan, 1991), p. 9, table 2.

10. Earlier studies focused on intellectuals and their ideas in the twentieth century such as D. Fleming and B. Bailyn, *The Intellectual Migration: Europe and America, 1930–1960* (Cambridge: Belknap, 1969), whereas recent works adopt a broader approach. See R. Scazzieri and R. Simili (eds.), *The Migration of Ideas* (Sagamore Beach: Science History, 2008).

11. Malzberg, 'Are immigrants psychologically disturbed?', pp. 491, 399–400.

12. R. Littlewood and M. Lipsedge, *Aliens and Alienists: Ethnic Minorities and Psychiatry* (London: Unwin Hyman, 1989), pp. 87, 90.

13. D. Wright, J. Moran, and S. Gouglas, 'The confinement of the insane in Victorian Canada: The Hamilton and Toronto asylums, c.1861–1891', in R. Porter and D. Wright (eds.), *The Confinement of the Insane: International Perspectives, 1800–1965* (Cambridge: Cambridge University Press, 2003), p. 120.

14. E. Delaney and D. M. MacRaild (eds.), *Irish Migration, Networks and Ethnic Identities Since 1750* (London: Routledge, 2007).

15. A. Scull, *The Most Solitary of Afflictions: Madness and Society in Britain, 1700–1900* (New Haven, CT: Yale University Press, 1993); J. Walton, 'Lunacy in the industrial revolution: A study of asylum admissions in Lancashire, 1848–50', *Journal of Social History*, 13 (1979), pp. 1–22.

16. R. Adair, J. Melling, and B. Forsythe, 'Migration, family structure, and pauper lunacy in Victorian England: Admissions to the Devon County pauper lunatic asylum, 1845–1900', *Continuity and Change*, 12:3 (1997), pp. 373–401.

17. J. Melling and B. Forsythe, *The Politics of Madness: The State, Insanity and Society in England, 1845–1914* (London: Routledge, 2006), p. 77.

18. 'Wanderers' also feature in the work of historians interested in other colonial settings, including J. H. Mills, *Madness, Cannabis and Colonialism: The 'Native-Only' Lunatic Asylums of British India, 1857-1900* (Basingstoke: Macmillan, 2000).

19. Littlewood and Lipsedge, *Aliens and Alienists*, p. 104.

20. See, however, M. Wyman, *Round-Trip to America: The Immigrants Return to Europe, 1880–1930* (Ithaca, NY: Cornell University Press, 1993).

21. See, for instance, the lives of around 1,000 medical students in M. A. Crowther and M. W. Dupree, *Medical Lives in the Age of Surgical Revolution* (Cambridge: Cambridge University Press, 2007).

22. Ibid.

23. See W. Anderson, 'Postcolonial histories of medicine', in F. Huisman and J. H. Warner (eds.), *Locating Medical History: The Stories and Their Meanings* (Baltimore, MD: Johns Hopkins University Press, 2004), pp. 292–95.

24. Mahone and Vaughan, *Psychiatry and Empire*, p. 3.

25. H. Deacon, 'Racial categories and psychiatry in Africa: The asylum on Robben Island in the nineteenth century', in W. Ernst and B. Harris (eds.), *Race, Science and Medicine, 1700–1960* (London: Routledge, 1999), pp. 104, 102.

26. W. Ernst, *Mad Tales from the Raj: Colonial Psychiatry in South Asia, 1800–58* (London: Anthem, 2010; first published 1991), pp. 14, 63, 118.

27. J. Leckie, 'Unsettled minds: Gender and settling madness in Fiji', in Mahone and Vaughan, *Psychiatry and Empire*, pp. 103, 109.

28. Ibid., p. 108.

29. R. Menzies and T. Palys, 'Turbulent spirits: Aboriginal patients in the British Columbia psychiatry system, 1879–1950', in Moran and Wright (eds.), *Mental Health and Canadian Society*, p. 162.

30. L. Barry and C. Coleborne, 'Insanity and ethnicity in New Zealand: Māori encounters with the Auckland mental hospital, 1860–1900', *History of Psychiatry*, 22:3 (2011), pp. 285–301.

31. Littlewood and Lipsedge, *Aliens and Alienists*, pp. 95–96.

32. K. N. Conzen, D. A. Gerber, E. Morawska, G. E. Pozzetta, and R. J. Vecoli, 'The invention of ethnicity: A perspective from the U.S.A.', *Journal of American Ethnic History*, 12:1 (1992), p. 28.

33. D. Handelman, 'The organization of ethnicity', *Ethnic Groups*, 1 (1977), pp. 187–200.

34. See, for instance, McCarthy, *Scottishness and Irishness*.

35. Leonard D. Smith, 'Insanity and ethnicity: Jews in the mid-Victorian lunatic asylum', *Jewish Culture and History*, 1:1 (1998), p. 33.

36. A. McCarthy, 'Ethnicity, migration and the lunatic asylum in early twentieth-century Auckland, New Zealand', *Social History of Medicine*, 21:1 (2008), pp. 47–65.

37. A. McCarthy, 'Exploring ethnicity and ethnic identities in New Zealand lunatic asylums before 1910', in R. McClean, B. Patterson, and D. Swain (eds), *Counting Stories, Moving Ethnicities: Studies from Aotearoa New Zealand* (2011, forthcoming).

38. W. Ernst, 'Colonial policies, racial politics and the development of psychiatric institutions in early nineteenth-century British India', in Ernst and Harris *New Zealand* (Hamilton: University of New Waikato, 2011) , *Race, Science and Medicine*, p. 91.

39. See, for instance, S. Garton, *Medicine and Madness: A Social History of Insanity in New South Wales, 1880–1940* (Kensington: New South Wales University Press, 1988); M. Finnane, 'Asylum, families, and the state', *History Workshop Journal*, 20 (1985), pp. 134–48; B. Labrum, 'Looking beyond the asylum: Gender and the process of committal in Auckland, 1870–1910', *New Zealand Journal of History*, 26 (1992), pp. 125–44.

40. See F. Condrau, 'The patient's view meets the clinical gaze', *Social History of Medicine*, 20:3 (2007), pp. 525–40.

41. C. Coleborne, 'Families, insanity and the psychiatric institution in Australia and New Zealand, 1860 to 1914', *Health and History*, 11:1 (2009), pp. 65–82. See also D. Wright, 'Getting out of the asylum: Understanding the confinement of the insane in the nineteenth century', *Social History of Medicine*, 10 (1997), pp. 137–55.

42. G. Risse and J. H. Warner, 'Reconstructing clinical activities: Patient records in medical history', *Social History of Medicine*, 5 (1992), pp. 183–205.

43. B. Brookes and J. Thomson (eds.), *'Unfortunate Folk': Essays on Mental Health Treatment, 1863–1992* (Dunedin: University of Otago Press, 2001), p. 17.

44. Malzberg, 'Are immigrants psychologically disturbed?', p. 408.

45. Coleborne, *Madness in the Family*, pp. 137–42.

2 Mental Health and Migration
The Case of the Irish, 1850s–1990s

Elizabeth Malcolm

'There is scarcely any human act so important in its consequences as that of exchanging one country for another'.[1]

INTRODUCTION

In her controversial study of mental illness in the west of Ireland, first published in 1979 and provocatively entitled *Saints, Scholars and Schizophrenics*, the American anthropologist Nancy Scheper-Hughes asked somewhat facetiously with regard to migration: 'Do the Irish have it coming and going, or rather going and staying? In short, are the Irish susceptible to schizophrenia, depression, and alcoholism *wherever* they live?' And answering her own question, she stated, 'Available data indicate that the Irish vulnerability to mental illness has, in fact, crossed the Atlantic'. Scheper-Hughes was suggesting that the high rates of mental illness she had found among Irish people during the 1970s were also evident among Irish immigrants in the United States.[2] But what Scheper-Hughes did not mention was the fact that the United States was not the only country to which the Irish went where the phenomenon occurred: it was to be found also in England and Australia.[3] Thus, in seeking to understand the mental health of the Irish, we must venture beyond the island of Ireland and encompass the Irish diaspora as well.

This chapter adopts a broad approach canvassing the topic of mental illness among the Irish both at home and overseas during both the nineteenth and twentieth centuries. Whereas there have been a number of studies of Ireland itself, such as Scheper-Hughes's book, and of some diasporic communities, there has not as yet been a systematic effort to compare rates of mental illness among the Irish in both Ireland and the diaspora. Nor has a comparative study been attempted of the explanations offered by different disciplines, such as psychiatry, anthropology, and history, for the apparently high rates of mental illness among the Irish. The first part of the chapter provides a brief, largely statistical picture of psychiatric institutionalisation among the Irish during the period from the 1850s to 1990s, looking first at Ireland and then at three of the major Irish diaspora countries: the United States, England, and Australia. The second part of the chapter then explores some of the theories and explanations advanced by different disciplines since the 1850s for Irish mental health problems. Ireland, the United States, England, and Australia are again considered, but they are also compared, as explanations have increasingly transcended national boundaries.

THE RISE OF PSYCHIATRIC
INSTITUTIONALISATION IN IRELAND

Although 'madhouses' of various sorts had operated in Britain and Ireland for centuries, large-scale institutionalisation of the mentally ill only began in the early nineteenth century. This was true also for many British colonies, and for the United States as well.[4] Nowhere, however, was the rise of psychiatric institutionalisation more evident than in Ireland. The country's first state-built public asylum opened in Dublin as early as 1815; an additional nine asylums were erected between 1824 and 1835, a further six between 1852 and 1855, and another six between 1865 and 1869. All these buildings were enlarged at different times, while at the end of the century three auxiliary asylums had to be built to relieve overcrowding at the Dublin, Belfast, and Cork asylums: Portrane in 1895, Antrim in 1899, and Youghal in 1904. By 1912 the four largest Irish asylums were Cork with 1,798 patients; Ballinasloe with 1,450; Belfast with 1,252; and dwarfing them all, Dublin and Portrane with together 3,264 patients.[5] Yet this growing public asylum network served a country that, since the late 1840s, had a steadily declining population, high rates of emigration, and relatively low levels of industrialisation and urbanisation.

Institutionalisation for mental illness on a large scale in fact continued in Ireland up to the 1980s. The absolute number of patients resident in mental hospitals peaked in 1914 at 25,180. This reflected a rate of 4.96 per 1,000 of population; in the same year the comparable rate in England and Wales was 2.98.[6] However, the rate of psychiatric institutionalisation did not actually peak in the Irish Republic until 1956, when it reached 7.49 per 1,000. In 1955 the comparable figure for England and Wales was 3.49 per 1,000—less than half the Irish rate. For the United States and Australia it was even lower at 3.38 in 1955 and 3.10 in 1960, respectively.[7] By the 1950s and 1960s, it was widely recognised that the Irish Republic had one of the highest rates of institutionalisation for mental illness in the world.[8]

Other aspects of Irish mental health were also distinctive. Unlike most Western countries, the majority of Irish psychiatric patients were males. These men were overwhelmingly unmarried, mainly between ages thirty and fifty, and often came from rural areas; around 32 per cent of them had been diagnosed as suffering from schizophrenia, with a further 20 per cent considered to be alcoholics. In 1969 a remarkable 12.9 per 1,000 single adult males were resident in mental hospitals in the Irish Republic. A somewhat similar though less extreme picture was evident among female patients in the 1960s, with 58 per cent being single or widowed and 25 per cent being diagnosed with schizophrenia.[9] By 1971 it was estimated that 2 out of every 100 men living in the west of Ireland were in mental hospitals, with the majority suffering from schizophrenia.[10] Discussing these figures in 1973, an anthropologist concluded that 'mental breakdown' was 'almost a routine part' of life in Ireland's west.[11]

Experts began speculating as to whether either epidemic or endemic schizophrenia was ravaging the west of Ireland—an area from which large numbers of immigrants had come.[12] The controversial American expert on schizophrenia, E. F. Torrey, went so far as to suggest in 1980 that 'if we could fully explain the high prevalence of schizophrenia in Ireland, we could probably explain schizophrenia'.[13] A study he conducted in the west of Ireland, which was published in 1984, showed an incidence rate of schizophrenia of 12.6 per 1,000, which was more than double the rates evident in other parts of the country at the time. Noting that schizophrenia was also 'common among Irish immigrants to the USA', Torrey argued that the high rates in the west therefore could not be explained, as some had attempted to do, by postulating that many of the healthiest members of the community had emigrated.[14]

Some studies during the late 1980s and early 1990s suggested that rates of schizophrenia in Ireland and elsewhere might have been falling.[15] An interesting 1994 investigation of schizophrenics, living in hospitals and in the community in County Cavan, certainly identified a marked fall in rates over the previous half-century, but the authors found that this fall in schizophrenia was only significant among women, not among men.[16]

At the same time that a vast network of psychiatric institutions was being built in Ireland and filled to overflowing with thousands of patients, Irish people were also leaving their country in unprecedented numbers for a variety of foreign destinations. In light of the alarming rates of psychiatric institutionalisation in Ireland, from an early date experts in various parts of the world began to ponder the links between Irish migration and mental health in their own countries.

A DIASPORIC APPROACH TO IRISH MENTAL ILLNESS

In the century from 1801 to 1900 approximately 7.58 million people left Ireland, and another 2.47 million followed between 1901 and 2000. Thus the population of the whole island, which was approaching 5 million in 1800 and had probably peaked at around 8.5 million in 1845, was only a little over 5.5 million in 2000, for it had fallen consistently in the period between 1846 and 1961. In per capita terms, no other Western country experienced such massive emigration or such a population collapse between the 1840s and the 1960s. These huge demographic shifts had profound effects, not only on the sending country, but also on the main immigrant-receiving countries. The principal destinations of Irish immigrants during the nineteenth century were North America (76 per cent), Britain (18 per cent), and Australasia (5 per cent); during the twentieth century the majority went to Britain (65 per cent), followed by North America (28 per cent), and Australasia (5 per cent).[17]

In the last twenty years historians have begun to conceptualise Irish migration in terms of a diaspora—a loosely linked international network of individuals and communities sharing a common sense of identity—and to compare the experiences of Irish immigrants in various destination countries.[18] The topic of mental health lends itself to such an approach partly because, from the mid-nineteenth century, the Irish were identified internationally as having particularly severe mental health problems. In fact, wherever the Irish went their propensity to be committed to psychiatric institutions became notorious. In trying to explain this phenomenon nineteenth-century psychiatric experts, including asylum superintendents, doctors, and medical writers, began to investigate the types of people who emigrated from Ireland, where they went, and what happened to them. They compared the Irish in different countries, swapped information, and published trans-national studies. In this regard a diasporic approach to the question of Irish mental health was pioneered long before the concept of a diaspora entered Irish studies at the end of the twentieth century.

THE IRISH AND MENTAL ILLNESS IN THE UNITED STATES

In 1854 Dr. Edward Jarvis was asked by the Massachusetts legislature to investigate the state's apparently rising rates of mental illness. Massachusetts was to the fore in the treatment of insanity, having established the country's first public asylum at Worcester in 1833 and hosted the first meeting of the American Psychiatric Association in 1844.[19] Jarvis's report, *Insanity and Idiocy in Massachusetts*, delivered in 1855, has been described as the 'single most important study of mental illness and public policy in nineteenth-century America'.[20] He investigated the insane in both institutions and the community, identifying nearly 3,000 such people and dividing them into native and foreign born as well as what he termed 'pauper' and 'independent'. His conclusions were that insanity was far more prevalent among paupers and the foreign born; or to use his own distinctive terminology, the 'greater liability of the poor . . . to become insane seems to be especially manifested among these strangers dwelling among us'. These 'strangers'—that is foreign-born immigrants—numbered a little over a quarter million people, or 20.5 per cent of Massachusetts's population, and nearly 75 per cent of them were Irish. Thus, as early as the 1850s, a clear connection was established in American psychiatric literature between the Irish and mental illness.[21]

High rates of institutionalisation for mental illness continued to be a feature of Irish communities in the United States well into the twentieth century. For example, in 1900 the Irish made up 15.6 per cent of foreign-born whites in the United States, but they composed 29.6 per cent of foreign-born whites in asylums—in other words, nearly double the proportion that might have been predicted. Moreover, the 1905 annual report of the New York Commission in Lunacy showed that from 1888 to 1904, 3.4 per cent of the state's Irish-born population had been committed to asylums. This suggested an extraordinary committal rate of 34 per 1,000, when the rate in Ireland at the time was claimed to be 5.6 per 1,000. The British *Journal of Mental Science* in reporting these figures described them as 'truly appalling' and 'sinister', and the Irish inspectors of lunacy worried that they were 'of grave portent to the welfare of our race'.[22]

If at the turn of the century the Irish born had by far the highest rates of first admissions to New York state mental hospitals of any white ethnic group, the situation remained much the same fifty years later, for in 1951 the Irish still topped the list of foreign-born committals. However, by then, statistics were suggesting that even the American-born children of Irish immigrants were likely to be admitted to New York psychiatric institutions at rates comparable to those of their parents, and well above the rates for the children of other immigrant groups.[23] So it appeared that poor mental health could extend beyond those who actually left Ireland into the second generation of Irish Americans.

THE IRISH AND MENTAL ILLNESS IN ENGLAND

A similar picture was evident in England. During the nineteenth century, outside of London, the largest Irish immigrant communities lived in Lancashire, especially in the cities of Liverpool and Manchester.[24] There too the Irish were vastly over-represented in asylums. For example, in 1871, fully 43 per cent of the inmates of Liverpool's Rainhill Asylum were Irish born, whereas they made up only 15.5 per cent of the city's population. In 1870 the London *Times*, commenting on the Rainhill situation, had complained of the 'enormous expense' the English were being burdened with in order to maintain what it termed Ireland's 'vagrant lunatics'. The situation was similar in Manchester in 1871, with 25 per cent of the inmates of the city's Prestwich Asylum being Irish born, whereas they made up only 9.7 per cent of the general population.[25]

As in the United States, apparently disproportionate rates of psychiatric institutionalisation for Irish immigrants continued in England throughout the twentieth century and, indeed, are still evident today. In 1971, for example, 4.94 per 1,000 people born in England and Wales were admitted to mental hospitals. The comparable figure for Northern Ireland immigrants living in England and Wales was 12.42, and for immigrants born in the Irish Republic it was 11.10. No other major immigrant group resident in England at the time had rates of hospitalisation for mental illness even approaching these levels.[26] Moreover, the figures suggested that it did not matter on which side of the border created in 1921 that Irish people had been born—all had high admission rates in England. Mind, the major British mental heath advocacy organisation, currently has a lengthy fact sheet on its website devoted to the mental health problems of Irish people living in Britain.[27] In addition, studies in recent decades have also confirmed the American pattern of mental illness being disproportionately evident in the children of Irish immigrants as well.[28]

THE IRISH AND MENTAL ILLNESS IN AUSTRALIA

In a recent book comparing Irish immigrants in Australia and the United States, Malcolm Campbell commented that 'Australia's Irish did not consider themselves subject to hardships and privations on a scale at all comparable to those present in the northeastern United States or Great Britain'.[29] Some Irish may well have taken this view, but outside observers, including many doctors working with the insane, were certainly convinced that the Irish in Australia were very similar to those who had gone to the United States and England.[30] For example, at a major medical congress held in Melbourne in 1889, Dr. Frederic Norton Manning, the New South Wales inspector of the insane and the country's leading alienist, pointed out that the largest ethnic group in Australasian asylums were the Irish born, comprising 27 per cent of all inmates in Australia and 28 per cent in New Zealand.[31] Census figures in 1891 showed that there were nearly 230,000 Irish-born immigrants living in Australia, but they made up only 7.2 per cent of the country's total population. Manning's figures suggested that a little over 1 per cent of Australia's Irish-born population was resident in asylums. This was a very high figure, but it was in line with committal rates around the turn of the century in some Irish counties.[32]

Not a great deal of research has been carried out by historians on the Irish and mental illness in colonial Australia, although Irish patients do figure in many of the general histories of asylums.[33] However, a recent study of the inmates of Victoria's main public asylum during the 1850s and 1860s has shown that around 36 per cent were Irish born, whereas at the time the Irish made up from 14 to 16 per cent of the colony's total population.[34] Similarly, Trevor McClaughlin, in a study of women, crime, and madness in late nineteenth-century eastern Australia, found that by 1901 Irish-born women were apparently over-represented threefold- to fivefold in asylums. Whereas they made up 4.5 per cent, 5.1 per cent, and 8.2 per cent, respectively, of the general female populations in New South Wales, Victoria, and Queensland, they made up 21.2 per cent, 18.5 per cent, and 36.4 per cent, respectively, of these colonies' female asylum populations.[35]

Unfortunately, we know little about the mental health of Irish immigrants in twentieth-century Australia. However, sparse data collected indicate that disproportionate numbers of Irish-born immigrants, especially single men and many increasingly elderly, were to be found in Australian mental hospitals at least into the 1930s.[36] In addition, a study published in 1971 appeared to demonstrate that Irish-born immigrants in Australia had significantly higher suicide rates than did the home population in Ireland.[37]

These apparently high rates of mental illness among the Irish—and certainly high rates of psychiatric institutionalisation—have led, not surprisingly, to much study and even more speculation, and frequently to intense debate. Explanations have come in many forms. The remainder of this chapter will survey some of the main explanations for this phenomenon offered by experts during both the nineteenth and twentieth centuries.

EXPLAINING MENTAL ILLNESS IN
IRELAND AND THE DIASPORA

Concern about the levels of mental illness in Ireland had been expressed throughout the nineteenth century, but there was particularly intense debate from about 1890 up to 1914, when the Irish asylum population peaked. Various explanations were offered by the medical profession for the apparent rapid rise in Irish asylum committal rates towards the end of the century, but many highlighted poverty and harsh living conditions, especially in rural Ireland. As for emigration, there was disagreement, but some, including the Irish lunacy inspectors, argued that the brightest and most capable were leaving in large numbers, and behind them in dwindling, impoverished, rural communities remained those particularly susceptible to mental illness.[38] This discussion was not restricted to Ireland, however, but spilled over into medical and popular journals in Britain and America as well, because it was hoped that explaining the situation in Ireland would throw light on the reasons for the high committal rates found also among Irish immigrant populations.

New Irish lunacy inspectors were appointed in 1890, the previous two inspectors, appointed in 1847 and 1857, having been inactive due to age and ill health for a number of years.[39] Drs E. M. Courtney and G. P. O'Farrell were asked by Dublin Castle to provide a report explaining why committal rates had jumped in just ten years from 2.5 per 1,000 of population in 1880 to 3.44 in 1890. In their 1894 report, by which time committals had reached 3.85 per 1,000, the inspectors stressed what they termed 'accumulation', arguing that Irish asylums had relatively low discharge and death rates, and that inmates were long lived. Thus in Ireland, unlike other countries, once admitted, few patients were released and so long-stay populations built up in asylums. Although this might explain high residence rates, of course it did not explain rising committal rates. So the inspectors went on to argue that asylums were numerous and long established and the Irish were therefore very familiar with them. Increasingly, lunatics who would have been looked after by their families in the past were being committed.

As well, workhouses were transferring their elderly and chronic inmates to asylums, and significant numbers of returned migrants were also ending up in them.[40] Statistics in their annual reports provided some evidence in support of the inspectors' arguments. Whereas 63.7 per cent of lunatics in 1851 were in asylums, with 21.1 per cent being 'at large'—that is, mainly in the care of their families—by 1891 75.4 per cent were in asylums, with only 5.9 per cent 'at large'. However, while the Irish population had declined by 28.2 per cent during these forty years, the number of lunatics had jumped by 194.5 per cent.[41]

In light of these figures, the inspectors could not totally deny that an actual increase in insanity appeared to be occurring. This they explained in terms of four key factors: heredity; consanguineous marriages, especially between cousins; the consumption of nervous stimulants, in particular alcohol and tea; and the economic depression, which had been afflicting rural Ireland since the late 1870s.[42] But not everyone agreed with them. The medical superintendent of one of the asylums the inspectors had responsibility for, Dr. Thomas Drapes of Enniscorthy, published a long article in 1894 questioning the inspectors' four key factors largely because there was not sufficient statistical evidence to demonstrate conclusively the impact of any of them.[43]

The inspectors also drew attention to emigration as a significant issue. They speculated that it was those 'healthy and strong, in both mind and body' who were most likely to depart, leaving behind disproportionate numbers of the 'weak and infirm'. But at the Medico-Psychological Association annual conference, held in Dublin in July 1894, Dr. Daniel Hack Tuke, a leading English alienist, gave a paper on the 'Increase of Insanity in Ireland' in which he dismissed as 'absurdly illogical' the claim that 'emigration from Ireland has caused an increase of lunacy'. Drapes, while noting that 13 per cent of the male inmates of Mullingar Asylum were returned migrants, also doubted the significance of emigration, considering it to have been 'over-estimated'.[44] Tuke certainly recognised that the increase in insanity over the previous decade was greatest in those counties with the highest rates of emigration, but he argued that this did not mean that migration caused mental illness; rather, it was a reflection of the fact that these were the poorest counties in the county. It was poverty that boosted both emigration and insanity. For Tuke, the 'precarious living' conditions of poor tenant farmers were 'calculated to produce mental weakness and insanity'.[45] He suggested in addition that emigration was an influential factor in two particular ways: first, that the departure of so many of the young and strong from struggling communities inevitably put more pressure on those left behind; and second, that Ireland was now having to deal with a large influx of insane emigrants sent back from the United States.[46] During the first decade of the twentieth century, it was estimated that around 7 per cent of the inmates of Irish asylums were returned migrants.[47]

In an influential paper delivered in 1911, at another Medico-Psychological Association annual meeting in Dublin, a new lunacy inspector, Dr. William Dawson, offered a statistical study correlating asylum committals on a county basis with rates of poverty, emigration, crime, disease, drunkenness, death, population density, and land value. He identified only a 'trifling' correlation between insanity and emigration, but there was 'some little relation' to crime and alcoholism. However, insanity shared a 'close relation' with poverty. Dawson, like Tuke nearly twenty years earlier, saw poverty as the key to understanding the poor mental health of the Irish.[48] But neither saw fit to investigate exactly how poverty produced mental illness.

After 1922 the newly independent south of Ireland demonstrated little interest in mental health matters, and indeed, no significant legislation was passed until 1945.[49] However, by the 1950s and 1960s there was growing alarm among psychiatrists and sociologists at the extraordinarily high rates of admission to psychiatric hospitals. It was in this context that historians finally entered the debate during the 1970s and 1980s.

Mark Finnane's *Insanity and the Insane in Post-Famine Ireland*, completed as a doctoral thesis under the supervision of Oliver MacDonagh, and published in 1981, remains, thirty years later, the seminal study.[50] But MacDonagh had also made major contributions to the history of British government. He argued that successive British governments had used Ireland as a laboratory in which to experiment with highly interventionist social policies that were later applied, in modified form, in Britain itself. Health care was one such policy, and within health care one of the most 'startling' breaks with past practice was the establishment of a large, centrally controlled asylum system. However, this 'bureaucratisation of the treatment of the insane in Ireland', MacDonagh wrote in 1977, 'worked against the patient's immediate interests'.[51]

Finnane echoed some of MacDonagh's arguments, claiming that 'what England saw only in 1845 . . . Ireland had already witnessed in its essentials in 1817: the legislative provision of public asylums for the entire country'. He stressed the 'advanced state of public provision for the insane in nineteenth-century Ireland', arguing that by 1914 'Ireland had a quite massive provision of asylum beds'. This 'generosity' on the part of the British, this 'apparent excess of social welfare', plus the 'broadening of insanity's boundaries' by doctors eager to claim new territory and enhance their power and prestige, opened the way for a great confinement of those deemed insane that continued into the twentieth century.[52] According to Finnane's analysis it was the 'massive' and 'excess' provision that had helped generate the 'massive' and 'excess' demand—not the other way round.

During the 1970s and 1980s, under the influence of the writings of Michel Foucault, the anti-psychiatry movement, social control theorists, and especially the work of Andrew Scull on Britain and David Rothman on the United States,[53] those in Ireland pondering the high rates of psychiatric institutionalisation were inclined to lay the responsibility at the door of politicians and doctors, especially during the period of British rule up to 1922.

Joseph Robins, in his 1986 history *Fools and Mad*, argued that Ireland was not unique, for in 'other western countries, too, the introduction of special provisions for the insane had set off an unexpected demand'. According to him, however, Ireland was 'an extreme example' of this trend. Robins suggested that the poverty of the Irish meant that it was often impossible for families to support a sick relative and the asylum lacked the stigma associated with the workhouse. Quoting Scull to the effect that nineteenth-century alienists left the boundary between the normal and the pathological 'extraordinarily vague', Robins claimed that many 'took advantage' of the 'comparative ease' of committal 'to rid themselves of relatives and friends who were a burden and a nuisance'. Yet, despite abuse of the system, Robins seemed prepared to believe that the lunacy inspectors' reports were 'reasonably honest' and that the 'great majority of admissions had at least some manifestation of insanity'.[54] In effect Robins attempted to cover all the bases by arguing that, during the nineteenth century, the existence of such an extensive system and its lax regulation encouraged poor people to abuse it, while at the same time maintaining that most of those committed were in fact mentally ill. The continuance of high rates of committal into the late twentieth century, Robins ascribed to the carry over of 'deeply rooted' nineteenth-century habits: 'what contemporary Ireland has inherited', he concluded, 'is not a high level of mental illness but an excessive commitment to the mental hospital'. And summing up, he said succinctly, 'Ireland is hospital prone'.[55]

Such historical interpretations of course fitted neatly with—and indeed, offered intellectual justification for—contemporary mental health policies in Ireland and elsewhere that advocated de-institutionalisation and community care: that is, the closing down of most of the large nineteenth-century mental hospitals and the dispersal of their inmates to live in managed community accommodation.

Anthropologists, though, took a rather different line. They blamed Ireland's high rates of psychiatric institutionalisation, not on an excess of British-built hospitals, but on the Irish themselves, or at least on the impoverished and repressive society and culture that existed in the west of Ireland where committal rates were highest. In the 1970s two studies both based on extensive fieldwork in the west were particularly influential. One, published in 1973, was by the British anthropologist Hugh Brody; the other, which appeared in 1979 and has been mentioned already, was by the American anthropologist Nancy Scheper-Hughes.

Brody conducted his research during the late 1960s among rural communities in the west of Counties Clare and Cork. He was critical of Arensberg and Kimball's famous study of Clare rural life in the 1930s, seeing it as 'functionalist' and excessively optimistic.[56] Although he thought life in rural Ireland had become much worse since the 1930s, largely due to contact with the outside world, he traced some problems, like mass emigration of the young, back to the mid-nineteenth century. Brody found traditional society 'demoralised'; the people were 'lonely and withdrawn'; they felt that their society did 'not function for them'; they had lost faith 'in the social advantages and moral worth of their own small society'. And one of the consequences of this alienation, isolation, and depression was mental breakdown. Of the 231 households that Brody studied, aside from those with members in a psychiatric hospital, 5.2 per cent were caring for mentally ill relatives at home.[57]

Scheper-Hughes, who conducted her research in County Kerry, melodramatically announced at the beginning of her book: 'rural Ireland is dying'. And she went on to describe a people infused 'with a spirit of anomie and despair'. She also identified a 'pattern of dependency on "total" institutions'. Characterising herself as 'heir to the insights of Foucault', Scheper-Hughes described madness as a 'projection of cultural themes'. For her, Irish schizophrenics offered 'eloquent testimony to the repressed fears, longings and insecurities of the group', and especially the 'miseries of adult life in devitalised rural Ireland'. As already mentioned, Scheper-Hughes also drew attention to the high levels of mental illness among Irish immigrants in United States, which by implication challenged the argument that it was the provision of excess hospital beds in Ireland that was the cause of high rates of institutionalisation among the Irish. She compared the experience of living in the rural west to the experience of migration: both, she argued, entailed 'social disorganisation'.[58]

These historical and anthropological studies published during the 1970s and 1980s leave us with some obvious questions. Did the lavish provision of psychiatric institutions by the British during the nineteenth century inevitably invite Irish society to over-use them; or were large numbers committed to these hospitals due to an economically and culturally dysfunctional post-Famine rural society? In fact, this is really a classic 'chicken-and-egg' question. Put bluntly: were the hospitals responsible for high mental illness rates, or were high mental illness rates responsible for the hospitals? Such a question is probably unanswerable, or is only answerable in terms of concluding that both factors almost certainly played a significant role.

If historians and anthropologists produced differing explanations during the 1970s and 1980s, so did psychiatrists. In 1984, for example, a much-quoted study of schizophrenics in County Roscommon, published by a group of leading American and Irish psychiatrists, revived Tuke and Dawson's arguments about poverty. The study found a high schizophrenia prevalence rate of 12.6 per 1,000 of population. Examining both emigrants who had returned due to illness and those prevented from emigrating by illness, the researchers calculated that 'emigration accounts for a maximum of one-third of the schizophrenia prevalence rate in the study area'. They then turned for explanations of the other two-thirds to a variety of factors, including: consanguineous or late marriage; mother-son relationships; lack of communication in families; stress; celiac disease; and alcoholism. None, they concluded, were convincing. However, it was their 'impression' that 'a strong correlation exists between rural lower socio-economic status and high rates of psychosis'.[59] But as with the theories of Tuke and Dawson around the beginning of the twentieth century, the exact process by which poverty gave rise to schizophrenia in the 1980s was not explained.[60]

EXPLAINING IRISH MENTAL ILLNESS IN THE UNITED STATES

In line with the scientific and pseudo-scientific preoccupations of the time, during the late nineteenth and early twentieth centuries a significant number of mental health experts came to stress the perceived inferior racial origins and defective genetic characteristics of the Irish. Skull sizes and brain capacity, heredity, and later eugenics, all began to figure prominently in psychiatric discourse.[61] But such thinking was already evident in Jarvis's 1854/1855 survey of insanity in Massachusetts. It is no coincidence that in 1854 a candidate representing the nativist Know-Nothing Party had been elected governor of the state. Jarvis conducted his research in an atmosphere of intense hostility to immigrants—or 'strangers', as he repeatedly called them—who were perceived to be a major threat to 'our' superior way of life.[62]

Jarvis believed that poverty was the consequence of what he termed 'less vital force'. This was an hereditary condition, which gave rise to poor physical and mental health, as well 'less self respect, ambition and hope' and 'more crime'. Those, like impoverished Irish immigrants, afflicted with 'weak and unbalanced minds' and also very prone to intemperance, were especially vulnerable to the peculiar stresses of migration, as they were unable to adapt to 'our institutions and customs' and also suffered severely from 'home-sickness'.[63] Migration was calculated to exacerbate the pre-existing mental defects of the Irish. Jarvis obviously perceived Irish 'strangers' as 'other'. In fact, he saw them as so alien in terms of American society, he recommended in his report that separate asylums be built for them staffed by Irish people, or at least by people familiar with Irish habits. To house insane persons from 'these two races [Irish and American], with such diversity of cultivation, tastes and habits' who had always 'stood aloof from each other' when well, in the same wards was, according to him, calculated to worsen the illnesses of both.[64] Similar arguments were being applied at the time to African-American patients, for whom separate asylums were actually built. In the case of the Irish, some asylum managers tried to exclude them altogether, whereas others, such as at Massachusetts's Worcester State Asylum, decided to confine them in separate wards.[65]

However, recent re-examinations of Jarvis's statistics have shown that they do not prove what he claimed they did. He highlighted migration and 'race' as causes of the increasing rates of mental illness among the population of

Massachusetts. Yet his own figures demonstrated a higher statistical correlation between mental illness and class, especially poverty, than mental illness and place of birth; and his foreign-born Irish paupers actually had a slightly lower incidence of insanity than did his native-born American paupers.[66] The grave shortcomings of Jarvis's analysis and the negative stereotyping of the Irish and other ethnic immigrant groups in the United States and elsewhere during the nineteenth century offer salutary lessons in how prejudice can warp supposedly objective medical and scientific research.

But not all American alienists followed Jarvis into race-based theories; some advanced altogether more prosaic explanations. When contemplating the fact that, between 1849 and 1859, some 75 per cent of those committed to New York's Blackwell's Island Asylum were immigrants, of whom around 66 per cent were Irish, the hospital's resident physician suggested that the American born were more likely to care for mentally ill relatives at home, whereas immigrants lacked such family support networks. But at the same time, he also suspected that families in Ireland and other European countries might have been shipping their insane relatives overseas during 'a lucid interval'.[67] Others also suspected a deliberate attempt by Irish families and even by the lunacy inspectors themselves to export some of Ireland's many lunatics.[68]

Blackwell Island's medical superintendent, Dr. Ralph Parsons, entertained a rather different explanation for the large numbers of Irish patients in his institution—one more in line with Jarvis's thinking. In 1870 he wrote that the Irish exhibited a 'low order of intelligence', and that very many had 'imperfectly developed brains'; they were a 'most indigent class' whose physical health had been 'broken down' by hard labour, poor diet, and intemperance; should they become insane, the prognosis was therefore 'peculiarly unfavourable'.[69]

Such views were widespread, not only in the United States, but in England and Australia as well, fed by beliefs in hierarchies of races which situated the Celts, and the Irish in particular, well below the dominant Anglo-Saxon race in terms of brain capacity.[70] Charles Darwin lent his considerable authority to these ideas when, in 1871 in *The Descent of Man*, he referred to the Irish as 'reckless, degraded, often vicious', a 'careless, squalid, uninspiring' race, but one that 'multiplies like rabbits'. At the same time, he worried that 'we civilised men . . . build asylums for the imbecile, the maimed and the sick. . . . Thus the weak members of civilised societies propagate their kind . . . this must be highly injurious . . . [as it can only lead to] the degeneration of a . . . race'.[71]

EXPLAINING IRISH MENTAL ILLNESS IN ENGLAND

Some of those attempting to explain the apparently high rates of mental illness among Irish immigrants in England have pointed to the 'curious' position the Irish occupy in that country, given the long history of conflict and animosity between the two peoples. In 1989, for example, the historian David Fitzpatrick described the Irish in the mid- and late nineteenth century as 'reluctant' immigrants to Britain: most would have preferred, had they the means, to go to the United States or Australia. Instead in Britain they were a 'restless' people, 'concentrated in the most menial, casual . . . sectors of manual employment'; they 'clustered in the most congested and decaying sections of most British towns'; they were 'alienated from British culture' yet were 'not cushioned by the creation of an immigrant "community" with [an] autonomous sub-culture'. And they were characterised by high levels of pauperism, crime, and ill health.[72]

In 1992 Liam Greenslade, an English-born sociologist and psychologist of Irish descent, offered a more radical interpretation of the situation of the Irish in twentieth-century England, based especially on the work of the Algerian psychiatrist and post-colonial theorist Franz Fanon. Greenslade echoed the anti-psychiatry views of R. D. Laing and Thomas Szasz, stating that the 'vast majority of mentally ill people are not "ill" in the sense proposed by the medical model of illness and its social practices'. Such people were, according to Greenslade, the 'physical manifestation' of the 'oppression, contradictions and pathologies in the society in which they live'. On this point he was in agreement with Scheper-Hughes. Turning to Ireland, he argued that the country, like many other British colonies, had suffered 'violence, oppression and expropriation' over centuries and, at the time he was writing, part of it was 'still engaged in a struggle for liberation against British imperialism'.[73] To Greenslade, then, the Irish were in effect 'forced' immigrants, driven from their homeland by British mis-rule. But whether at home or working as immigrants in England, they were liable to experience the insidious and destructive effects of colonialism.

Fanon had argued that colonialism had not only major political and economic effects but psychological ones as well. According to him, powerless colonial subjects were forced to turn their anger at the coloniser in upon themselves, and thus they experienced a sense of inferiority, worthlessness, and dependence. Nor was leaving the colonial society a solution. Indeed, immigration only made the situation worse, for the colonised then had to make their way in the world of the coloniser, largely cut off from their own kind.[74] Greenslade applied such theories to the Irish in England. Following Fanon's lead and echoing some of Fitzpatrick's remarks about the nineteenth century, he argued that the Irish were prevented from 'forming a stable cultural identity': they could not fully preserve their Irish identity in a non-Irish society, yet the English regarded them as an inferior 'other', so they could not fully embrace Englishness either.[75] They were thus left as deeply conflicted people in a hostile world. Little wonder, then, that so many of them had succumbed to mental illness.

During the second half of the twentieth century the international literature on migration and mental illness was much influenced by the work of O. Ödegaard. In a key study published in 1932 Ödegaard investigated psychiatric admission rates in his native Norway and among Norwegian immigrants in the United States, and he found that the immigrants had significantly higher rates. This led him to consider two hypotheses, usually known as 'social selection' and 'social causation', or 'stress'. The selection hypothesis proposes that the mentally unstable are more likely to emigrate; the stress hypothesis proposes that the trauma of migration and re-settlement can produce mental illness. Ödegaard, like some nineteenth-century alienists, favoured selection as an explanation because his study had suggested that immigrants tended to be discontented people, and few became ill immediately upon arrival.[76]

Greenslade dismissed both these hypotheses as inadequate to explain the high rates of mental hospital admission among the Irish in Britain. They were unconvincing because a study conducted by Cochrane and Stopes-Roe in the early 1970s had shown that whereas Irish immigrants' rates of first admission were significantly higher in England and Wales than the native-born rates—more than double in the case of men—they were still lower than the rates then prevailing in Ireland. This contradicted the selection hypothesis, which suggested that the immigrants should have had higher admission rates than the Irish at home, as was found in Ödegaard's Norwegian study. In addition, the longer immigrants lived in England and Wales, the more likely they were to be admitted. This contradicted the stress hypothesis for, according to it, newly arrived immigrants should have had higher admission rates.[77]

But instead of dismissing selection and stress in favour of a post-colonial explanation, as Greenslade did, Cochrane and Stopes-Roe had actually claimed that both were significant. Other, more recent researchers have also argued that a wide range of factors must have been at play in order to produce the consistently poor mental and physical health that is characteristic of Irish immigrants in England.[78]

Patricia Walls, in her important studies of the mental health of Irish communities in turn-of-the-century London, offered five possible explanations for poor Irish mental health. First was selection, in other words, the theory that the most vulnerable members of a community are more likely to emigrate. Second came stress, that is, the argument that the migration experience itself is traumatic, especially for young, single Irish people from close-knit rural communities. Third in Walls's list was material deprivation, which refers to the fact that large numbers of Irish immigrants have been poor, often engaged in unskilled and insecure jobs and living in substandard accommodation. Then there was colonialism, meaning that the Irish in Britain suffer from identity problems as a result of their colonial past. Fifth and last was racism, that is, the deeply engrained and long-standing anti-Irish prejudices which exist in England.[79]

Walls accepted both selection and stress as important factors; added poverty, which many nineteenth-century observers of Ireland had highlighted;

and as well Greenslade's arguments about colonialism. In addition, she included racism, or prejudice against the Irish as a group, which had been so evident in England and the United States during the nineteenth century and was heightened in England during the late twentieth century due to the Troubles in Northern Ireland.

The factors that Walls highlighted reflect approaches taken by what is called cross- or trans-cultural psychiatry, which deals with mental health problems in different cultures, and especially among immigrant ethnic groups.[80] Since the World Health Organisation's 1979 International Pilot Study on Schizophrenia found that schizophrenia was more of a problem in 'developed' than 'developing' countries, there has been a great deal of debate about and research into the cultural contexts of mental illnesses and their diagnosis.[81] The work of Walls and also Greenslade marks a step towards trying to understand how the different and sometimes antagonistic cultures of Ireland and England affected Irish mental health.

EXPLAINING IRISH MENTAL ILLNESS IN AUSTRALIA

Australia's leading late nineteenth-century alienist, English-born Frederic Norton Manning, was convinced that the Irish were deliberately shipping their lunatics overseas, and thus the answer to the problem of the large numbers of Irish immigrants in colonial asylums was restrictive migration legislation.[82] But like his friend Daniel Hack Tuke, Manning also believed that there was a link between poverty and madness. According to him, the poor were largely composed of people who could not cope with the stresses of modern civilisation, and the large families of the poor inevitably inherited the defective temperaments of their parents.[83]

A rather more nuanced analysis was offered by one of Manning's protégés, Dr. Chisholm Ross, who was his successor as medical superintendent of Sydney's Gladesville Asylum. During the years between 1878 and 1887, according to Ross, 1 in 93 of the Irish-born population of New South Wales had been committed to Gladesville, compared to only 1 in 579 of the Australian-born population. But Ross cautioned against jumping to conclusions on the basis of such figures, for he recognised that those born overseas and the white Australian-born population were different: in particular, there were far more children among the Australians. As children were rarely committed to asylums, this made statistical comparisons on the basis of general population figures questionable: like was not being compared with like. Yet at the same time, Ross described the Irish inmates of his asylum as 'altogether disproportionate' in number and noted that the 'excess' insanity among the Irish had been 'very variously' explained. He believed that the Irish were characterised by an 'abeyance of will power' and that they were much 'more demonstrative' than other nations. When insane they were therefore more difficult to manage and so their families were more likely to commit them. In terms of their disorders, the largest number by far, 38 per cent, were suffering from 'paranoia' and 'delusions'. Ross believed that 'foreigners' were generally prone to paranoia, for being in a new and strange country bred suspicion and 'false beliefs'.[84] Ross was in effect employing a stress hypothesis, arguing that migration was calculated to produce psychosis, but at the same time he selected the Irish as a group different from other 'nations' and more prone to mental breakdown and committal.[85]

Patrick O'Farrell, the leading twentieth-century historian of the Irish in Australia, did not have a great deal to say on the topic of Irish mental health. He was, however, convinced that there was 'no simple explanation' for the high Irish committal rates during the late nineteenth century. Although he referred to a number of factors, like Ross, he endorsed a stress hypothesis. According to O'Farrell, 'the migration process itself commonly induced some degree of trauma, placing on the individual expectations and pressure to succeed, adapt, make decisions, which may have been beyond the capacities of those used to the lesser demands of Irish situations'. That some collapsed under these strains was not surprising, especially if they found themselves 'isolated' and 'friendless' in Australia. Like Manning, O'Farrell also thought poverty important, though in practical ways. He claimed that it was 'impossible to disentangle mental illness and poverty', yet he did make some attempt to do so by pointing out that asylums were largely pauper institutions because the poor were probably least able to care for mentally ill relatives at home. This would account, in part at least, for the high committal rates found among the Irish. At the same time, though, he again followed Manning in believing that Irish families 'deliberately dispatched to Australia relatives with mental problems'. [86]

As we have already seen, Trevor McClaughlin produced figures seemingly showing that Irish women were over-represented in eastern Australian asylums at the beginning of the twentieth century by a factor of three to five. But McClaughlin recognised, as Ross had a century earlier, that the age structure of the immigrant population was very different from that of the native-born population: whereas adults comprised about 90 per cent of most immigrant populations, they were only about 50 per cent of the Australian-born population. This makes statistical comparisons unreliable and tends to inflate Irish committal rates. As well, the Irish were more likely to be single adults, and again this increased their chances of committal, for the majority of asylum inmates were unmarried. Nevertheless, like Ross, McClaughlin did accept that the Irish were over-represented in asylums to some degree at least. He dealt particularly with women and, among other things, pointed out that Irish women often married older men and thus endured long widowhoods. Elderly working-class widows were especially vulnerable to psychiatric institutionalisation. And like O'Farrell, McClaughlin stressed poverty, quoting a number of instances of Irish women entering mental hospitals in a destitute and emaciated state.[87]

The relatively few Australian studies undertaken have therefore tended to highlight the fact that Irish immigrants were an 'at risk' population in terms of committal to nineteenth-century asylums because most were poor, single, and adult, and asylums were institutions catering largely for these types of people. And indeed, being an immigrant was in itself another major risk factor, for throughout most of the second half of the nineteenth century Australian asylums were largely populated by immigrants.[88]

CONCLUSIONS

As Dr. Chisholm Ross remarked in Melbourne in 1889, the apparently high rates of mental illness among Irish immigrants have been 'variously explained'. The same is true of the apparently high rates among the Irish in Ireland. There is no clear consensus of opinion among psychiatrists, anthropologists, and historians about the reasons for this situation. This is perhaps not surprising as no one factor, or even small group of factors, could possibly account for a phenomenon so widespread—one evident for well over a century in a number of different countries. Many variables must be borne in mind and care taken in assessing them, for some variables may be time and place specific whereas others are not. First, however, we must always remember that psychiatric committal rates are not an accurate measure of the mental health of any community—and particularly not during the nineteenth century. There were many reasons why people were institutionalised, some of them having little to do with insanity. Thus we should avoid the trap, which many earlier commentators fell into, of using admission statistics as reliable measures of the incidence of mental illness among a particular group. Second, the statistics on Irish committals and admissions, and especially their relationship to the general Irish-born population and to other populations, require thorough scrutiny. Comparisons are vital, but we must always ensure that we are comparing like with like. It may well be that the apparent over-representation of the Irish is in some, if not many, instances largely a statistical artefact that does not reflect an actual difference.

A narrow focus only on the Irish may have its problems as well. Is place of birth the key variable?[89] Many studies of the Irish in both the nineteenth and twentieth centuries identified their poverty rather than their ethnicity as the crucial causal factor in their institutionalisation, although there was disagreement over exactly how the poverty factor operated. Yet ethnicity could be significant in indirect ways. As an immigrant ethnic minority, the Irish were subjected to stereotyping, prejudice, and discrimination, which were especially severe in England and during the nineteenth century in the United States. Hostility to them as an ethnic group and often also a religious group was important in that it contributed to their marginalisation and poverty.

Other immigrant ethnic and religious minorities in various countries have shared the Irish experience of poverty and prejudice and some—though by no means all—have manifested high psychiatric admission rates as well.[90] This is where the insights of trans-cultural psychiatry can be valuable and where the selection and stress hypotheses also remain relevant. It is not only that people belong to a different ethnic and religious group or that they are poor which is important, but that they are newcomers—or 'strangers', as Edward Jarvis preferred to call them. Many immigrants are discontented with their place of birth and leave with high hopes of a better life elsewhere. Some are able to fulfil their dreams to their own satisfaction, but some find that their new homes do not live up to their expectations at all: instead of living a dream, they find themselves trapped in a nightmare. Migration inevitably involves risk-taking behaviour, and immigrants gamble not only on their economic prospects but also on their mental well-being.

ACKNOWLEDGMENTS

I would like to thank the Australian Research Council for funding the research upon which this chapter is based, and also Dr Dianne Hall for her research assistance.

NOTES

1. R. Howitt, *Impressions of Australia Felix, during Four Years' Residence in that Colony* (London: Longman, Brown, Green and Longmans, 1845), p. 205.
2. N. Scheper-Hughes, *Saints, Scholars and Schizophrenics: Mental Illness in Rural Ireland* (Berkeley: University of California Press, 1979), p. 71.
3. Due to constraints on space, this chapter will focus only on the United States, England, and Australia, but studies undertaken of Canada and New Zealand suggest a similar picture as regards the mental health of Irish immigrants. See D. Wright, J. Moran, and S. Gouglas, 'The confinement of the insane in Victorian Canada: The Hamilton and Toronto asylums, c. 1861–91', in R. Porter and D. Wright (eds.), *The Confinement of the Insane: International Perspectives, 1800–1965* (Cambridge: Cambridge University Press, 2003), pp. 100–28; A. McCarthy, 'Ethnicity, migration and the lunatic asylum in early twentieth-century Auckland', *Social History of Medicine*, 21 (2008), pp. 47–65.
4. H. C. Burdett, *Hospitals and Asylums of the World: Their Origin, History, Construction, Administration, Management and Legislation*, vol. 1 (London: J. and A. Churchill, 1891), pp. 51–77.
5. M. Finnane, *Insanity and the Insane in Post-Famine Ireland* (London: Croom Helm, 1981), p. 227; *The Sixty-Second Annual Report of the Inspectors of Lunacy (Ireland), being for the Year ending 31st December 1912* (Dublin: E. Ponsonby, 1913), pp. 5–6.
6. Finnane, *Insanity and the Insane in Post-Famine Ireland*, pp. 224, 233.
7. E. F. Torrey and J. Miller, *The Invisible Plague: The Rise of Mental Illness from 1750 to the Present* (New Brunswick, NJ: Rutgers University Press, 2001), pp. 346–50.

34 Elizabeth Malcolm

8. For Northern Ireland, see P. Prior, *Mental Health and Politics in Northern Ireland* (Aldershot: Ashgate, 1993).
9. A. O'Hare and D. Walsh, *Activities of Irish Psychiatric Hospitals and Units, 1965–9* (Dublin: Medico-Social Research Board, 1969), pp. 14–17, 28.
10. A. O'Hare and D. Walsh, *Irish Psychiatric Hospital Census, 1971* (Dublin: Medico-Social Research Board, 1974), pp. 9–11.
11. H. Brody, *Inishkillane: Change and Decline in the West of Ireland* (Harmondsworth: Penguin Books, 1974), p. 100.
12. D. Walsh, 'The ups and downs of schizophrenia in Ireland', *Irish Journal of Psychiatry*, 13 (1992), pp. 12–16.
13. E. F. Torrey, *Schizophrenia and Civilization* (New York: Aronson, 1980), p. 131.
14. E. F. Torrey, 'Prevalence studies in schizophrenia', *British Journal of Psychiatry*, 150 (1987), p. 602.
15. J. M. Eagles, 'Is schizophrenia disappearing?', *British Journal of Psychiatry*, 158 (1991), pp. 834–35. Others have argued that it is increasing: see Torrey and Miller, *The Invisible Plague*, pp. 1–5.
16. J. L. Waddington and H. A. Youssef, 'Evidence for a gender-specific decline in schizophrenia in rural Ireland over a 50-year period', *British Journal of Psychiatry*, 164 (1994), pp. 171–76.
17. P. Fitzgerald and B. Lambkin, *Migration in Irish History, 1607–2007* (Basingstoke: Palgrave Macmillan, 2008), pp. 251–55.
18. D. Hall and E. Malcolm, 'Diaspora, gender and the Irish', *Australasian Journal of Irish Studies*, 8 (2008/9), pp. 6–10.
19. D. J. Rothman, *The Discovery of the Asylum: Social Order and Disorder in the New Republic* (Boston: Little, Brown, 1971), pp. 271–73, 283–85.
20. G. N. Grob, *Edward Jarvis and the Medical World of Nineteenth-Century America* (Knoxville: University of Tennessee Press, 1978), p. 2.
21. N. Dain, *Concepts of Insanity in the United States, 1789–1865* (New Brunswick, NJ: Rutgers University Press, 1964), pp. 99–104, 129–30; J. W. Fox, 'Irish immigrants, pauperism, and insanity in 1854 Massachusetts', *Social Science History*, 15 (1991), pp. 315–36; A. Vander Stoep and B. Link, 'Social class, ethnicity and mental illness: The importance of being more than earnest', *American Journal of Public Health*, 88 (1998), pp. 1396–1402.
22. 'Supplement to the fifty-fourth report of the Inspectors of Lunatics on the district, criminal, and private lunatic asylums in Ireland; being a special report on the alleged increase of insanity', *Journal of Mental Science*, 53 (1907), p. 160.
23. Scheper-Hughes, *Saints, Scholars and Schizophrenics*, pp. 72–73.
24. For the Irish in a London asylum during 1843–53, see V. Bhavsar and D. Bhugra, 'Bethlem's Irish: Migration and distress in nineteenth-century London', *History of Psychiatry*, 20 (2009), pp. 184–98.
25. E. Malcolm, '"A most miserable looking object": The Irish in English asylums, 1851–1901: Migration, poverty and prejudice', in J. Belchem and K. Tenfelde (eds.), *Irish and Polish Migration in Comparative Perspective* (Essen: Klartext Verlag, 2003), pp. 125–26.
26. R. Cochrane, 'Mental illness in immigrants to England and Wales: An analysis of mental hospital admissions, 1971', *Social Psychiatry and Psychiatric Epidemiology*, 12 (1977), pp. 23–35.
27. M. Tilki, 'The mental health of Irish people in Britain', Mind Fact Sheet, 2008, available at: http://www.mind.org.uk/help/people_groups_and_communities/mental_health_of_Irish_people_in_britain (accessed 25 September 2010).
28. P. J. Bracken, L. Greenslade, B. Griffin, and M. Smyth, 'Mental health and ethnicity: An Irish dimension', *British Journal of Psychiatry*, 172 (1998), pp. 103–5.

29. M. Campbell, *Ireland's New World: Immigrants, Politics and Society in the United States and Australia, 1815–1922* (Madison: University of Wisconsin Press, 2008), p. 87.

30. One important point to emerge from recent research into the history of nineteenth-century Australian asylums is that Irish involvement in the mental health system went well beyond their role as patients: the Irish also figured prominently among the doctors and attendants who staffed psychiatric institutions and among the police who played a key role in the Australian committal process. The Irish as managers of mental health services in the diaspora is a topic that requires further investigation. L. Monk, *Attending Madness: At Work in the Australian Colonial Asylum* (Amsterdam: Rodopi, 2008); D. Wilson, *The Beat: Policing a Victorian City* (Melbourne: Circa, 2006).

31. F. N. Manning, 'President's address: Psychology section', in *Intercolonial Medical Congress of Australasia. Transactions: Second Session, Melbourne, January 1889* (Melbourne: Stillwell, 1889), p. 818, table IV.

32. In 1911 Dr. William Dawson, one of the Irish inspectors of lunatic asylums, identified the highest committal rate in Ireland as 9.2 per 1,000, not in the west, but in County Waterford. W. R. Dawson, 'The presidential address on the relation between the geographical distribution of insanity and that of certain social and other conditions in Ireland', *Journal of Mental Science*, 57 (1911), pp. 578–79.

33. For an important exception, see M. Finnane, 'Asylums, families and the state', *History Workshop*, 20 (1985), pp. 134–48. For general studies that mention Irish asylum inmates, see C. Coleborne and D. MacKinnon (eds.), *'Madness' in Australia: Histories, Heritage and the Asylum* (Brisbane: University of Queensland Press, 2003); C. Coleborne, *Reading 'Madness': Gender and Difference in the Colonial Asylum in Victoria, Australia, 1848–88* (Perth: Network, 2007).

34. E. Malcolm, '"Our fevered past": Irish immigrants in a colonial lunatic asylum during the Australian gold rushes, 1848–69', in P. Prior (ed.), *Asylums Mental Health Care and the Irish: Historical Essays, 1800–1910* (Dublin: Irish Academic Press, forthcoming).

35. T. McClaughlin, '"I was nowhere else": Casualties of colonisation in eastern Australia during the second half of the nineteenth century', in T. McClaughlin (ed.), *Irish Women in Colonial Australia* (Sydney: Allen and Unwin, 1998), p. 156.

36. S. Garton, *Medicine and Madness: A Social History of Insanity in New South Wales, 1880–1940* (Sydney: UNSW Press, 1988), pp. 103–4.

37. F. A. Whitlock, 'Migration and suicide', *Medical Journal of Australia*, 2 (1971), pp. 840–48. Most immigrant groups in the mid-1960s had suicide rates around 50 per cent higher than the Australian-born population; British, New Zealand, and Polish immigrants, in addition to the Irish, had rates in excess of those of their home populations. R. Broome, *The Victorians: Arriving* (Sydney: Fairfax, Syme and Weldon, 1984), p. 215.

38. For parallels between emigration and committal, see E. Malcolm, '"The house of strident shadows": The asylum, the family and emigration in post-famine Ireland', in E. Malcolm and G. Jones (eds.), *Medicine, Disease and the State in Ireland, 1650–1940* (Cork: Cork University Press, 1999), pp. 185–86.

39. E. Malcolm, '"Ireland's crowded madhouses": The institutional confinement of the insane in nineteenth- and twentieth-century Ireland', in Porter and Wright (eds.), *The Confinement of the Insane*, p. 321.

40. 'The forty-third report (with appendices) of the Inspectors of Lunatics (Ireland)', *Journal of Mental Science*, 41 (1895), pp. 324–25.

41. *Forty-Ninth Report of the Inspectors of Lunatics (Ireland), for the Year ending 31st December, 1899* (Dublin: Alex Thom, 1900), p. xiv.
42. 'The forty-third report (with appendices) of the Inspectors of Lunatics (Ireland)', p. 325.
43. T. Drapes, 'On the alleged increase of insanity in Ireland', *Journal of Mental Science*, 40 (1894), pp. 533–36. Drapes did, however, agree with the inspectors that lunatics were accumulating in Irish asylums, and he argued this was 'pre-eminently' caused by low Irish asylum death rates. English asylums had significantly higher death rates due largely to general paralysis of the insane caused by syphilis, which was endemic in English cities. In rural Ireland, on the other hand, syphilis was rare.
44. Ibid., p. 536.
45. D. Hack Tuke, 'Increase of insanity in Ireland', *Journal of Mental Science*, 40 (1894), pp. 551–52.
46. Ibid., p. 555.
47. H. M. Henry, *Our Lady's Psychiatric Hospital, Cork* (Cork: Haven, 1989), p. 240.
48. Dawson, 'The presidential address', p. 587.
49. Malcolm, '"Ireland's crowded madhouses"', p. 328.
50. Finnane, *Insanity and the Insane in Post-Famine Ireland*. The thesis was completed at the Australian National University in Canberra. MacDonagh was a leading historian of nineteenth-century Irish political history.
51. O. MacDonagh, *Early Victorian Government, 1830–70* (London: Weidenfeld and Nicolson, 1977), pp. 180–81, 186–87.
52. Finnane, *Insanity and the Insane in Post-Famine Ireland*, pp. 14, 222–23.
53. Torrey and Miller, *The Invisible Plague*, pp. 300–13.
54. J. Robins, *Fools and Mad: A History of the Insane in Ireland* (Dublin: Institute of Public Administration, 1986), pp. 109–11.
55. Ibid., pp. 203, 201.
56. C. M. Arensberg and S. T. Kimball, *Family and Community in Ireland*, 3rd ed. (Ennis. Co. Clare: Clasp, 2001), pp. 116–17.
57. Brody, *Inishkillane*, pp. 4–16, 100–7.
58. Scheper-Hughes, *Saints, Scholars and Schizophrenics*, pp. 4, 13, 191.
59. E. F. Torrey, M. McGuire, A. O'Hare, D. Walsh, and M. P. Spellman, 'Endemic psychosis in western Ireland', *American Journal of Psychiatry*, 141 (1984), pp. 966–70.
60. This study has attracted a good deal of criticism: see, for example, T. J. Fahy, 'Is psychosis endemic in western Ireland?', *American Journal of Psychiatry*, 142 (1985), pp. 998–99.
61. S. J. Gould, *The Mismeasure of Man*, rev. ed. (New York: W. W. Norton, 1996), pp. 87, 98–99; D. J. Kevles, *In the Name of Eugenics: Genetics and the Uses of Human Heredity* (Harmondsworth: Penguin, 1985), pp. 76, 132, 134.
62. D. T. Knobel, *Paddy and the Republic: Ethnicity and Nationality in Ante-Bellum America* (Middletown, CT: Wesleyan University Press, 1986), pp. 84–90; N. Ignatiev, *How the Irish Became White* (New York and London: Routledge, 1995), p.162.
63. 'Proceedings of the twelfth annual meeting of the Association of Medical Superintendents of American Institutions for the Insane', *American Journal of Insanity*, 14 (1857), p. 103.
64. Quoted in Vander Steep and Link, 'Social class, ethnicity and mental illness', pp. 1399–1400.
65. Dain, *Concepts of Insanity in the United States*, pp. 100–1.
66. Vander Steep and Link, 'Social class, ethnicity and mental illness', p. 1398.

67. A. M. Kraut, 'Illness and medical care among Irish immigrants in antebellum New York', in R. H. Bayor and T. J. Meagher (eds.), *The New York Irish* (Baltimore, MD: Johns Hopkins University Press, 1996), p. 159.
68. These suspicions were not without foundation: see P. Prior, 'Emigrants or exiles? Female ex-prisoners leaving Ireland, 1850–1900', *Australasian Journal of Irish Studies*, 8 (2008/9), pp. 34–43.
69. 'Proceedings of the Association for Medical Superintendents', *American Journal of Insanity*, 27 (1870), pp. 158–59.
70. S. Garner, *Racism in the Irish Experience* (London: Pluto, 2004), pp. 123–29.
71. C. Darwin, *The Descent of Man, and Selection in Relation to Sex*, reprint 2nd ed. (London: Penguin, 2004), pp. 164, 159; P. B. Rich, 'Social Darwinism, anthropology and English perspectives of the Irish, 1867–1900', *History of European Ideas*, 19 (1994), pp. 777–85.
72. D. Fitzpatrick, '"A curious middle place": The Irish in Britain, 1871–1921', in R. Swift and S. Gilley (eds.), *The Irish in Britain, 1815–1939* (London: Pinter, 1989), pp. 10, 15–16, 25–29.
73. L. Greenslade, 'White skins, white masks: Psychological distress among the Irish in Britain', in P. O'Sullivan (ed.), *The Irish World Wide*, vol. 2, *The Irish in the New Communities* (Leicester: Leicester University Press, 1992), pp. 202–3.
74. F. Fanon, *The Wretched of the Earth*, trans. C. Farrington (Harmondsworth: Penguin, 1967), pp. 31–32, 42, 200.
75. Greenslade, 'White skins, white masks', p. 215.
76. O. Ödegaard, 'Emigration and insanity: A study of mental disease among the Norwegian-born population in Minnesota', *Acta Psychiatrica et Neurologica Supplementum*, 4 (1932), pp. 1–206; R. Littlewood and M. Lipsedge, *Aliens and Alienists: Ethnic Minorities and Psychiatry* (Harmondsworth: Penguin, 1982), pp. 88–90.
77. Greenslade, 'White skins, white masks', pp. 209–10; R. Cochrane and M. Stopes-Roe, 'Psychological disturbance in Ireland, in England and in Irish emigrants to England: A comparative study', *Economic and Social Review*, 10 (1979), pp. 301–20.
78. P. J. Bracken and P. O'Sullivan, 'The invisibility of Irish migrants in British health research', *Irish Studies Review*, 9 (2001), pp. 41–51; E. Malcolm, *Elderly Return Migration from Britain to Ireland: A Preliminary Study*, Report No. 44 (Dublin: National Council for the Elderly, 1996).
79. P. Walls, *Researching Irish Mental Health: Issues and Evidence: A Study of the Mental Health of the Irish Community in Haringey* (London: Muintearas, 1996); P. Walls, *The 2006 Irish in Brent Health Profile Report* (London: Brent Irish Advisory Service, 2006).
80. J. Bains, 'Race, culture and psychiatry: A history of trans-cultural psychiatry', *History of Psychiatry*, 16 (2005), pp. 139–54.
81. A. Kleinman, 'Anthropology and psychiatry: The role of culture in cross-cultural research on illness', *British Journal of Psychiatry*, 151 (1987), pp. 447–54; R. B. Edgerton and A. Cohen, 'Culture and schizophrenia: The DOSMD challenge', *British Journal of Psychiatry*, 164 (1994), pp. 222–31.
82. For a more extensive discussion of Manning's influence, see C. Coleborne, *Madness in the Family: Insanity and Institutions in the Australasian Colonial World, 1860–1914* (Basingstoke: Palgrave Macmillan, 2010), pp. 20–23, 32–40, 68–70.
83. Garton, *Medicine and Madness*, pp. 104–5.
84. C. Ross, 'Race and insanity in New South Wales, 1878–87', in *Intercolonial Medical Congress of Australasia*, pp. 851–52, 855–56.

85. While not linking migration to any particular illness, many modern psychiatrists have agreed with Ross in identifying paranoia or a sense of persecution as a feature of immigrant psychosis. Littlewood and Lipsedge, *Aliens and Alienists*, pp. 90–91.
86. P. J. O'Farrell, *The Irish in Australia, 1788 to the Present*, 3rd ed. (Sydney: UNSW Press, 2000), pp. 169–70.
87. McClaughlin, '"I was nowhere else"', pp. 150, 154–61.
88. Broome, *The Victorians: Arriving*, p. 126.
89. For a recent attempt to assess the relative contributions of ethnicity and socio-economic factors to the poor general health of the Irish in England, see M. Clucas, 'The Irish health disadvantage in England: Contribution of structure and identity components of Irish ethnicity', *Ethnicity and Health*, 14 (2009), pp. 553–73.
90. R. Cochrane and S. S. Bal, 'Migration and schizophrenia: An examination of five hypotheses', *Social Psychiatry and Psychiatric Epidemiology*, 22 (1987), pp. 181–91.

3 Migration, Madness, and the Celtic Fringe

A Comparison of Irish and Scottish Admissions to Four Canadian Mental Hospitals, c. 1841–91

David Wright and Tom Themeles

INTRODUCTION

John Prindiville was 'dead from his waist down'. Or so the fifty-six-year-old Irishman confided to Dr. Griffen, the medical practitioner who was called to certify him as a lunatic in November 1887 in Wentworth County, Ontario. The married Catholic carpenter and father of three was described in his admission documents as having lived a 'sober and industrious' life both before and after his migration to Canada. But clearly he had been troubled by his intermittent unemployment, particularly during the previous winter. For the month previous Prindiville had become preoccupied with unusual bodily (somatic) delusions such as imagining 'that he has no use of his bowels or urinary organs'. Little is known of the various attempts by his family and local community to accommodate his increasingly erratic behaviour. We do know that he began refusing to go outside due to 'enemies in waiting' who wanted to 'do him injury'. The incidents precipitating institutional committal to the Hamilton Lunatic Asylum appear to have been his recent attempt to 'get [an] axe and to kill himself' and his 'repeated threats to kill his family'. Searching for a possible cause, the doctors certifying him alluded to the fact that his sister, who had emigrated from Ireland to Australia, had also been insane, a not-so-subtle hint of hereditary illness. Prindiville passed away on 15 June 1888, ostensibly as a result of 'heart disease'.[1]

Prindiville was but one of almost 3,000 Irish immigrants who found themselves confined in lunatic asylums in Victorian Ontario. In some respects, this is hardly noteworthy, as the Irish constituted, at mid-century, the largest non-indigenous group in Ontario.[2] But the presence of Irish and other 'foreign' patients became a major public policy controversy as the mental hospitals grew dramatically in size and cost. By the end of the nineteenth century, Canadian commentators were decrying the explosive growth of public lunatic asylums and the huge costs associated with their maintenance. C. K. Clarke, the paterfamilias of Canadian psychiatry at the time, would lament that 'an enormous current of alien degenerates' would ruin the young

Dominion.[3] Much of the anger was directed at immigrants who, critics were claiming, were innately mentally enfeebled and clogging up what were supposed to be therapeutic institutions. The assumption that the rate of insanity was being fuelled by unrestricted immigration fed a growing eugenic discourse in Canada that became enshrined in turn-of-the-century legislation ensuring mental testing and the repatriation of feebleminded and insane new arrivals to their countries of origin.[4] This case study of migration, madness, and institutional confinement provides an important socio-demographic context leading up to this debate and sheds some important light (and raises further questions) on the complex interaction of poverty, migration, mental health, and institutional confinement in the past.

Migration has always loomed large in the historiography of the lunatic asylum. Gerald Grob first wrote about this phenomenon four decades ago. In his study of the patients in the Worcester mental hospital in Massachusetts, he suggested that, by 1851, more than 40 per cent of the patients were foreign born, a figure that was higher than one would expect from the surrounding communities.[5] The rapid construction of purpose-built asylums for the insane coincided in many European and North American jurisdictions with explosive population growth and urbanisation. The commingling of peoples in close proximity to each other, yet who did not share a common past or community understanding, would be bound to heighten tensions and anxieties. In addition, the urban landscape made strange behaviour more visible, and in settings where individuals were less likely to know each other (or one's family), such behaviour would be perceived as threatening. As Grob summarised in one of his first works on the rise of the mental hospital in the United States:

> Such demographic changes exercised a profound impact on the issue of mental illness. The care of the insane proved to be far more complex in an urban than a rural environment. Not only was there a far greater concentration in the number of cases of insanity, but more people were able to witness and feel threatened by the aberrant and seemingly bizarre behaviour of insane persons.[6]

Pursuing a similar line of inquiry, John Walton found that it was the dislocating process of urbanisation that undermined the family and kin resources of those who had left the countryside for work in the developing English industrial city of Lancaster. The interplay of industrialisation and rural depopulation thus placed strains on households which, in turn, became eager to find non-domiciliary options to care for their relatives. Walton uncovered ambiguous findings, with admissions from the 'emerging conurbations' of Lancashire over-represented when compared to the adult population of the 1851 census but also that many 'agricultural districts [also] provided a higher proportion or admissions, relative to population, than did these industrial centres'.[7]

Richard Fox, in his landmark study of the institutionalisation of the insane in late nineteenth-century California, also identified migration as an important factor in the complex process of institutionalisation. He concluded that there was a disproportionately higher rate of foreign-born inmates (and male inmates) when compared to the regular population. Like Walton, he hypothesised that this was because they were less likely to have networks of kin support: 'for it seems likely that disturbed individuals without relatives in the city would be more liable to come to the attention of the court'.[8] Stephen Garton and Harriet Deacon also discovered that new immigrants were over-represented in the asylums of New South Wales and South Africa, respectively.[9] The question of new immigrants in lunatic asylums, however, was inextricably linked with gender and marital status. As Fox cautioned in his case study of California, as foreign-born individuals were older than the general population into which they migrated and were disproportionately men, the raw figures may exaggerate the 'foreign' contribution to increasing rates of insanity.[10] Yet Bronwyn Labrum demonstrated, in her study of the Auckland Asylum, that men were more than 50 per cent more likely to be committed even when one factors in the over-abundance of men in that colony.[11] Ultimately, then, the reality of institutional confinement in settler societies was a complex interaction of gender, geography, marital status, household structure, and of course the psychological and behavioural status of the individuals concerned.

Although most researchers have identified migration as an important factor in the vulnerability of individuals being confined in mental hospitals, there have been some disagreements over the emphasis on the relationship between urban life and the rise of the asylum. Andrew Scull, for example, challenged Gerald Grob's connection between the rise of industrial cities and institutional confinement by reminding readers that the first institutions in Britain and the United States were established in predominantly rural and less demographically explosive counties and states. He identified Nottinghamshire and South Carolina as Anglo-American examples of rural jurisdictions that were, paradoxically, at the forefront of asylum construction. Scull argued that it was not the rise of the industrial city per se—what Grob had identified as the volatile commingling of strangers—that led inevitably to the mental hospital as a product of the industrial city; rather, the 'roots of institutional demand lay in the advent of a mature capitalist economy'.[12] For Scull it was the ethos of capitalism—which placed emphasis on individualism and economic productivity—that was taking hold in rural *and* urban jurisdictions that spelt the end of the previously compassionate attitudes to the mentally ill and other dependent members of society.[13]

A recurring theme in the inter-relationship between migration and madness has been the symbolic role occupied by the Irish. The Irish had the dubious distinction of having the highest reported rate of institutional incarceration at home while simultaneously constituting the most conspicuous of inmate populations in settler societies. Contemporaries, as well as historians, have repeatedly drawn attention to the remarkable number of Irish in public luna-tic asylums in England, Australia, and New Zealand. Mark Finnane, one of the first to hypothesise as to why this was the case, suggested that the great emigration of the Irish during and following the Great Famine may well have left dependent family members with fewer household and familial resources to care for them, thus accounting for the very high rates of incarceration in their home communities.[14] Because the Irish themselves were considered to be a different 'race' from the English, some authors have suggested that ethnic stereotypes played into the attitudes of judicial authorities. Elizabeth Malcolm has comprehensively summarised the arguments that might have, independently or in conjunction with each other, led to excessively high rates of Irish pauper lunatics. Factors identified by a range of authors include the impact of migration; poverty, particularly the extreme privation associated with the Famine; prejudice against the Irish both as Irish and as Catholics; and most controversially, an innate Irish predisposition to insanity.[15]

These historical arguments can be usefully explored looking at the experience of patients in Canadian asylums, institutions which were not immune to a heavy Irish presence. Indeed, research two decades ago by Wendy Mitchinson and Cheryl Krasnik Warsh observed the high number of Irish-born admissions to the Toronto Asylum in the 1840s, 1850s, and 1860s, and to the London Asylum in the 1860s.[16] They drew logical infer-ences about the poverty, social dislocation, and malnutrition of the Irish in the wake of the Great Famine. This chapter builds on their important work and tests some of the theses summarised by Malcolm. First, it will provide the results of a complete study of the admission registers of the four public lunatic asylums in the province (Toronto, Kingston, London, and Hamil-ton) over five decades, a database incorporating over 12,000 admissions. Second, it will broaden the analysis by juxtaposing the Irish and the Scots in an attempt to assess and disentangle the relative importance of pov-erty, migration, religion, and ethnicity. Because the Scots also emigrated to Canada in significant numbers at the same time and were also numerous in Ontario asylums, they constitute a useful group with which to compare the Irish experience. The chapter will demonstrate that the disproportionately high rates of Irish and, to a lesser extent, Scottish admissions that existed in the early decades of the asylum system in Ontario declined steadily over the second half of the nineteenth century. It will question the 'exceptionalism' of the Irish by highlighting the very similar socio-demographic characteris-tics of both Irish- and Scottish-born patients. Moreover, it will utilise medi-cal evidence from patient-level cause of death data to demonstrate that the Irish did not appear to be dying of nutritional or poverty-related causes any more than the rest of the patient population. Two variables that did with-stand the statistical analysis—age and religion—raise interesting questions as to whether the apparent over-representation of Catholics was indeed a reflection of Protestant hegemony and discrimination in Ontario or rather a proxy for the relative poverty of these nineteenth-century Irish migrants.

THE CULTURE OF ASYLUM USE AMONG
IRISH AND SCOTTISH IMMIGRANTS

In a now famous review article, Mark Finnane affirmed that the asylum should be seen 'as an institution whose role and function was mapped out by a lengthy process of popular usage and custom as much as by the legal and financial imperatives which the state erected around it'.[17] So it is appropriate to begin by examining to what extent the Irish and Scottish migrant families came from communities where the lunatic asylum, as a social institution, was part of 'popular usage and custom'. It is noteworthy that the Irish and the Scottish had left jurisdictions that, by the middle of the nineteenth century, had extensive networks of lunatic asylums already in place. We will use the date 1841 as a convenient snapshot, being both the first year of the temporary asylum in Toronto (the future Provincial Asylum) as well as a census year in Britain and, the following year, in Ontario. By 1841, Ireland had asylums in Richmond, including in order of establishment one near Dublin (1814), in Derry (1827), Limerick (1827), Belfast (1829), Carlow (1832), Ballinasloe (1833), Maryborough (1833), and Clonmel (1834). There was a pause in the 1840s until another surge of asylum construction began in the 1850s and 1860s. Although given the population of Ireland at the time, this was an impressive number of institutions by the 1840s, one must not forget that asylums were being constructed rapidly throughout the British Isles and the continent at the same time. Scotland also had eight institutions by 1841: Montrose (1782); Aberdeen (1800); Edinburgh (1813); Gartnavel, near Glasgow (1814); Dundee (1820); Perth, a.k.a. 'James Murray' (1827); Elgin (1830); and Dumfries, a.k.a. 'Crichton Royal' (1839). By contrast, English patients, who are not the subject of this chapter, were served by nineteen county institutions by 1845; France, meanwhile, had made all seventy *départements* responsible for asylums for their poor insane under the Lunatics Act of 1838, dozens of which were constructed in the 1840s. This is all to suggest that many Irish were familiar with the asylum system by mid-century, but so too, for that matter, were the Scottish, English, and the French.[18]

The historiography of Irish migration to Canada in the nineteenth century has long been influenced by stereotypes about the Irish experience in 'America'. The long-standing narrative of the Irish immigrant depicts unskilled, uneducated, and destitute Irish Catholics fleeing an impoverished island that was suffering under direct rule of the British from 1801. Emigration from Ireland, according to this narrative, was accelerated by the Great Famine of 1845–52, precipitating a mass exodus, particularly to the United States. The Irish became synonymous with immigration and the hardscrabble life of nineteenth-century urban America. The reality, at least as far as Upper Canada (Ontario) goes, differed significantly from this stereotype. As Donald Akenson's path-breaking study *The Irish in Ontario* has demonstrated, Irish migrants to Upper Canada predated the

Famine, migrating to Ontario throughout all decades of the nineteenth century. Nor were they unskilled, poor, or even overwhelmingly Catholic. In many cases, these Irish in Ontario were disproportionately Protestant, skilled, educated, relatively well-off families who settled in the countryside. In fact, according to Akenson, even at the time of the Great Famine, the Irish in Ontario had attained social hegemony in the rural townships as the largest immigrant community, and were politically dominant and successful entrepreneurs.[19] Little appeared to change as a result of the Great Famine. As Cecil Houston and William Smyth observe, the Great Famine exodus represents 'a temporary aberration in the long-established history of Irish emigration to British North America'.[20] Akenson hypothesised that the poor and landless (and overwhelmingly Catholic) labourers migrated largely to England because North America was simply too expensive for them. These data are important for placing in context the following results of an analysis of Irish inmates sent to the four Ontario lunatic asylums. There can be no reflexive assumptions that they were Catholic, poor, urban-settled castoffs of the Famine.[21]

Arriving earlier and in considerably smaller numbers, the Scottish migrant story to Ontario was more complicated. The first Scottish migrants actually migrated not directly from Scotland but from New York State in 1784. Following the conclusion of the War of Independence, British North America had a policy of encouraging 'Loyalists' to settle in Upper Canada (Ontario) and Lower Canada (Quebec), especially along strategic lands near the St. Lawrence and Ottawa Rivers. Approximately 4,000 Loyalists settled in what would become the eastern extremity of Upper Canada between 1784 and 1803, a small percentage of the total Upper Canada population of 71,000 in 1806. [22] Throughout the nineteenth century, the twin pressures of land consolidation and clearances in the Highlands to make room for sheep grazing and industrialisation in the Lowlands were the major incentives for migration directly from Scotland. Following the War of 1812, the British government once again wanted to keep bolstering its defences against the encroaching Americans and realised that the only proper barrier was to populate the long border that Upper Canada shared with its southern neighbour.[23] Once the Glengarry Settlement, the area populated by Scots just west of Montreal around present-day Cornwall, was mostly occupied (the Irish began arriving in large numbers after about 1825 as well), Scots moved further west and north, especially around the Lake Simcoe district, and into the south-western peninsula. J. M. Bumsted suggests that the post-1815 migrants were a mix of both Highlanders and Lowlanders and included a significant proportion of middle-class individuals, among them teachers, religious leaders, doctors, and lawyers.[24]

The 1842, 1871, and 1881 censuses of Ontario provide a snapshot of the approximate number of residents claiming Ireland or Scotland as their place of birth. Modelled on the contemporary British decennial censuses, the 1871 and 1881 censuses in Ontario enumerated households through

Table 3.1 Number and Proportion of 'Irish' and 'Scottish' Residents in Ontario, c. 1842, 1871, and 1881, as Reported in Censuses

Country of birth	Number of people, 1842	Approx. %	Number of people, 1871	Approx. %	Number of people, 1881	Approx. %
'Canada'	261,634	45–54	1,178,510	65	1,493,518	70
Ireland	78,255	16–18	153,000	9	130,094	7
Scotland	39,781	8–10	90,807	6	82,173	4

Sources: (For 1842) Akenson, *The Irish in Ontario*, p. 16, table 3; *Census of Canada 1870–71*, vol. 2 (Ottawa: I. B. Taylor, 1873), pp. 364–65; *Census of Canada 1880–81*, vol. 2 (Ottawa: Maclean Rogers, 1882), p. 394.

schedules, asking for name, age, occupation, and place of birth. Table 3.1 summarises the proportion of Irish by birth, which declined from 16 per cent to 18 per cent mid-century to about 9 per cent in 1881. The Scottish by birth comprised a smaller proportion of the population—somewhere between 8 per cent and 12 per cent mid-century to about 4 per cent of the general population by the end of the period under study. These figures are of course approximations and speak only of places of birth rather than ethnicities and familial cultures. Although the asylum admission register asked explicitly for 'nativity', one cannot discount some inaccuracies in the compiling of information at the time of admission. Moreover, censuses were notoriously inaccurate, due to a significant rate of illiteracy among residents at the time, fears over taxation and retribution against minorities, and human error. They must be taken as a broad measure.

IMMIGRANTS AND THE ONTARIO LUNATIC ASYLUMS

The temporary asylum in Toronto[25] was established in the very year of the Union between Upper Canada and Lower Canada (1841), the first major step towards Confederation. The Provincial Asylum (later the Asylum for the Insane, Toronto) was temporarily located in the abandoned city gaol, only to be relocated to a large purpose-built institution just outside the western most boundaries of the city in 1850. By the 1860s the Provincial Asylum for the Insane—as it was then known—became severely overcrowded, in part a response to a rapidly expanding general population which had reached 1 million residents by the early 1850s. Consequently, Ontario[26] established an asylum in Kingston (1853), followed by two other regional provincial asylums, one in the south-west of the province in London (1867) and another around the lake in Hamilton (1875). The Kingston Asylum doubled as a regional asylum for eastern counties and a provincial institution for criminal lunatics. Thus by the late 1870s, the Toronto Asylum was largely reduced to an institution serving what was then the second largest city in Canada and the central region of the province. Finally, the province also established a separate asylum for 'idiots' in the northern town of Orillia (1876). Without a poor law system in the English manner, the legal and administrative dimensions of confinement operated similar to that of New South Wales and other colonial jurisdictions, falling under the jurisdiction of an Inspector of Prisons and Asylums. Individuals were either admitted directly by family members, or they came to the attention of magistrates through the criminal justice system. Local jails thus often operated as a filter for those who were both mentally ill and judged to be dangerous to themselves or others, or in need of institutional treatment.[27]

The four Ontario lunatic asylums grew dramatically in size and influence, admitting a reported 12,596 individuals between 1841 and end of 1891. Some of the general socio-demographic characteristics of the patients admitted to these institutions have been discussed elsewhere and need not be detailed extensively here.[28] In summary, the patients appear to have conformed to the results of the new quantitative research that have emerged in the last two decades of scholarship, with a balance of men and women, admissions from across the age spectrum, poor but previously employed individuals working as labourers and skilled tradesmen, and even members of the middle class. Half of these admissions were discharged; half died in the institution. The proportion of the general population resident in public lunatic asylums also conformed to the pattern in the English-speaking world, rising to about 1 in 400 persons by the end of the century. As the institutions 'regionalised', with unofficial catchment areas, the religious composition reflected the communities from whence the patients came. Finally, there was a small Jarvisian effect to admissions, meaning that those living closer to the institution had a slightly higher rate of committal to the institutions than those living in the more remote parts of the provincial counties.[29] To date, however, there has been little sustained historical analysis of immigration and confinement, as derived from 'Name, Nativity and Place of Residence' entries in the Ontario Asylum admission registers.

In terms of 'nativity', almost exactly 50 per cent of the patients admitted over the fifty-year period under study were born in Canada (as then defined), whereas the censuses of 1871 and 1881 suggest that somewhere closer to 60 per cent of the general population, rising to 70 per cent in 1881, were born in Canada. Approximately 40 per cent of admissions to the Ontario mental hospitals listed England, Ireland, Scotland, or Wales as the place of birth; a further 10 per cent were from Europe, America, or elsewhere. Only 3 per cent had a place of birth that was unknown, or at least was unrecorded in the admission records. By any measure, then, the proportion of non-native-born admissions was higher than a random sample of the adult population of Ontario would predict, but not as dramatically as some historical literature, and contemporary anti-immigrant and eugenic treatises, would lead us to believe. However, these aggregate numbers conceal the dramatic shift in the composition of new admissions to the institutions over the half-century under study. For the first twenty years (1841 to 1861), foreign-born admissions made up over 75 per cent of all admissions, dipping to below 50 per cent during the 1870s and continuing this downward trend by the final decade of the century. The decline over time in the proportion of non-native-born admissions is illustrated in chart 3.1, reflecting a dramatic shift from non-native-born Canadians to 'Canadians' in the asylum that has rarely been captured in smaller cohort studies.

There were 2,830 Irish-born admissions to the four asylums during the five decades of this study, constituting approximately 22 per cent of all admissions to the provincial lunatic asylum over the half-century. The aggregate data, however, occludes the dramatic change over time. The Irish proportion of all admissions topped 40 per cent in the first decade of the asylum system in the province, double what one would expect. Gradually, their over-representation diminished (see chart 3.2). By the last decade of the nineteenth century, the admission rate to the asylum of those born in Ireland was, in a demographic sense, less remarkable. In the last decades under study (1881 to 1891) they represented only 12 per cent of admissions, compared to an 'expected' 9 per cent.[30] These numbers reflect more closely the findings for New South Wales, where the Irish were over-represented, but more in the order of 30 per cent to 40 per cent above the 'random' expectation.[31] The Scottish, by contrast, do *not* see a comparable decline in their *relative* over-representation. In the

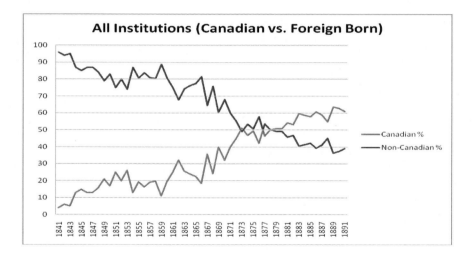

Chart 3.1   Proportion of foreign-born admissions to Ontario lunatic asylums versus Canada-born admissions (three-year moving average).
Source: Database compilation of (first) admissions to the following provincial asylums from their inception to 31 December 1891, inputted from microfilm copies provided by the Archives of Ontario (AO): Toronto Asylum [AO: RG 10-20-B-3 Registers and Rolls, 1841-1980]; Hamilton [AO: RG 10-20-F-3 Registers and Rolls, 1855-1923]; London [AO: RG 10-20-C-3 Registers, Rolls and Books, 1870-1970]; and Hamilton [AO: RG 10-20-D-3 Registers, Rolls and Books, 1876-1951]. Known transfers were excluded.

1840s they numbered more than twice what one would assume from crude estimates of the Scottish born in the 1842 Census (approximately 8 per cent to 10 per cent). In the final decade (1881 to 1891) they constituted 7 per cent of admissions, still about twice as much as the representation of Scottish born in the 1881 Ontario Census (see chart 3.2).

The sheer size of the database allows for greater scrutiny variable by variable (see appendixes 3.2 through 3.7). Indeed, by exploring in greater detail the socio-demographic characteristics of the Irish and Scottish patients admitted to the Ontario asylums, one can test some of the aforementioned hypotheses about the over-representation of the Irish in British World mental hospitals. There were no anomalous findings of admission by sex, with a more or less equal number of Scottish and Irish men as women being admitted. The marital status of patients was also predictable, with Irish and Scottish inmates reflecting the now widely recognised pattern across the English-speaking world of an over-representation of unmarried persons. The first surprising and somewhat counter-intuitive variable was age on admission. Here, the Irish *and* Scottish immigrants to Canada admitted relatives across the age spectrum. One observes, however, a much higher proportion of older admissions (defined as those aged fifty years or older) among the Scottish and the Irish. Approximately 30 per cent of the admissions of Irish and the Scots were aged fifty and over, with no statistically

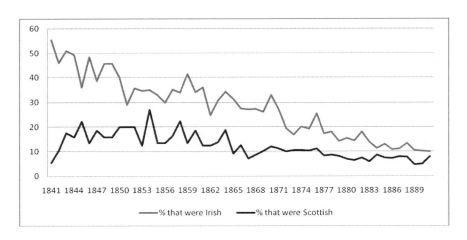

Chart 3.2   Proportion of admissions to Ontario lunatic asylums who claimed Irish or Scottish birth (three-year moving average).
Source: Database compilation of (first) admissions to the following provincial asylums from their inception to 31 December 1891, inputted from microfilm copies provided by the Archives of Ontario (AO): Toronto Asylum [AO: RG 10–20-B-3 Registers and Rolls, 1841–1980]; Hamilton [AO: RG 10–20-F-3 Registers and Rolls, 1855–1923]; London [AO: RG 10–20-C-3 Registers, Rolls and Books, 1870–1970]; and Hamilton [AO: RG 10–20-D-3 Registers, Rolls and Books, 1876–1951]. Known transfers were excluded.

significant difference between them or between men and women. This higher rate of admitting 'elderly' patients could reflect a cultural usage of mental hospitals for the care of the aged that the Irish and the Scots brought with them to Upper Canada. But they do not appear to conform to any of the predominant hypotheses outlined in previous studies.

The other striking finding—one that does intersect with the work of previous scholars—concerns religion. The Irish who migrated to Upper Canada did so in a 2:1 ratio of Protestants to Catholics.[32] With only a third of Ontario Irish-born residents being Catholics, the fact that 50 per cent of Irish-born asylum admissions were Catholic does deserve further comment and investigation. Akenson and others have argued that, relatively speaking, the Catholics tended to 'linger' in the cities for longer before settling in rural areas in Ontario.[33] Their presence in the principal cities (where the asylums were located) may have, combined with the aforementioned Jarvisian effect, contributed somewhat to their over-representation. Of course, one cannot dismiss the effect of anti-Catholicism in Ontario, yet the fact that the Scottish in Ontario did *not* see an over-representation of Catholic Scots in asylums does make this a particularly compelling argument.

Finally, a more popular hypothesis, dating back to Nancy Scheper-Hughes,[34] that the Irish were somehow 'predisposed' to insanity, or other hypotheses about the psychogenetic impact of the Famine, finds only marginal support in this large database analysis. The proportion of the Irish who were diagnosed with psychotic disorders, the length of stay of Irish patients, and the proportion of Irish dying from certain conditions suggests little out of the ordinary. Looking at the more than 12,000 records, the Irish appeared to be dying of malnutrition-related causes (such as 'marasmus') or of complications related to general paresis (tertiary syphilis) at the same rate as other ethnic groups. If anything, the Irish men appear to have had significantly lower rates of general paresis (8 per cent compared to the average male rate of 14 per cent). They also had no higher rates of readmission. Yes, in *absolute* numbers the Irish were being admitted at a higher rate for most years than the non-Irish, but to define this as biological would require greater evidentiary support.

CONCLUSIONS

Migration and madness have always been intertwined in Canadian society. The 1869 Immigration Act (Canada) explicitly banned the admission of insane immigrants, and eugenic discourse at the turn of the century was fuelled by the dramatic increase in the sheer number of immigrants at the turn of the century, which had quintupled from a decade before, and the shift in source country from Britain and Ireland to southern and eastern Europe. Leading psychiatrists, such as C. K. Clarke, the superintendent of the Kingston Asylum, warned of the disastrous intersection of tainted heredity and unrestricted immigration. Between 1896 and 1914,

Canada would admit 3 million immigrants. As the level of immigration accelerated in the last few years of the nineteenth century, this anxiety reached a crescendo.[35]

The Irish were certainly part of this Canadian discourse about immigration and asylum admissions, although the Canadian eugenicists were becoming somewhat more concerned about the southern European immigrants, or in the case of British Columbia, the impact of Chinese immigration, than they were the 'Celtic' fringe. And it should occasion little surprise that of the 4 million Irish who emigrated to other English-speaking jurisdictions in the second half of the nineteenth century, they would represent an important and identifiable group who found themselves residing in British World asylums. In Ontario, the Irish were over-represented during the course of the first decades under study (1841 to 1871); but as the nineteenth century drew to a close, their over-representation diminished. By the dawn of the twentieth century, their rate of admissions was more closely aligned to what a 'random' selection of community members in Ontario might produce. The Scottish followed a similar trajectory of being over-represented (based on contemporary census data), and also witnessing a relative decline by the turn of the century. The Irish and Scottish, along with the other non-native Canadians, were being joined, over two generations, by more and more native-born Canadians, something that might well reflect the growing acceptance of the mental hospital as an option for middle-class Canadian families. The very similar pattern of the Scottish and the Irish suggests that the accusation of racism or ethnic stereotyping in the British World asylums, although not to be excluded entirely, has poor evidentiary support in this Ontario case study. Even the cause-of-death data does not appear, at first glance, at least, to support an exceptionalism hypothesis as it relates to the Irish. It appears that the Irish in the asylum were not dying from different diseases or at different rates than the non-Irish.

The results from this study suggest that it was the Irish as *immigrants*— rather than as Irish per se or as Catholics—that played some role in their over-representation in the asylum in the first decades of the asylum system in Ontario. Poor and often isolated from kin networks, it makes sense that Irish and Scottish migrants might find themselves vulnerable to institutional confinement, in a manner analogous to the findings of researchers who have explored comparable situations in California, New Zealand, or New South Wales. And perhaps, like institutions in those jurisdictions, the mental hospitals became culturally accepted by 'native' members of the community over time. For the Irish, the Ontario situation represents a contrast to what was going on in their native island, where admissions continued to escalate in the last decades of the nineteenth century and where the Protestant Irish tended to stay clear of the public/pauper institutions, frequenting the few private and philanthropic institutions in Ireland. In Ontario, although not in Quebec, Protestants, and Catholics comingled in the public mental hospitals, bridging in an unusual manner the sectarianism that so divided their coreligionists back home.[36]

Table 3.2   Age at Time of Admission (First Admissions Only), Male Admissions, Ontario Asylums, 1841–91

Age	Irish	%	Scottish	%	Other	%	TOTAL
<20	47	4%	7	1%	321	7%	375
20–29	268	20%	114	18%	1605	33%	1987
30–39	313	23%	159	25%	1186	25%	1658
40–49	304	23%	139	22%	805	17%	1248
50–59	198	15%	111	17%	425	9%	734
>59	166	12%	96	15%	332	7%	594
n/a	36	3%	14	2%	139	3%	189
TOTAL	1332	100%	640	100%	4813	100%	6785

Table 3.3   Age at Time of Admission (First Admissions Only), Female Admissions, Ontario Asylums, 1841–91

Age	Irish	%	Scottish	%	Other	%	TOTAL
<20	59	4%	15	3%	240	6%	314
20–29	279	19%	92	16%	1299	33%	1670
30–39	356	24%	141	25%	1092	27%	1589
40–49	345	23%	128	22%	713	18%	1186
50–59	255	17%	115	20%	314	8%	684
>59	182	12%	69	12%	232	6%	483
n/a	22	1%	9	2%	82	2%	113
TOTAL	1498	100%	569	100%	3972	100%	6039

Table 3.4   Marital Status at Time of Admission (First Admissions Only), Male Admissions, Ontario Asylums, 1841–91

	Irish	%	Scottish	%	Other	%	TOTAL
Unmarried	660	60%	306	48%	2859	59%	3825
Married	576	43%	294	46%	1741	36%	2611
Widowed	65	5%	29	5%	128	3%	222
n/a	31	2%	11	2%	85	2%	127
TOTAL	1332	100%	640	100%	4813	100%	6785

ACKNOWLEDGMENTS

This chapter has received generous funding from Associated Medical Services, Inc. of Toronto and McMaster University through the endowed Hannah Chair. Grant funding for the larger project from which this chapter has

Table 3.5 Marital Status at Time of Admission (First Admissions Only), Female Admissions, Ontario Asylums, 1841–91

	Irish	%	Scottish	%	Other	%	TOTAL
Unmarried	523	35%	212	37%	1718	43%	2453
Married	784	52%	278	49%	1945	49%	3007
Widowed	157	10%	69	12%	272	7%	498
n/a	34	2%	10	2%	37	1%	81
TOTAL	1498	100%	569	100%	3972	100%	6039

Table 3.6 Stated Religion at Time of Admission (First Admissions Only), Male Admissions, Ontario Asylums, 1841–91

	Irish	%	Scottish	%	Other	%	TOTAL
Protestant	689	52%	608	95%	3543	74%	4840
Catholic	607	46%	17	3%	800	17%	1424
Other	17	1%	7	1%	244	5%	268
n/a	19	1%	8	1%	226	5%	253
TOTAL	1332	100%	640	100%	4813	100%	6785

Table 3.7 Stated Religion at Time of Admission (First Admissions Only), Male Admissions, Ontario Asylums, 1841–91

	Irish	%	Scottish	%	Other	%	TOTAL
Protestant	716	48%	526	92%	3053	77%	4295
Catholic	759	51%	26	5%	593	15%	1378
Other	5	0%	7	1%	165	4%	177
n/a	18	1%	10	2%	161	4%	189
TOTAL	1498	100%	569	100%	3972	100%	6039

been written came from the Arts Research Board of McMaster University and the Canadian Institutes of Health Research. We are grateful to Caitlin Dyer for research in support of this article and for critical feedback from Angela McCarthy, Catharine Coleborne, and Oonagh Walsh.

NOTES

1. Archives of Ontario (Canada), Admissions to the Asylum for the Insane, Toronto, Reg. No. 1620 (John Prindiville), from the Case Files, Hamilton Asylum/Hospital (RG 10–20-D 1–3).

2. D. H. Akenson, *The Irish in Ontario: A Study in Rural History*, 2nd ed. (Montreal: McGill-Queen's University Press, 1999), p. 15.
3. As quoted in I. Dowbiggin, '"Keeping this young country sane": C. K. Clarke, immigration restriction, and Canadian psychiatry, 1890–1925', *Canadian Historical Review*, 76 (1995), p. 608.
4. This debate was particularly intertwined with the issue of child immigration and the extent to which children (such as those from the Barnado homes in England) were fostering a future generation of asylum admissions. See Dowbiggin, '"Keeping this young country sane"', pp. 605–6 and passim. For the broader North American context, see I. Dowbiggin, *Keeping America Sane: Psychiatry and Eugenics in the United States and Canada, 1880–1940* (Ithaca, NY: Cornell University Press, 1997).
5. Although Grob demonstrated how this was not the case prior to the 1880s. See G. Grob, *The State and the Mentally Ill: A History of Worcester State Hospital in Massachusetts, 1830–1920* (Chapel Hill: University of North Carolina Press, 1966), table V. This finding was also acknowledged in D. Rothman, *The Discovery of the Asylum: Social Order and Disorder in the New Republic* (Toronto: Little, Brown, 1971), p. 273.
6. G. Grob, *Mental Institutions in America: Social Policy to 1875* (New York: Free Press, 1973), p. 37.
7. J. Walton, 'Lunacy in the Industrial Revolution: A study of asylum admissions in Lancashire, 1848–1850', *Journal of Social History*, 13 (1979), pp. 7–8, table 2, and passim.
8. R. Fox, *So Far Disordered in Mind: Insanity in California, 1870–1930* (Berkeley: University of California Press, 1978), p. 108.
9. S. Garton, *Medicine and Madness: A Social History of Insanity in New South Wales, 1880–1940* (Kensington: New South Wales University Press, 1988); H. Deacon, 'Insanity, institutions and society: The case of the Robben Island Lunatic Asylum, 1846–1910', in R. Porter and D. Wright (eds.), *The Confinement of the Insane: International Perspectives* (Cambridge: Cambridge University Press, 2003), pp. 20–53. Although the South American experience is outside the scope of this chapter, the concern over immigrant inmates also seems to have been important in Argentina and elsewhere. See J. Ablard, *Madness in Buenos Aires: Patients, Psychiatrists, and the Argentine State, 1890–1983* (Calgary: University of Calgary Press, 2008), p. 133.
10. Fox, *So Far Disordered in Mind*, pp. 107–8.
11. Women only represented, in absolute terms, 36 per cent of all admissions to the Auckland lunatic asylum between 1870 and 1910. B. Labrum, 'Looking beyond the asylum: Gender and the process of committal to Auckland, 1870–1910', *New Zealand Journal of History*, 26 (1992), pp. 553–74.
12. A. Scull, *Museums of Madness: The Social Organization of Insanity in Nineteenth-Century England* (London: Allen Lane, 1979), p. 30.
13. Ibid., passim.
14. M. Finnane, *Insanity and the Insane in Post-Famine Ireland* (London: Routledge, 1981).
15. E. Malcolm, '"A most miserable looking object": The Irish in English Asylums, 1851–1901: Migration, poverty and prejudice', in J. Belchem and K. Tenfelde (eds.), *Irish and Polish Migration in Comparative Perspective* (Essen: Klartext Verlag, 2003), pp. 115–26.
16. W. Mitchinson, 'Reasons for committal to a mid-nineteenth-century Ontario insane asylum: The case of Toronto', in W. Mitchinson and J. D. McGinnis (eds.) *Essays in the History of Canadian Medicine* (Toronto: McClelland and Stewart, 1988), p. 93; C. Warsh, '"In charge of the loons": A portrait of the London, Ontario Asylum for the Insane in the nineteenth century', *Ontario History*, 74 (1982), pp. 138–84.

17. M. Finnane, 'Asylums, families and the state', *History Workshop Journal*, 20 (1985), p. 136.

18. The section of the asylum admission registers that details place of birth does not consistently list the county in Ireland, Scotland, England, or Wales in order to determine whether there was an unusual number of admissions of Ontario patients from Irish counties that already had their own lunatic asylums.

19. D. H. Akenson, *The Irish in Ontario: A Study in Rural History*, 2nd ed. (Montreal: McGill-Queen's University Press, 1999).

20. C. Houston and W. Smyth, *Irish Emigration and Canadian Settlement: Patterns, Links and Letters* (Toronto: University of Toronto Press, 1990), p. 27.

21. Akenson, *The Irish in Ontario*, pp. 31–34, 43.

22. Approximately 50 per cent of the early pioneers were Catholics, although they tended to settle in Catholic-dominated Lower Canada (Quebec). L. H. Campey, *The Scottish Pioneers of Upper Canada, 1784–1855: Glengarry and Beyond* (Toronto: Natural Heritage, 2005), pp. 3–5.

23. Campey, *Scottish Pioneers*, ch. 3 and 4.

24. J. M. Bumsted, *The Scots in Canada* (Ottawa: Canadian Historical Association, 1982), pp. 7–13. Campey, *Scottish Pioneers*, pp. 64, 171–72.

25. Like the province, Toronto also went through name changes over the course of the nineteenth century, and was referred to in the early decades as York or Fort York. This chapter will use 'Toronto' throughout so as not to confuse readers.

26. Ontario was formally known as Upper Canada from 1792 to 1841 and as Canada West between 1841 and 1867. This chapter shall hereafter use the term 'Ontario'.

27. For a survey of the rise of asylums in Ontario and Quebec, see J. Moran, *Committed to the State Asylum: Insanity and Society in Nineteenth-Century Quebec and Ontario* (Montreal: McGill/Queen's University Press, 2000).

28. See D. Wright, J. Moran, and S. Gouglas, 'The confinement of the insane in Victorian Ontario', in Porter and Wright (eds.), *The Confinement of the Insane*, pp. 100–28.

29. C. Smith, D. Wright, and S. Day, 'Distancing the mad: The spatial distribution of admissions to the Hamilton (Ontario) Asylum, 1876–1902', *Social Science and Medicine*, 64 (2007), pp. 2362–77; D. Wright, S. Day, and N. Flis, 'A Janus-like asylum: Urbanization and the institutional confinement of the insane in Victorian Ontario', *Urban History Review*, 36 (2008), pp. 43–52.

30. Compare these to the figures cited by Malcolm of 40 per cent to 50 per cent Irish composition of residential populations of lunatic asylums in New York state and Massachusetts, c. 1900. Malcolm, '"A most miserable looking object"', p. 115.

31. Garton, *Medicine and Madness*, pp. 102–5.

32. Scholars have suggested a range of figures, from 30 per cent to 38 per cent Catholic. See P. Magosci (ed.), *Encyclopedia of Canadian Peoples* (Toronto: University of Toronto Press, 1999), p. 744 and 774, table 4.

33. Akenson, *The Irish in Ontario*, p. 26, fn 30.

34. N. Scheper-Hughes, *Saints, Scholars and Schizophrenics: Mental Illness in Rural Ireland* (Berkeley: University of California Press, 1979). For a different perspective, see E. Malcolm, '"The house of strident shadows": The asylum, the family and emigration in post-famine Ireland', in E. Malcolm and G. Jones (eds.), *Medicine, Disease and the State in Ireland, 1650–1940* (Cork: Cork University Press, 1999), pp. 177–91.

35. Dowbiggin, '"Keeping this young country sane"', pp. 604–8 and passim.

36. We are grateful to Oonagh Walsh for this illuminating point.

4 Migration and Madness in New Zealand's Asylums, 1863–1910

Angela McCarthy

Most studies of migrant groups, particularly nineteenth-century migrants, generally emphasise the successful adjustment and settlement of new-comers. But what do we know about those migrants who struggled with their relocation abroad? Attempted suicide, heavy drinking, violence, and domestic disharmony were all possible outcomes of dysfunction, despair, and hardship, and were among the reasons for committal to an asylum. Yet were such explanations the result of antecedent experience, the process of migration, or of conditions encountered in the new land? Such questions are a central puzzle in studies of migration. Historians of medicine also grapple with the role of migration and mental health, specifically whether movement enhanced the prospect of admission to an asylum. For instance, Andrew Scull and John Walton perceive a link between long-distance migration and committal whereas other scholars refute any correlation between long-distance migration and admission to the asylum.[1] The physical and cultural differences of migrants and the absence of kin networks are also cited as reasons for committal, with the cultural background of migrants a particular factor in explanations of mental health proffered by transcultural psychiatrists.[2]

Drawing on institutional data from the Auckland Asylum (founded in 1853) and the Dunedin and Seacliff asylums (established in 1863 and 1877, respectively), together with official immigration files, this chapter considers aspects relating to antecedent experience, the migration process, and conditions abroad in generating committal to an asylum in New Zealand. This is not to detract from other explanations for committal but to reveal that for some migrants these aspects were held to have played a part in their admission to the asylum. What follows also highlights the importance of records relating to mental health for historians of migration. Among the themes examined are details about a migrant's time spent in other countries and admission to other asylums before and/or after departure from their homeland. Whether foreign-born patients had relatives confined to asylums in New Zealand and/or in the homeland is also occasionally noted. Such information was gathered by institutions as part of a concern about the hereditary nature of mental disease in the imperial and colonial context.

Additionally, the length of time between arrival in New Zealand and committal to an asylum is occasionally reported in patient case books revealing whether migrants were more prone to be admitted shortly after arrival or years after settlement. That New Zealand was predominantly an immigrant society for much of the period under consideration means, however, that such analyses are only relevant to particular individuals, for if migration did result in stresses leading to committal, more migrants would likely have entered asylums. The issue of return migration is also briefly considered.

In addressing these aspects, the analysis that follows is theoretically underpinned by Nancy Green's comparative models of migration. A divergent comparative model emphasises the importance of the destination in shaping migrant behaviour, whereas a convergent model aids the investigation of different migrant groups in one place of settlement, advancing the migrants' national background as the starting point for explaining differences and recognising the distinctiveness of each group. Also relevant is Green's linear model which offers a perspective on past and present by comparing developments in the new world with experiences in the old, thereby promoting scrutiny of continuity and change.[3]

As with scholars elsewhere, historians of the lunatic asylum in New Zealand have predominantly examined aspects of gender and the family.[4] Also traversed in the historiography of specific asylums are themes such as the treatment of patients, social attitudes to lunatics as a response to changing legislation, the presence and absence of family in asylum archives, and the experience of Māori patients.[5] To date, the utilisation of New Zealand asylum records to explore issues of migration is rare.[6] Before considering this under-researched aspect in relation to asylum records, what do we know about asylum committals in New Zealand?

STATISTICAL OVERVIEW

Analysis of the published data relating to asylum admissions in New Zealand, printed regularly in the *Appendices to the Journals of the House of Representatives*, reveals the following returns for country of birth for the major groups admitted to New Zealand asylums (table 4.1). At first glance, the admission of English-born patients in New Zealand asylums rose during the nineteenth and earlier twentieth centuries, whereas the Scottish presence in asylums generally increased until the end of the nineteenth century before beginning a small decline; Irish migrants took the middle ground. Yet when comparing the presence of these foreign-born groups in the asylum with their presence in the population at large, the findings are quite similar with all groups being increasingly confined. Unsurprisingly, there is an increase in admissions of New Zealand–born patients over time, but because of issues relating to age and asylum committals their presence in the asylum compared to the wider population is low.

Table 4.1 Place of Birth for Patients in New Zealand Asylums at Year End, 1879–1909

Year	England	Scotland	Ireland	Germany	China	Australia	NZ
1879	379	208	288	29	6	13	48
1882	438	217	373	26	16	18	79
1885	543	256	437	33	20	18	95
1888	569	274	476	34	25	20	125
1891	618	295	540	41	17	30	198
1894	647	318	559	53	20	33	294
1897	745	373	597	38	25	50	432
1900	788	409	631	46	31	58	539
1903	846	402	664	47	26	85	704
1906	843	386	621	41	26	100	988
1909	923	381	611	38	21	121	1255

Source: Appendices to the Journals of the House of Representatives

In reality, then, the ethnicity of patients and composition patterns are not quite as clear-cut as table 4.1 suggests. First, the published asylum statistics are snapshots in time and so are of comparatively little value in terms of establishing the overall numbers of patients and their backgrounds. A focus on official annual returns also excludes how many of these admissions were repeat or long-stay patients. Large-scale statistical studies using admission registers, such as those undertaken on Canadian asylums, would assist in clarifying these issues.[7] Notable discrepancies also exist in terms of the patients' birthplace when comparing the original patient registers with case books. Evidence from the Auckland Asylum, for instance, reveals that some patients listed in the admissions registers as having been born in Germany were recorded with other ethnic designations in the case books. Axel, although registered on admission as born in Germany, was listed as a Swede in the case books, and Gabriel's country of origin was Germany in the admission registers as opposed to him being considered a native of Hungary in the case books.[8] Such discrepancies may reflect transcription errors, possibly due to confusion arising from language differences. More likely, they suggest that greater knowledge of the patient was ascertained between their listing in the initial admission register and their inclusion in the patient casebook.

These complications aside, comparing the admission of foreign-born migrants to asylums with published census data (table 4.2) reveals a number of interesting trends that deserve consideration. Scots, for instance, entered asylums in proportion to their representation among the foreign-born in New Zealand society. Irish migrants, by contrast, were over-represented

Table 4.2   Foreign-born Percentages in the New Zealand Census and Asylums, 1878–1906

Census Year	Scotland born		Ireland born		England born	
	Census per cent	Asylum per cent	Census per cent	Asylum per cent	Census per cent	Asylum per cent
1878	20.0	21.9	18.2	29.0	44.3	38.5
1881	19.8	18.3	18.5	31.7	44.7	36.8
1886	19.7	17.9	18.5	32.1	45.2	37.9
1891	20.0	18.1	18.3	33.0	45.0	37.8
1896	19.3	18.1	17.6	31.0	44.5	38.0
1901	18.6	19.0	17.0	29.7	43.6	38.1
1906	16.9	17.7	15.0	28.4	41.3	38.6

while English migrants were under-represented. In terms of population patterns and migratory trends, therefore, the most striking anomalies in terms of asylum confinement relate to the Irish and to the English.

This is a point worth pausing over as international analyses of the differences in the ethnic composition of lunatic asylums also identify the over-representation of Irish migrants generating a number of theories to explain their disproportionate incarceration as Elizabeth Malcolm outlines in her chapter in this volume. Although speculative, a possible explanation for the divergent utilisation of asylums in New Zealand (and elsewhere) may relate to the experiences of institutional care in the homelands. In Ireland, for instance, admission rates were disproportionate compared to elsewhere in the UK.[9] In Scotland, by contrast, chartered asylums, lunatic wards in poorhouses, private asylums, and boarding out were initially favoured over large-scale publicly-funded institutional care, which developed after 1860.[10] Despite these broad national differences, it is important to note that even within each national context, there were regional differences.[11] Although more study is needed, the issue does raise the importance of considering antecedent experiences before migration in shaping some individuals' tendency to be admitted to an asylum.

ANTECEDENT EXPERIENCE

Prior Admissions

Throughout the nineteenth century, medical officials were deeply disturbed about the arrival in New Zealand of the insane and published accounts reveal a number of cases where newcomers to New Zealand were considered of unsound mind before leaving their homelands. In the mid-1870s, for instance, the inspector of Sunnyside Asylum 'noticed three admissions, since my visit made a month previously, of patients recently arrived from England, all of whom I had reason to presume were not of sound mind when they left. One of them, at all events, the medical officer entered on the register as suffering from congenital dementia. It is not unreasonable to presume that this person was fraudulently palmed off on the agents at home to become a permanent burden on the colony'.[12] The inspector of asylums in 1884 also expressed concern that patients in home asylums or showing 'insane tendencies' were shipped to New Zealand to escape 'the burden of their maintenance at home'.[13] In New Zealand, for instance, asylums were government institutions, and care of the insane was provided by the provincial governments before 1876 and by central government thereafter, although attempts were made to secure financial support from the families of those committed.[14] In Britain and Ireland, by contrast, maintenance of the insane was a local charge with central government only providing some financial relief after 1874.[15] This situation allegedly generated the accumulation of chronic harmless lunatics in the colony which 'is greatly exaggerated by the impossibility of getting families to take charge of such cases, as is so extensively done in Britain'.[16]

Patient case books and completed questionnaires as well as official publications similarly document the prior admissions of migrants to asylums before arrival in New Zealand. It was discovered of Margaret S. from Glasgow 'that her parents took her out of an asylum at home & brought her out here'.[17] Data contained in patient case books is often treated sceptically by scholars who question the accuracy of such information. Although Margaret's admission to a Scottish asylum, probably Gartnavel, has yet to be established, preliminary investigation confirms the authenticity of several other prior homeland admissions. Married farmer Andrew T., for instance, was committed to Seacliff Asylum in Dunedin in 1881, five years after his arrival in New Zealand. His case notes reveal that he was illegitimate, had worked as a gamekeeper with the Earl of Airlie, and was confined six years previously at the Montrose Asylum for a period of three months.[18] Research on the Montrose Asylum records confirms that Andrew, a gamekeeper, was admitted in November 1873. He was apparently illegitimate 'and his father, a heartless wretch, though perfectly in good Circumstance refused to have anything to do with his mother'. The record indicates that Andrew provided for his mother and was kind and attentive to her. His friends, however, worried about Andrew committing suicide and were responsible for his admission to the asylum. By March 1874 Andrew escaped the asylum, and he left for New Zealand within the next two years.[19] Another admission at Seacliff, this time in 1887, was married forty-seven-year-old Ann P., of whom it was noted was confined eighteen years previously in Montrose Asylum and ten years earlier at Dundee.[20] Research confirms her previous confinements, despite slight discrepancy with dates and ages. When confined at Montrose at thirty years of age in 1874 with a case of puerperal mania, it was noted that Ann entered the Dundee Asylum eight years earlier. She left the Montrose Asylum at the end of January 1875 and was readmitted a week later, only to be removed by her husband in March against the wishes of the superintendent.[21] These cases highlight the importance of prior confinement before migration as a factor in asylum admission abroad. In other words, prior experience of committal at home may have prompted family members of patients to utilise asylums abroad. Consequently, asylum admissions cannot simply be viewed solely as the result of conditions encountered abroad, such as experiences of dislocation or isolation, for continuities existed between old-world experiences and new-world lives.

Hereditary Insanity

The issue of hereditary insanity, that is, whether family members of the patients were labelled insane, also connects to antecedent experience. Nineteenth-century medical authorities in New Zealand, as in Britain and elsewhere, expressed on-going concern with the issue of hereditary insanity. As reported in 1880, 'that hereditary predisposition was only ascertained to exist in 40 cases is rather a proof of the difficulty of getting information than a reason for supposing that it was not present in a great many more'.[22] Case books substantiate such concerns. Despite the patchy data, the case books for Dunedin's public asylums show that of the sample so far analysed, 8.6 per cent (n=64) of patients were recorded as having a history of insanity in the family. Sometimes it was simply observed that a family member was odd or insane. On other occasions, however, the name of an asylum in the homeland or in the colony where a relative was confined was provided. While these figures are yet to be analysed by ethnicity, the current statistic mirrors the findings of patients labelled with hereditary insanity at the Connaught District Lunatic Asylum in Ireland.[23]

Again, examples serve to demonstrate the attribution of insanity to hereditary factors for some migrants. Andrew B., a sixty-five-year-old single labourer, entered Seacliff in 1891. According to his report, 'melancholy moods run in the family', and an unidentified sister was noted as having been 'wrong in the head', having spent time in the Perth Asylum.[24] Records of the Perth Asylum reveal that his sister was admitted in 1841 and 'is hereditarily predisposed to Insanity and one of her sisters died Insane'. It was noted that her brother removed her later that year.[25] In 1901 Scotswoman Annie R., a fifty-three-year-old married Presbyterian housewife from Balclutha, was committed to the Seacliff Asylum. According to her case book entry, this was not Annie's first attack of insanity, as three years earlier she spent seven months at Dunedin's private asylum, Ashburn Hall. Born at Wick, Annie had spent two years in Tasmania and ten years in New Zealand. The asylum case book also holds a letter Annie wrote to her husband in February 1911, a decade after her admission, declaring, 'Had I been at Home the doctors would not have dared to as this upon me, but here, advantage has been taken of me as I have nobody in the colony but yourself that knows anything about me'. After thirteen years in the asylum, Annie was eventually discharged in January 1914, and apparently left for England, the medical official noting that relatives at home had been agitating for her removal and had paid for a nurse to accompany her.[26] Annie's case book entry also reveals that her sister Catherine was confined at the Montrose Asylum in Scotland while her brother John, an imbecile from birth, was boarded out. Research on the Montrose records confirms Catherine's admissions, where she was termed a 'suspicious, scheming deluded creature, a most persistent letter-writer—she misconstrues the simplest acts into deeds of malice and persecution'. Catherine's case book record also reveals that her sister Annie was residing in Glasgow in 1924 and had written to the asylum seeking information about Catherine.[27]

Margaret W., admitted to Seacliff in 1901 after thirty-nine years in New Zealand, was another migrant with relatives recorded as patients in homeland asylums. Her mother was said to have spent time in an asylum in Edinburgh while her sister was currently confined there.[28] Again, consultation of overseas records confirms such admissions. Margaret's mother, also Margaret, 'a case of old standing dementia', was admitted to the Royal Edinburgh Hospital (Morningside) in 1870 from the Smeaton Grove Asylum.[29] Meanwhile, Margaret's sister Mary was admitted several times to Morningside. Her first two admissions cited the cause as hereditary insanity, noting that in 1868 her mother was in the lunatic wards of St. Cuthbert's Poorhouse and in 1872 was also in Morningside.[30] Again, for the historian of migration and mental health, these examples underscore the influence of factors other than the experience of migration and conditions encountered in new lands of settlement in determining asylum confinement.

THE MIGRATION PROCESS

Migration Pathways

If scholars of migration increasingly incorporate the experiences in the homeland as well as the country of settlement, the migration process itself is less explored because of a dearth of sources. Yet if prior admissions and hereditary insanity were experienced by some migrants before departure, migration pathways also must be considered, including time spent in other destinations. Institutional data is helpful in illuminating these migration pathways. In questionnaires that family and friends completed for asylum authorities, the length of time spent in New Zealand and whether time had been spent in other destinations was one of the questions asked. The latter question might reflect changes in civil registration from 1880, but such information was contained in asylum records prior to that legislative development. This suggests that the role of migration on mental health was of considerable interest to some medical professionals.

From an initial sample of foreign-born patients taken from Dunedin's public asylums, data relates to 176 who recorded whether or not they had spent time in other countries before arriving in New Zealand. Of that number, 62 per cent (n=109) sojourned elsewhere, and 38 per cent came directly to New Zealand.[31] Of those who spent time elsewhere, an overwhelming majority of those, four-fifths, were in Australia before arrival in New Zealand, either solely in Australia (71 per cent; n=77) or in Australia as well as another destination (9 per cent; n=10). Analysis of data at the Auckland Asylum for a later time period, that of 1903 to 1910, also shows that one-third of the 389 foreign-born committals during that period resided elsewhere before arriving in New Zealand with Australia again the favoured destination (41 per cent having spent time there).[32]

This was the case with Christian, of whom it was stated in 1867, 'is a native of Germany and had accumulated some money from the Victoria gold-diggings'. Although successful in Victoria, Christian's concern for his family in Germany seems to have contributed to his less than smooth integration in New Zealand. As his records further document, 'coming over to Auckland the first thing which he did was to send this money to a brother at home leaving himself without any means of support upon which he suffered much privation'.[33] One of the more elaborate cases of such migration routes, however, was that of Theodore D., raised at Risely in Bedfordshire. Noting that the 'patient comes of very insane stock' (his brother and cousin were insane), his case note goes on to outline his move to Edinburgh where he allegedly studied medicine between 1884 and 1890. Theodore then proceeded to the Hughes settlement in Tennessee to undertake farm work before living in poverty in New York for a year. Following this he proceeded to his brother in South Africa before departing in a 'huff' for New Zealand.[34] These migration trajectories were presumably also of interest to asylum officials who sought financial maintenance for patients from their family members around the world and in some cases, their return to places of origin.

The Voyage

By contrast with a relative dearth of studies relating to migration pathways, scholars of migration have undertaken sustained investigation of the voyage process. Yet such analyses typically concentrate on issues of power, and gender and class segregation on-board ship.[35] Meanwhile, international, health-related explorations largely focus on issues of quarantine and shipboard mortality rates.[36] The effect of the voyage on the mental state of some migrants is generally missing from the analysis. Yet examples can be found from asylum patients and their family members who indicated that the voyage was held to have played a part in the mental suffering of some migrants. As one male patient put it, 'I did not enjoy the Voyage out very much and have been rather queer since I have been here'.[37] In some cases explanations related to the physical hardship of the voyage out. Janet R., a thirty-three-year-old housewife, for instance, experienced seasickness and sleeplessness. Her condition was also influenced by the loss of her baby a few months before the voyage.[38] Of another migrant, Catherine M., it was said that she 'fell into Melancholia on voyage'.[39] Even those making the short crossing from Australia to New Zealand suffered from the physical symptoms arising from the transition. As Jeannie's case notes reveal, she 'left Melbourne because of the hot weather' and 'was very seasick all the way over and felt very weak and wretched on landing'.[40] In other cases, the behaviour of fellow passengers was held to have contributed to a migrant's condition during the passage. During her 1876 voyage, twenty-year-old Catholic Eliza from Londonderry, who migrated with one of her brothers, 'became insane and was taken here. She says she was very badly treated by the other girls on board'.[41]

In most cases, however, the voyage played a role in conjunction with other factors. As one brother commented in 1890 of his fifty-year-old Greenock-born sister Margaret M., a dressmaker, 'I may mention that after my sister's arrival in the colony she lived with me for about ten months—and she became insane but recovered in about three months. I lived in a very solitary place at that time and I thought the solitude coupled with the life on board ship might be the cause'.[42] Jane from Lanarkshire, meanwhile, lost a child at sea and 'says it was leaving home that "Crabbet her brain" seems to have been upset at beginning of voyage'.[43] Mary Ann B. from County Kerry, a twenty-year-old single Catholic, was also considered to be 'depressed since landing here'. According to her case notes, 'at first she was very cheerful on board ship, but after a few weeks she became sullen. On landing in N.Z. she at first refused to speak to her uncle, who met her [and] took her by train to his residence'. It was further noted that 'she admits that she was dull and wretched on the voyage out'.[44] Separation from family and friends, however, was cited as the overarching cause of Mary Ann's mental state, also evident in the case of Charles M., a twenty-five-year-old Catholic farm labourer from County Cavan. According to his wife, Charles had 'no cause for grief unless leaving home and parting with friends. He was very anxious to get to NZ and never showed any sign of grief'. Nevertheless, as his wife further testified, the anxieties associated with the voyage to New Zealand via Australia on the *Oruba* in 1893 seemingly contributed to Charles's state of mind: 'He was not strange or essentic only he began talking about religion and as pious as the people were at home compared to the people in the ship he commenced talking about piety ten days before he got insane'. The medical officer also noted that Charles's wife 'informs me that his mind was troubled on board ship by his protestant fellows jeering him about religion'. According to the medical remarks, Charles 'Tells many queer and incoherent stories about the passage from Britain to Australia'.[45]

Apart from case book entries, accounts of mental distress prior to and during the voyage also appear in official immigration reports and in accounts from surgeon superintendents. One such case concerned Catherine M. who, while waiting at Gravesend for the departure of the *Waipa* in 1876, showed signs of being noisy and turbulent. The ship's matron 'could not say whether it proceeded from mental weakness or ignorance'.[46] The surgeon superintendent, meanwhile, 'considered the girls behaviour was in a great measure from excitement arising from the annoyances of the other girls & that he then saw no objection to her proceeding in the ship'.[47] Following the voyage the surgeon superintendent divulged that Catherine 'has conducted herself fairly well during the passage. She is at times very excitable and inclined to be abusive. Her general manner is also strange and capricious being as a rule moody and reserved. At times she will refuse to answer questions. She has often for days together sat in her bunk resisting every inducement offerred for her to leave it'. He concluded, 'I consider her case to be one of Dementia with excitement'.[48]

In many cases like Catherine's, where a new arrival was considered to be insane, the issue of maintenance arose, generating the scorn of officials in New Zealand towards those in the homeland for arranging these departures. For example, in the case of Jane T., who travelled to the colony in 1875 from Devon on the *Merope*, the surgeon superintendent felt 'it is perhaps another of those cases where the Parochial authorities have tried to rid their Parish and the rate-payers of the charge of a Pauper or Lunatic by persuading her to emigrate—a practice which cannot be too strongly condemned'.[49] Not only did the potential expense of maintenance in the colony justify her return to England, but so too did the fear that Jane would marry and be 'the mother of children suffering the same mental defect'.[50] Such alarm triggered investigations with home authorities, but no evidence surfaced to suggest that Jane suffered 'from mental derangement' prior to her emigration.[51]

One of the more extensive cases surrounding the activities of family members in facilitating the migration of supposedly insane siblings is that of Bridget O. who travelled on the *British Empire* in 1875. According to the commissioners who investigated the case, her brother Michael 'states that he had no knowledge before emigrating of his sisters liability to the malady in question. He is reported to have spoken otherwise on board ship to some of his fellow passengers'. They concluded, 'it is to be regretted that there are no available means provided by law for the punishment of frauds of this description by which the colony is subjected either to heavy permanent charges for maintaining such persons for life, or put to the serious cost of returning them again to the Mother Country'.[52] This case resembled others in Ireland which appeared 'suspiciously as though brothers were trying to rid themselves of unwanted female dependents by having them committed'.[53]

By contrast with lay accounts which testify to the role of the voyage in shaping a migrant's mental health, there is evidence of medical testimony endorsing the voyage out and settlement abroad as a cure for mental and physical health. In the case of English woman Elizabeth B., a thirty-year-old single teacher, it was noted that 'nine months before leaving for N. Zealand was spent with relations in the Highlands of Scotland. In the meantime her father died, the voyage out here was taken as a last hope for her recovery'.[54] That medics encouraged the return home of patients who would not harm or alarm their fellow passengers also suggests that the voyage was not perceived as detrimental as conveyed in lay testimony. On the other hand, this downplaying by medics of the voyage's detrimental effects may have been a way of reassuring family members back in the homelands who had agreed to receive the patient back home—and accept financial responsibility for them.

Although speculative, the voyage to New Zealand may account for the admission of 8 per cent (n=29) of a sample of foreign-born patients to Dunedin's public asylum within their first year of arrival in New Zealand, a factor also noted in the *AJHR* for 1879: 'as many as 9 patients were admitted within a month after their arrival in the colony, 3 of whom were sent straight from their ships'.[55] Alternatively, these may have been individuals who had exhibited symptoms of insanity at home and, in such cases, efforts were made to return the migrant. If the captain or owner of a vessel refused to return the migrant, then specific legal acts, such as the Imbecile Passengers Act, were enforced against the ship's owner or captain requiring them to pay a bond of £100. If a passenger was then admitted to an institution within five years, the bond was taken as payment for their maintenance.[56] Curiously, however, there appears to be no official acts of repatriation as evident with indentured migrants in Fiji discussed by Jacqueline Leckie in this volume, and insane migrants in India.[57] Instead, return migration was usually undertaken in consultation with networks of family and friends in New Zealand and back home. In many cases patients also desired to return home, and 'anxiety' was a key term connected with their longing.[58]

SETTLEMENT

If some migrants were admitted to an asylum shortly after their arrival, then at what stage were other migrants committed? Of a sample of 350 foreign-born patients at the Dunedin and Seacliff public asylums for whom there is information on the number of years spent in New Zealand, 44 per cent (n=154) were confined having spent ten or less years in New Zealand, 34 per cent (n=118) spent between eleven and twenty years in the colony, and 18 per cent (n=64) spent twenty-one to thirty years in New Zealand. Just 4 per cent (n=14) were in New Zealand for more than thirty-one years before admission to Dunedin's public asylums. This differs from the analysis of later admissions at Auckland where one-quarter were resident for ten years or less before committal while half were confined having spent between eleven and twenty years in New Zealand.[59] Nevertheless, despite a strong contingent entering the asylum in their first year in New Zealand, migrants were more likely to be admitted some years after settlement. For scholars who focus on migration, this seems to provide support for Roland Littlewood and Maurice Lipsedge's thesis which contends that mental illness among migrants is more evident after several years of settlement when 'the new life in the adopted country has fallen short of expectations'.[60]

Such dissatisfaction may have generated behaviours and responses which were then cited as causes for admission to an asylum such as drink, disappointment, religious fervour, and solitude. Congenital and heredity factors, masturbation, childbirth, epilepsy, and senile decay were also among the official published causes of insanity.[61] Again, however, such factors must be examined before and after migration. One potential influence deserving consideration is the existence and operation of networks of family and friends. This is an important avenue of enquiry, as both scholars of migration and psychiatry have emphasised the difficulties of migrant adjustment abroad and how this may be connected to dislocation and isolation. Importantly, an enduring narrative in the New Zealand context is that of atomisation promoted by Miles Fairburn. Eschewing ethnicity as a governing category, Fairburn contends that 'the scantiness of kinship ties deprived colonists of a base for the development of community ties'. As a result, he argues, 'community structures were few and weak. . . . Bondlessness was central to colonial life'. A significant cause of this atomisation, Fairburn maintains, was that 'most colonists . . . had already severed their links with place, family, friends, community in the great uprooting that led them to New Zealand'. As such, 'this deficient framework of association' resulted in extreme loneliness, aggression, and intoxication.[62] Recent scholarship on the Irish, however, casts doubt on Fairburn's thesis, documenting instead the existence and strength of kinship ties.[63]

Asylum records provide information relevant to this debate. Family information was often sought because of medical concerns surrounding hereditary insanity. According to a cousin of John from Donegal, a brother of John's was insane and committed suicide by drowning in Wellington after discharge from the asylum there.[64] It was also reported of Kate from Ireland that 'her sister Mary [surname removed] is at present a patient here, so there is evidently [*erased:* an] insane tendency in the family'.[65] Historians of medicine, however, have generally focused on the role of the family in generating asylum admissions and discharges.[66] Apart from concerns about heredity, information about family networks was also sought for the purpose of securing the financial maintenance of a patient, despite asylums being centrally maintained.

Recently, Joseph Melling and Bill Forsythe utilised census manuscripts to ascertain household structures, demonstrating that most admissions to Devon County Asylum in England were from deeply rooted, physically less mobile families.[67] No such analysis is possible in New Zealand where original census manuscripts were destroyed. We are therefore reliant on sources such as data in case books which point to the presence or absence of kin ties. Although quantitative analysis is required to give statistical substance to what follows, qualitative data reveals a variety of kin connections, although the extent to which these were simple household structures of parents and children rather than extensive networks of siblings remains to be verified.

Family networks are evident in discussions of a patient's migration, either in accompanying the patient abroad or encouraging them to the colony. Londoner William, for instance, voyaged to Otago on the *Carnatic* with one of his brothers, whereas Scotswoman Ann, allegedly 'assaulted and violated by two ploughmen', moved to New Zealand on the *Parsee* with her unmarried sister.[68] Another Londoner, George, arrived in Dunedin on the *Peter Denney* two years prior to his admission, having 'emigrated to New Zealand at the advice of his brother'.[69] Of Maria from Galway: 'her uncle sent for Maria & her sister & paid their passages'.[70] Other cases document the migration of families including that of Glaswegian Samuel who moved to New Zealand in 1871 with his parents.[71] Malcolm also arrived in the colony with his parents and although visited by his father and brother in 1883 would not converse with them.[72]

Yet while such connections were noted, it is difficult to discern how extensive such contact was. Scotsman William, for instance, had a strong bond with his sister with whom he and his two children resided 'in a lonely part of the country'. William, however, was only home once a week and fell into a melancholy state on learning that his sister had borne an illegitimate child.[73] While childbirth was attributed as the cause for Irishwoman Margaret's admission to Seacliff, her husband reported that 'she has being in a qui*te* plase 4 years in the township but No hause very Near'.[74] Isolation also seemingly contributed to the admission to the asylum of Peter from Stirlingshire, eight months after his arrival in the colony. As his half cousin put it: 'Melancoly. Being strange in a foreign country. Not knowing where to find a friend'.[75] Irishwoman Catherine also had a sister in the colony but was reluctant for her to know of her admission.[76] Indeed, it is likely that migrants found their way to asylums because of extant family networks rather than their absence.[77]

Such cases echo broader claims that 'landing here among strangers and placed in the midst of forceful conditions of life such as they had never been accustomed to, and with the necessity laid upon them to rely upon their own resources, they earlier or later broke down under a pressure too great for them'.[78] Indeed, some case files mention the difficult circumstances of colonial life. Mary from Galway, for instance, 'found colonial life too hard for her'.[79] Medical superintendents of asylums clearly considered the challenges of colonial life an impediment to the mental health of some patients, like Bridget, of whom it was reported to relatives in 1889: 'If she had enough money to pay the passage I should not hesitate to send her away at once for she is mentally fit . . . and a good worker, but I do not think it could be well for her to go from here to stay in Dunedin because she would be better among friends—a struggle to earn a living directly she left might make her health break down again. . . . Bridget has applied to you for fifteen pounds and I think it could be well if you could spare that sum'.[80]

Conflict between family members is a further indicator of the existence of kin ties in the colony. Whereas Fairburn has argued that violence emerged from a 'deficient framework of association',[81] asylum records provide an alternative insight. For the most part, however, such conflict seemingly revolved around marital discord or parent-child encounters rather than broader kin relationships. Englishman William, for instance, claimed to be unhappy in his married life, alleging that his wife's temper made him drink.[82] Similar claims were made by George, 'a native of Tasmania'. It was alleged that 'his wife appears to [*erased:* have] be a bit of a shrew & his home-life seems not to have been the brightest, in fact he just looks like a properly hen-pecked husband with all the spirit taken out of him'.[83]

We do, however, need to be alert to migrants who seemingly operated without such connections. It was explicitly noted of Fife-born Thomas, for instance, that he was without relatives in the colony, leading to his subsequent discharge in 1882 in order to return home on the *Marsala* accompanied by an attendant.[84] Meanwhile, Robert's wife had died and a nephew was embarking to England prompting the statement that there was no relative in the colony.[85] Mary was another who was without family in the colony. An orphan, she had worked as a servant in a boarding house in London, before her mistress sent her to New Zealand to better herself.[86] Despite such examples, initial impressions suggest that many of those confined to asylums had networks of family and friends in the colony, many of whom provided testimony relevant to a patient's committal. Further quantitative research in this area will inevitably confirm or reject this hypothesis.

CONCLUSION

Examination of a range of conditions in the new world, the divergent model according to Nancy Green's conceptualisation, is clearly needed in any study of migrant adjustment. This chapter has explored one particular aspect of those conditions: the existence and operation of networks of family and friends, a key area of analysis for both historians of medicine and migration. Additional quantitative analysis is needed to more closely investigate the issues raised here, and more investigation is also required to identify whether behaviours which were cited as causes of admission to asylums including recourse to drink, religious fervour, and solitude were connected to the process of migration or tied to old-world behaviours. In other words, Green's linear model, which offers perspectives on the past and present, must be incorporated into any analysis. Indeed, despite the importance of conditions encountered in the new world in migrant adjustment, foreign-born admissions to asylums were also influenced by prior experience, including hereditary insanity and previous confinement to homeland asylums, as well as the process of migration itself, especially the voyage out and time spent in other destinations. Whether such factors differed according to migrants' backgrounds is outside the remit of this chapter, although the over-representation of Irish migrants in asylums indicates the need to also engage with Green's convergent model. This chapter's focus on issues of migration, however, is not designed to detract from other explanations for admission to asylums, but does offer insight into aspects relating migration process. Furthermore, this focus is also of benefit for historians of migration, with asylum records shedding light on important and often under-explored areas of analysis.

NOTES

1. A. Scull, *The Most Solitary of Afflictions: Madness and Society in Britain, 1700–1900* (New Haven, CT: Yale University Press, 1993); J. Walton, 'Lunacy in the industrial revolution: A study of asylum admissions in Lancashire, 1848–50', *Journal of Social History*, 13 (1979), pp. 1–22; R. Adair, J. Melling, and B. Forsythe, 'Migration, family structure, and pauper lunacy in Victorian England: Admissions to the Devon County pauper lunatic asylum, 1845–1900', *Continuity and Change*, 12:3 (1997), pp. 373–401.
2. D. Wright, J. Moran, and S. Gouglas, 'The confinement of the insane in Victorian Canada: The Hamilton and Toronto asylums, c. 1861–1891', in R. Porter and D. Wright (eds.), *The Confinement of the Insane: International Perspectives, 1800–1965* (Cambridge: Cambridge University Press, 2003), pp. 100–28; R. Littlewood and M. Lipsedge, *Aliens and Alienists: Ethnic Minorities and Psychiatry*, 2nd ed. (London: Unwin Hyman, 1989).
3. N. L. Green, 'The comparative method and post-structural structuralism: New perspectives for migration studies', in J. Lucassen and L. Lucassen (eds.), *Migration, Migration History, History: Old Paradigms and New Perspectives* (Bern: Peter Lang, 1997), pp. 57–72, 57.
4. C. Coleborne, *Madness in the Family: Insanity and Institutions in the Australasian Colonial World, 1860–1914* (London: Palgrave Macmillan, 2010); B. Labrum, 'Looking beyond the asylum: Gender and the process of committal in Auckland, 1870–1910', *New Zealand Journal of History*, 26 (1992), pp. 125-44.
5. See especially B. Brookes and J. Thomson (eds.), *'Unfortunate Folk': Essays on Mental Health Treatment, 1863–1992* (Dunedin: University of Otago Press, 2001); J. H. Bloomfield, 'Dunedin Lunatic Asylum, 1863–1876' (BA Hons essay, University of Otago, 1979); C. Hubbard, 'Lunatic Asylums in Otago, 1882–1911', (BA Hons, University of Otago, 1977); E. C. Spooner, 'Digging for the Families of the "Mad": Locating the Family in the Auckland Asylum Archives, 1870–1911' (MA, University of Waikato, 2006); L. J. Burke, '"The voices that caused him to become porangi:" Maori Patients in the Auckland Lunatic Asylum, 1860–1900' (MA, University of Waikato, 2006).
6. An exception is A. McCarthy, 'Ethnicity, migration and the lunatic asylum in early twentieth-century Auckland, New Zealand', *Social History of Medicine*, 21:1 (2008), pp. 47–65.
7. Wright, Moran, and Gouglas, 'The confinement of the insane in Victorian Canada'.

8. Archives New Zealand Auckland Regional Office (ANZ ARO), Auckland Carrington Hospital Files, Register of Admission (1885–96), YCAA 1021/2, p. 1226; Patient Casebook, YCAA 1048/4 (1885–87), p. 31; Register of Admission, YCAA 1017/1, p. 641; Patient Casebook, YCAA 1048/5, p. 108.
9. M. Finnane, *Insanity and the Insane in Post-Famine Ireland* (London: Croom Helm, 1981), p. 224.
10. J. Andrews, 'Raising the tone of asylumdom: Maintaining and expelling pauper lunatics at the Glasgow Royal Asylum in the nineteenth century', p. 201; and A. Scull, 'Rethinking the history of asylumdom', p. 308, in J. Melling and B. Forsythe (eds.), *Insanity, Institutions and Society, 1800–1914: A Social History of Madness in Comparative Perspective* (London: Routledge, 1999).
11. J. Melling, 'Accommodating madness: New research in the social history of insanity and institutions', in Melling and Forsythe (eds.), *Insanity, Institutions and Society*, p. 20.
12. *AJHR*, 1876, H-4, p. 11.
13. Ibid., 1884, H-7, p. 1.
14. See, for instance, Coleborne, *Madness in the Family*, ch. 5.
15. Finnane, *Insanity and the Insane*, pp. 54–59.
16. *AJHR*, 1874, H-2, p. 9.
17. Archives New Zealand Dunedin Regional Office (ANZ DRO), Seacliff Hospital Medical Casebook (1894–1895), DAHI/D264/19956/46, case 2829.
18. ANZ DRO, Dunedin Lunatic Asylum Medical Casebook (1877–1913), DAHI/D264/19956/39, fo. 460.
19. University of Dundee Archive Services (UDAS), Records of Sunnyside Royal Hospital, THB 23/5/3/3, fo. 417.
20. ANZ DRO, Seacliff Asylum Medical Casebook (1885–1915), DAHI/D264/19956/40, fo. 339.
21. UDAS, Records of Sunnyside Royal Hospital, THB 23/5/2/4, pp. 243, 257.
22. *AJHR*, 1880, H-6, p. 2.
23. O. Walsh, 'Gender and insanity in nineteenth-century Ireland', in J. Andrews and A. Digby (eds.), *Sex and Seclusion, Class and Custody: Perspectives on Gender and Class in the History of British and Irish Psychiatry* (Amsterdam: Rodopi, 2004), p. 73.
24. ANZ DRO, Seacliff Hospital Medical Casebook (1891–1892), DAHI/D264/19956/43–3, case 2459.
25. UDAS, Records of Murray Royal Lunatic Asylum, THB 29/8/6/1/3, p. 22.
26. ANZ DRO, Seacliff Hospital Medical Casebook (1900–1901), DAHI/D264/19956/53, case 3464.
27. UDAS, Records of Sunnyside Royal Hospital, THB 23/5/2/12, fo. 407.
28. ANZ DRO, Seacliff Hospital Medical Casebook (1900–1901), DAHI/D264/19956/53, case 3453.
29. Edinburgh University Library, Royal Edinburgh Hospital Casebooks (1870–73), LHB 7/51/22, fo. 74.
30. Ibid., 7/51/20, fo. 57; and 7/51/22, fo. 736. See also 7/51/24, fo. 498; and 7/51/37, fo. 393.
31. Evidence can also be found of these migration pathways in data from the Auckland asylum. See McCarthy, 'Ethnicity, migration and the lunatic asylum', pp. 47–65, 53–54.
32. Ibid., p. 54.
33. ANZ ARO, Auckland Carrington Hospital Files, Patient Casebook (1853–71), YCAA 1048/1, p. 74.
34. ANZ DRO, Seacliff Hospital Medical Casebook (1903), DAHI/D264/19956/56, case 3810.

35. The major book-length study for New Zealand is D. Hastings, *Over the Mountains of the Sea: Life on the Migrant Ships, 1870–1885* (Auckland: Auckland University Press, 2006). For chapters on the voyage, see C. Macdonald, *A Woman of Good Character: Single Women as Immigrant Settlers in Nineteenth-Century New Zealand* (Wellington: Bridget Williams, 1990); A. McCarthy, *Irish Migrants in New Zealand, 1840–1937: 'The Desired Haven'* (Woodbridge: Boydell, 2005), ch. 3.
36. K. Maglen, '"The first line of defence": British quarantine and the port sanitary authorities in the nineteenth century', *Social History of Medicine*, 15:3 (2002), pp. 413–28; and 'A world apart: Geography, Australian quarantine, and the mother country', *Journal of the History of Medicine and Allied Sciences*, 60:2 (2005), pp. 196–217.
37. ANZ DRO, Seacliff Hospital Medical Casebook (1897–1898), DAHI/D264/19956/49, case 3048.
38. Ibid., (1890–1891), DAHI/D264/19956/42, case 2354.
39. ANZ DRO, Dunedin Lunatic Asylum Medical Casebook (1877–1913), DAHI/D264/19956/39, 253.
40. ANZ DRO, Seacliff Hospital Medical Casebook (1897–1898), DAHI/D264/19956/49, case 3083.
41. ANZ DRO, Dunedin Lunatic Asylum Medical Casebook (1876–1913), DAHI/D264/19956/38, fo. 121.
42. ANZ DRO, Dunedin Lunatic Asylum and Seacliff Hospital Medical Casebook (1863–c.1920), DAHI/D265/19956/1, fo. 644.
43. ANZ DRO, Dunedin Lunatic Asylum Medical Casebook (1877–1913), DAHI/D264/19956/39, fo. 214.
44. ANZ DRO, Seacliff Hospital Medical Casebook (1893–1894), DAHI/D264/19956/45, case 2651.
45. Ibid., case 2718.
46. Archives New Zealand Wellington Regional Office [ANZ WRO], Papers relating to individual immigrants, ACFQ 8223, IM 3/3/1/3 (1875/1524–1876/980), 76/481, E. Redward, Matron, Immigration Depot to the Immigration Officer, Wellington, 21 April 1876.
47. Ibid., J. B. Robertson, Westminster, to E. A. Smith, 4 July 1876.
48. Ibid., C. H. Gibson, Surgeon Superintendent, *Waipa*.
49. Ibid., Papers relating to individual immigrants, ACFQ 8223, IM 3/3/1/3 (1875/1524–1876/980), 76/496, Dr. Hasard, Surgeon Superintendent, *Merope*, to J. E. March, Immigration Officer, Christchurch, 1 October 1875.
50. Ibid., Deputy Superintendent, 6 October 1875.
51. Ibid., Featherston, Agent General, London, to Minister for Immigration, Wellington, 18 February 1876.
52. Ibid., Commissioners Report on *British Empire*, Auckland, to Minister of Immigration, Wellington, 13 October 1875, IM/5/29/4/22 (1876/678–1876/780).
53. E. Malcolm, 'Women and madness in Ireland, 1600–1850', in M. MacCurtain and M. O'Dowd (eds.), *Women in Early Modern Ireland* (Edinburgh: Edinburgh University Press, 1991), p. 331.
54. ANZ DRO, Seacliff Hospital Medical Casebook (1893–1894), DAHI/D264/19956/45, case 2723.
55. *AJHR*, 1879, H-4, p. 2.
56. A. Hoult, 'Institutional responses to mental deficiency in New Zealand, 1911–1935: Tokanui Mental Hospital' (MA, University of Waikato, 2007), p. 17.
57. W. Ernst, *Mad Tales from the Raj: Colonial Psychiatry in South Asia, 1800–58* (London: Anthem Press, 2010; first published 1991).

58. For a fuller discussion, see A. McCarthy, 'Family networks among Irish migrants in New Zealand asylums', in P. Prior (ed.), *Mental Health Care and the Irish: Historical Studies* (Dublin: Irish Academic Press, 2012, in press).
59. McCarthy, 'Ethnicity, migration and the lunatic asylum', p. 54.
60. Littlewood and Lipsedge, *Aliens and Alienists*, p. 90.
61. These published causes of insanity can be found in the *AJHR*.
62. All previous quotes from M. Fairburn, *The Ideal Society and Its Enemies: The Foundations of Modern New Zealand Society, 1850–1900* (Auckland: Auckland University Press, 1989), pp. 11–12, 94, 192–93.
63. McCarthy, *Irish Migrants in New Zealand*.
64. ANZ DRO, Seacliff Hospital Medical Casebook (1897–1898), DAHI/D264/19956/49, case 3093.
65. Ibid., case 3340.
66. M. Finnane, 'Asylums, families and the state', *History Workshop Journal*, 20:1 (1985), pp. 134–48; D. Wright, 'Getting out of the asylum: Understanding the confinement of the insane in the nineteenth century', *Social History of Medicine*, 10:1 (1997), pp. 137–55.
67. J. Melling and B. Forsythe, *The Politics of Madness: The State, Insanity and Society in England, 1845–1914* (London: Routledge, 2006), p. 97.
68. ANZ DRO, Dunedin Lunatic Asylum Medical Casebook (1876–1913), DAHI/D264/19956/38, fo. 107, fo. 8.
69. Ibid., fo. 55.
70. Ibid., (1877–1913), DAHI/D264/19956/39, fo. 193.
71. Ibid., (1876–1913), DAHI/D264/19956/38, fo. 92.
72. Ibid., (1877–1913), DAHI/D264/19956/39, fo. 512.
73. Ibid., fo. 103
74. ANZ DRO, Seacliff Hospital Medical Casebook (1891–1892), DAHI/D264/19956/43, case 2456.
75. Ibid., (1894–1895), DAHI/D264/19956/46, case 2801.
76. ANZ DRO, Dunedin Lunatic Asylum Medical Casebook (1876–1913), DAHI/D264/19956/38, fo. 4.
77. Melling and Forsythe, *The Politics of Madness*, p. 84.
78. J. A. Torrance, *Picturesque Dunedin: Or Dunedin and its Neighbourhood in 1890* (Dunedin: Mills, Dick, 1890), p. 230.
79. ANZ DRO, Dunedin Lunatic Asylum Medical Casebook (1877–1913), DAHI/D264/19956/39, fo. 204.
80. ANZ DRO, Outwards Letters (2 October 1888–8 January 1890), Truby King to W Somerville, 7 June 1889, DAHI D264/3b.
81. Fairburn, *Ideal Society*, p. 12.
82. ANZ DRO, Dunedin Lunatic Asylum Medical Casebook (1876–1913), DAHI/D264/19956/38, fo. 51.
83. ANZ DRO, Seacliff Hospital Medical Casebook (1897–1898), DAHI/D264/19956/49, case 3072.
84. ANZ DRO, Dunedin Lunatic Asylum Medical Casebook (1877–1913), DAHI/D264/19956/39, fo. 500.
85. ANZ DRO, Seacliff Asylum Medical Casebook (1885–1915), DAHI/D264/19956/40, fo. 51.
86. ANZ DRO, Dunedin Lunatic Asylum Medical Casebook (1877–1913), DAHI/D264/19956/39, fo. 191.

5 Locating Ethnicity in the Hospitals for the Insane

Revisiting Case Books as Sites of Knowledge Production about Colonial Identities in Victoria, Australia, 1873–1910

Catharine Coleborne

By the 1870s, just a few decades following European settlement in the late 1830s, colonial Victoria in Australia was already home to thousands of new immigrants. As a relatively young settler society, it was forging a dark history of the displacement, dispersal, and segregation of its first peoples through violence, disease, and legislative measures.[1] Immigrants from Britain, Europe, and Asia had flocked to the goldfields in the 1850s and mingled in various states of harmony and disharmony, practising their cultural worlds in rough, temporary homes on frontiers and also in towns and in the growing city of Melbourne. Gold, argues David Goodman, provided a 'dislocated social setting in a society of immigrants'.[2] Wives had been left deserted; men had fallen victim to alcoholism; and the colony's web of welfare provisions was under noticeable strain. Yet many others had become wealthy through both prospecting and business. This vision of colonial Victoria as 'home' to all classes of person—from the 'poor, indigent [and] restless' to the 'sober and enlightened middle classes'—was one rehearsed over time by contemporaries.[3] The effects of immigration on the colony's history were profound, and histories of migrants as specific groups of people with a shared cultural purpose now provide insights into the rich layers of Australia's cultural heritage.[4]

However, imagining colonial Victoria as a site for the production of colonial identities such as those shaped by gender, class, and 'race' or ethnicity, which could both reinforce and transform relations of power in the colony, is a task yet to be fully undertaken by historians. This chapter argues that the institutional records of the mental hospital at the Yarra Bend, established in 1848 and one of several institutions in colonial Victoria by the 1870s, might yield some new ways of understanding these identities. The mental hospital was a place where those whose worlds had collapsed under the strain of the 'pressures of the colonising life' ended up.[5] It is also one of the only institutional sites which aimed to keep complete records of its population and its various social characteristics, and from these we can draw conclusions about society at large.[6]

Using these patient records to understand and interpret colonial identities, this chapter suggests a historical methodology of seeing and making visible 'ethnicity', recognising that the term itself belongs to a twentieth-century ontology of 'social identity'.[7] As the journal *Social Identities*, first published in the late 1990s, proclaims, scholarly concerns around identity including ethnicity and 'race' have arisen in tandem with social change and new forms of nationalism and racism. Understanding just how social identities have been formed and transformed over time has implications for the study of 'material exclusion and power'.[8] Along with 'gender' and 'class', 'ethnicity' is most readily understood by scholars across the disciplines as one aspect of the complex of ways in which social 'identity'—itself a slippery, contested term—is composed, proscribed, produced, performed, bodily inscribed, understood, and just possibly experienced, and it presents historians with critical interpretive challenges.[9] Jacqui Leckie calls ethnicity a 'subject location', and reminds us how far social differences important outside the asylum were reproduced inside the institutional context.[10] Other scholars comment on the flexibility and malleability of ethnicity—in fact, its very imprecision.[11] In this chapter, the concept is deployed both as a means to examine what contemporaries meant when they noted types, styles, behaviours, and characteristics of individuals and groups, and also somewhat more self-consciously as a critical tool of analysis.

The situation of ethnicity matters. Studies of 'race' and ethnicity have most recently been situated at the nexus between the nation, the empire, and discourses of racial hierarchy. Postcolonial scholarship has brought new perspectives to the study of past ethnicities, including the investigation of a dominant European ethnicity through the concept of whiteness. For example, the concept of 'whiteness' can be used to elucidate the meanings of the nation and its colonial past.[12] The identification of whiteness has considerably expanded the repertoire of historians working on the histories of settler colonies. Warwick Anderson shows us that medicine and the medical elite in the Australian colonies were preoccupied with the health of white settlers, developing theories about the health of the white 'race', feared to be under threat from the influx of all kinds of non-white 'others'.[13] Historical scholarship also identifies the discursive context for Australasian psychiatry as one shaped by ideas about whiteness.[14] However, ideas about ethnicity also have a history; not all whites were the same—for example, Irish could be considered 'black' in some contexts—with Ann Curthoys arguing that a new attention to whiteness cannot replace other forms of ethnic identification in the past, such as 'British'.[15] In fact, as John Comaroff suggests, the imperial world was based on 'ethnic subjection' and the hierarchical layering of peoples using ranks, categories, titles, and identities.[16]

In work more specific to the field of mental health, Angela McCarthy sets out the relationship between migration and ethnicity by using the patient case records of the Auckland Asylum in New Zealand in the early twentieth century, arguing that the contents of such records provide insights into settler society, as well as extending scholarly understandings of the ways in which ethnicity mattered in medical, institutional contexts.[17] Following McCarthy, this chapter is based on a selection of patient cases from colonial Victoria drawn from a large database created from a sample of records of patients confined at the Yarra Bend Hospital for the Insane between 1873 and 1910. From the 1850s, the Yarra Bend Asylum drew its substantive patient population from the suburban areas of Melbourne, as well as from rural areas to the east and north of the growing city. After institutions were established in the rural towns of Ararat and Beechworth in the late 1860s, and the metropolitan Kew Asylum was built in the 1870s, inmates at the Yarra Bend were most likely to be poor and living in the inner city areas, with many admitted from the poor inner city suburbs of Fitzroy, Collingwood, Carlton, North Melbourne, St. Kilda, and the central city itself.[18] The research database which provides the foundation for this study contains a sample of all patients at Yarra Bend for every three years from 1873, including both foreign-born and colonial-born inmates. In its design, the database aims to capture information about ethnicity. As well as containing information about places of birth, religion, and migration patterns, all mentions of ethnicity, language, and cross-cultural encounter are included. It is in fact the database design which has prompted some new questions about the project to locate and define past ethnicity, discussed in this chapter, as for some records created in colonial Victoria, no data on these themes exists. Indeed, in many cases, fields must be left blank, suggesting deep limitations in any exercise in data collection and its uses, reinforcing the contention that historians are constantly grappling with an unknowable past.[19]

This chapter sets out some ways we might proceed to find and understand ethnicity in all its manifestations through a qualitative assessment of these case book records. It seeks to extend McCarthy's discussion of ethnicity, insanity, and migration by elaborating on the possible methodology for the location of this unstable concept of 'ethnicity' in the past by arguing that the patient case book embodied an evolving system of meanings about colonial social identities. It first outlines some relevant examples of historiography in the field before going on to explore several ways in which we might locate ethnicity in the patient data. It discusses the 'counting' of ethnicity in the patient body, both in the nineteenth century and in the present, also reflecting on the practice and meanings of such enumeration; it then goes on to explore the potential use of themes including birthplace and origins, bodies and behaviours, including a discussion about the bodies of immigrant patients in the mental hospital, in order to identify the possible manifestation of contemporary meanings of ethnicity. It also examines the possibility of finding ethnicity in the traces left in the patient records by sound, language, gestures, and expressions. Finally, the chapter pays some attention to the analysis of the content of patient delusions, also linking these to notions of ethnicity.

ETHNICITY AND HISTORIES OF PSYCHIATRY

Ethnicity has, until recently, and with some major exceptions already noted, been a relatively neglected category in the study of psychiatric patient identities. In their edited collection *Sex and Seclusion, Class and Custody*, Jonathan Andrews and Anne Digby posit that ethnicities, along with gender and class, are highly relevant for a more 'inclusive' analysis of psychiatric confinement.[20] Despite the fact that the essays in their collection go on to explore gender and class in some detail whereas ethnicity is less visible, this view signals an awareness among scholars in the field that ethnicity as a category has been applied far less readily to the analysis of that most worked-over of archival materials: institutional patient records. Many historians have examined gender and class for the patient profiles of single institutions, but few have interrogated the utility of ethnicity to understand the processes of committal, treatment, and discharge of patients. Whether some groups were more likely than others to be admitted because of their ethnicity is a question explored in several contexts. In other accounts, the medical treatment and discursive constructions of some groups have received attention. For instance, Elizabeth Malcolm's exploration of Irish patients in four English psychiatric institutions based in Lancashire touches on a range of these themes and questions. She concludes that the Irish were more likely to end up inside institutions, in part because of their relationships to poverty and isolation, and to their relatively infrequent release or discharge.[21]

Historians of psychiatry in colonised settings where the white population was in a minority tend to raise the question of racial differences within asylum populations more readily. Waltraud Ernst refers to a 'colonial idiom' of madness in British India. Focused on British inmates, Ernst seeks to show that colonial identities derived from meanings of gender and 'race', and that aspects of colonial society, including immigration, produced 'mad' identities among British men and women.[22] Other studies of colonial India which explore the 'native only' asylums examine this colonial idiom of madness from another angle, showing that Indians confined in European institutions were caught in a peculiarly European framework for the construction of the identities of the insane.[23] In South Africa, in the Cape Colony, Harriet Deacon argues, white men's insanity 'threatened white supremacy and raised the spectre of degeneration and hereditary insanity', whereas black men's insanity was socially disruptive.[24] Peter McCandless also comments on the treatment and experiences of black patients in South Carolina, noting the high rates of mortality among black patients.[25]

Closer to Australia, at the St. Giles mental hospital in Fiji in the early twentieth century, Jacqui Leckie shows that more Indo-Fijians than Fijians and Europeans were admitted, which she suggests indicates the social and economic pressures on this community in the period. Mortality rates also were high among this group and among the group of indigenous Fijians.[26] Some work on the Māori insane at Auckland Mental Hospital to 1900 indicates that a careful reading and interpretation of patient case notes reveals Māori experienced forms of cultural alienation, which was reinforced by the institutional regimes of bodily examination, description, and reform (or 'civilising').[27] These ideas are explored to good effect by Robert Menzies and Ted Palys in the context of British Columbia.[28] Although relatively little scholarship about the Aboriginal insane exists in the Australian context, partly due to the relatively few Indigenous peoples institutionalised in mental hospitals in the colonies, similar arguments hold relevance there. Contemporaries considered the question. In 1889, leading mental health figure Dr. Frederic Norton Manning published his observations of insanity among thirty-two aboriginal patients, based on Aboriginal men and women confined in Queensland and New South Wales from the 1860s to the late 1880s. However, there were very few Aboriginal patients in Yarra Bend. Bain Attwood's account of Bratualung man Tarra Bobby, confined at Yarra Bend in 1877, provides an especially useful way into the stories of some cases of Aboriginal people, who were both dispossessed and institutionalised.[29] However, such accounts are rare, and little was known about most of the few aboriginal inmates. For example, one case in our database includes very little detail for a fifty-year-old Aboriginal man known simply as 'Charlie' and admitted to Yarra Bend from the Lake Condah Mission Station, located in western Victoria, in 1873.[30]

As Malcolm shows for the Irish in English asylums, the migration experience itself was also important. Malcolm highlights the way ethnic differences were assumed, portrayed, and experienced. In the case of the Irish, the motif of colonialism holds currency for Malcolm because the Irish were a colonised people at home and abroad. As this volume contends, immigration is another theme for studies of the colonial populations of the mad. David Wright, James Moran, and Sean Gouglas argue that different groups may have become vulnerable to confinement in Canada, whereas Jonathan Abelard comments on the phenomenon of mental disturbance among recent arrivals to Argentina.[31] This chapter draws on some of the ideas stemming from this literature, and it also introduces some other examples of ways in which historians have begun to find and interpret ethnicity, illustrating how these modes of inquiry might be applied to new research data for colonial Victoria.

WHO WERE THE INSANE? COUNTING ETHNICITY

In 1871, when the immigrant population formed around 51 per cent of the total population of Victoria, the combined population of the insane at institutions for the insane in the colony included 96 per cent who were born overseas, where information was known. By 1891, the immigrant population had dropped to 32 per cent of the total population, with 74 per cent of all asylum inmates born overseas. Even given the changing age composition of the colonial population, as Richard Broome points out, these differences are stark and are replicated in the percentages of those housed in other colonial welfare institutions.[32] In the Australasian setting, where migration patterns and the experiences of migrants were witnessed through the asylum populations across several decades, medical and social perceptions of ethnicity generated new questions about colonial identity, susceptibility to mental disease, and racial hybridity. Some of these questions were generated by fears about the colonial family, which was viewed as both a site of cure and a cause of mental breakdown. Colonial families were viewed, especially in the early decades of this study, as dislocated and atomised. How could systems of care be negotiated between families and inmates if families were barely whole? How could patterns of heredity be assessed if the colonial 'family tree' was 'not yet fully grown', as Dr. Manning put it?[33]

In addition, this interest in the nationalities of the insane was a global preoccupation and formed part of the asylum's tendency towards counting its population. In the system of official reporting maintained by institutional authorities and presented to parliament, the aggregation of 'nationalities and religious persuasions' in colonial asylums was presented annually. In 1887, the report tabled included Victoria, other colonies and British possessions, England, Scotland, Ireland, France, Germany, China, and other countries. Religions listed included Church of England, Presbyterian, Wesleyan, Lutheran, other Protestant denominations, Roman Catholic, Pagan, and Hebrew. By 1890, this list of religions included Mohammedan, with only one patient recorded in that category from an unspecified country. In subsequent reports the listed categories did not change, and at the end of the period, the report for 1909 made no reference at all to nationalities.[34]

This interest in the nationalities of the insane peaked during the 1880s and 1890s, when immigration patterns and colonial concerns about these were still fluctuating. At the Intercolonial Medical Congress of Australasia in 1889, colonial physicians displayed a preoccupation with the question of the 'race' and ethnicity of the insane in the colonies. The heritage of patients in hospitals for the insane proved to be a significant area of interest for Dr. Chisholm Ross, Medical Officer at Gladesville Hospital in Sydney. Ross examined the patient registers at Gladesville for the ten years between 1878 and 1887 to determine whether any particular patient nationalities dominated the admissions. He was puzzled by the identities of the colonial born, suggesting they were 'of no special race'.[35] Their 'marked hybridity' confused Ross, who wanted to apportion the incidence of insanity to racial categories. Given the structure of the population (more colonial born were young people, but asylum admissions tended to be older people), any quest to define insanity through 'race' was bound to be complex. He did find that more Irish were confined, comparatively speaking, than others from Britain. He had suspicions that more Chinese mad existed than asylum admissions revealed because they were 'harboured by their countrymen'.[36]

Ross put forward his theory that the hybridity of 'Australasians' possibly protected them from insanity, along with their environment, their diets, their conditions of life, and their lack of worry, all of which also shaped their responses to mental challenges. Like his contemporaries, he believed that 'self-reliance' and 'self-confidence' were two of the colonial attributes that held madness at bay.[37] These views were repeated by Ross a few years later in 1891, when fears about the preservation of the health of 'White Australia' were becoming more urgent. He noted that although there was a very low rate of insanity among Aborigines (counting only the institutionalised insane in New South Wales, a very low number of the recorded Aboriginal population at 8 in 8,280), the number of foreign-born insane constituted one-seventh of the asylum population, more than their proportion in the general population, which was less than one-twenty-seventh.[38] However, proving whether the presence of the foreign-born insane signalled a real or imagined threat to the mental health of the colonies is not the intention of this chapter. Rather, it suggests that the very preoccupation with counting peoples produced knowledge about nationality and therefore ethnicity, and provides historians with one avenue to finding out about the ethnicities of the insane in the past.[39]

NATIONALITY, BIRTHPLACE, AND ORIGINS

This concern over nationality and birthplace was captured in the official records for the patients at Yarra Bend under one term: 'native place'. The term 'native place' arguably stood in for 'ethnicity' in the case book's system of meaning in most colonial institutions. Native places of patients ranged from the names of countries to those of other colonies. Looking at the recorded data is suggestive: England, Scotland, and Ireland dominate among the countries listed, with finer calibrations in some cases, such as mentions of Yorkshire, Cornwall, Kilkenny, Clare, Galway, and sometimes Dublin; although rarely do the records mention all three categories of town, city or village, county and country. Where the patient cases do include such data, we have more opportunity to firmly categorise ethnicity, as a 'native place' might not always have been a birthplace, especially in the case of larger cities like London. Chinese patients formed another distinct ethnic group, with their native place noted as 'China', their religion usually recorded as 'Pagan' or 'Heathen', and the strong likelihood of poor English-language skills all signifying their otherness. Patients also came from Wales, Italy, Denmark, Holland, Germany or Prussia, Norway, Switzerland, France, Finland, Poland, Sweden, America, Canada, India, South Africa, and New Zealand, although in smaller numbers, reflecting migration patterns to the colonies.[40]

There were subtle meanings behind the recorded places of origin inside colonial institutions of this period, and these persisted into the early twentieth century. For instance, McCarthy shows that at Auckland Asylum in the early twentieth century, many patients spoke about local towns and villages, and conversed with assistant medical officer Alexander McKelvey about their birthplaces, also raising the question of the origins and ethnicities of the doctors and attendants in asylums who communicated with inmates.[41] Personal origins continued to have significance for patients at Yarra Bend, like the Englishman John G., confined with alcoholism at Yarra Bend in 1888, who commented that he had been in the colony for twenty-two years but had never had a 'settled residence'.[42] Matthew C., arrested for vagrancy, was anxious to return to Calcutta in India in 1888, where he was born and where his wife waited for him.[43] William R. recalled coming on a ship, but could not recall where from, although in 1894 his mother reported he was born in Nova Scotia and that he had been a sailor.[44] Letters to friends in Ireland warranted a mention in the 1873 case notes for James K., a thirty-year old labourer with delusional insanity.[45] Confused, and suffering from what the notes describe as 'imbecility', Robert R., aged forty, could remember people in Glasgow when questioned at Yarra Bend in 1900.[46]

Contemporaries also linked mental illness with the question of nationality, a theme which is the subject of Elizabeth Malcolm's chapter in this volume. Among the theories circulating about the Irish in Australia, for instance, was the suspicion that families back in Ireland sent family members with mental health problems to the colonies, a fear contradicted by the Irish Lunacy Commissioners themselves who worried about their own high rates of institutionalisation.[47] The enumeration and assessment of mental health populations in the international context had, then, produced ethnic stereotypes which continued to reproduce inside the institutional setting.

BODIES AND BEHAVIOURS

Interpreting the institutional representations of the bodies of the insane might therefore be another highly instructive mode of analysis.[48] Arguably, the colonial-born insane also took on social identities infused by ethnic and class stereotypes, with poor, slum-dwelling inmates inheriting the perceived unstable social patterns of their forebears. Concepts of social identity circulating in the colonies, such as the prejudices reported about some migrants who were perceived to be the 'social dregs', including Scottish Highlanders and southern Irish, and accompanied by accusations about rates of illiteracy and poor skills, were also reproduced in the institutional environment.[49] The very bodies of the insane were now being imagined through such differences. In some colonial contexts, including Fiji, the very embodiment of ethnicity among patients as witnessed in patient case records was stark.[50] Colonial asylums, argues Jim Mills, produced new forms of knowledge about the bodies of non-whites, a practice most explicit in sites where the British were in a minority, including British India.[51] Linked to this, gender was also a 'vehicle for the expression of ethnic otherness', as several historians note.[52] Research about colonial Australia also presents some evidence that physical and bodily differences began to shape the classification of patients beyond a simple gender classification, and it certainly characterised the case book representations of some patients.[53]

One pertinent signifier is found in the broken-down bodies of male patients transferred from the Immigrants' Home in Melbourne. By the 1870s, Australian historian Alan Atkinson writes, Melbourne was a 'chaos of humanity', a city which had grown nine times its size to 207,000 in the twenty years after the gold rushes of the 1850s.[54] Collingwood was 'poverty stricken and tightly packed', teeming with animals and coloured by 'brackish water'; the inner city was 'suffocating', full of rubbish and sewerage problems, with higher child mortality rates in the densely populated suburbs of North Melbourne, Fitzroy, and Collingwood than other areas of the city.[55] The city became, by the 1870s, sites for behaviour that Anderson calls 'the irresponsible conduct of others—especially other classes and other races', and places which were increasingly represented as crowded by uncontrolled 'displaced bodies'.[56] 'Foreigners' and new arrivals stood out among the groups who were recipients of charity in Victoria.[57] Immigrant men were among the 'outcasts of Melbourne'. Often bachelors, they mixed among the poor and criminal, and formed part of the 'itinerant street economy'.[58] These were men like Abrahaam A., who was confined at Yarra Bend in 1873. Aged forty-five, he was a street hawker who was described as 'Hebrew' in his patient case record. He had come to the colony from London, had been living in Collingwood, and his wife cited 'depression in business' as the cause of his illness. Other male hawkers living in the inner city were Italian, 'Mahomedan', Chinese, and British, and the patient case records for these men also suggest conflict and loss of income were causes for their hospitalisation.[59]

Located at Princes Bridge, St. Kilda Road, the Immigrants' Home was established in 1852 by the Immigrants' Aid Society, and by the middle of 1853, this home and other shelters had already provided temporary lodging for thousands of immigrants.[60] By the 1860s and 1870s, these included aged and infirm men waiting for admission to Benevolent Asylums, men suffering from chronic diseases, convalescents, single and pregnant women, and deserted wives and children. Cases of immigrants transferred from these homes provide us with some indicative evidence of the plight of immigrant men in colonial Victoria, as well the attempts of the colonial institutional authorities to find out more information about them.

We actually know very little about these immigrant men based on their patient records. William B., aged forty-four, was a labourer.[61] The cause of Thomas C.'s melancholia was said to be sunstroke, but he also suffered from tubercular disease.[62] Brian M., aged thirty, was from Dublin.[63] William R., aged seventy-two and originally from Glasgow, had suffered an accident to his head.[64] Joseph R., seventy-four, suffered from a form of dementia, and was described as a 'feeble old man'.[65] Charles J., twenty-seven, was also diagnosed with General Paralysis of the Insane (GPI), as was Brian M. John R. was covered in 'bruises and abrasions' when he arrived from the Immigrants' Home.[66] George S., formerly a ship's carpenter, although delusional, was quiet and well behaved, which possibly aided his later escape from Yarra Bend.[67]

The main feature of these records is that they are extremely brief. In none of these cases is there a note about family contacts in the colonies. In a few cases, police were involved in the transfer process. For 1874 the Immigrants Aid Society reported that the 'male adult inmates were of the most helpless class,— the majority suffering from disease, and requiring medical treatment and hospital care. The able-bodied who sought temporary relief with the Society as 'casuals' were comparatively few'.[68] In fact, throughout the 1870s, the annual reports of the society, including the reports of the medical officer and the special committees, began to complain, in particular, about the problem of men. Sick, disabled, living unstable lives, they were often 'utterly helpless' and were a burden on the community.

Such reportage perhaps accounts for some of these transfers of men who were not 'classic' cases of mental breakdown. By 1880, the medical officer's report for the Society noted 'revolting' cases among the ranks of the male immigrants, hinting at cases of GPI. The annual reports of the society between the 1870s and 1880s also shed light on the female population, noting the problem of women who were found to be 'sick and incompetent from mental defect'.[69] The women who relied on the support of the Immigrants' Home were either deserted wives with children; women who had become pregnant out of wedlock; or women who were sick, aged, or imbecile. One of these was an Irishwoman from Kilkenny, Kate H., who found herself hospitalised at Yarra Bend in 1885, and who preferred the asylum to the Immigrants' Home because its doors were locked.[70]

Chinese patients became a distinct bodily category of patient in a way that other groups of patients did not. In the Annual Inspector's Report for 1879, a broad discursive profile of the patients described new patients; those discharged; the number discharged; the rate of mortality; specific diseases; the number of epileptics and idiots; and the number of Chinese.[71] The wider social unease about Chinese immigration might explain this approach to the categorisation of the Chinese. But in this way, the report drew attention to only one ethnic group and seemed to ally it to a specific diagnosis or category of insanity.

Immigrant communities in colonial Victoria forged bonds and cultures though organised society, groups, religious worship, patterns of settlement and custom, with varying degrees of success.[72] However, once hospitalised, some new arrivals may have found their isolation dispiriting. Although by 1880 chaplains conducted regular services in the Church of England, Presbyterian, and Roman Catholic denominations, the dominant speaking language was English. It is not hard to imagine that Giovanni V. felt culturally alienated at Yarra Bend in 1891. Being both Catholic and Italian, he spent his time in constant prayer and was still deeply depressed in 1893, when he was described as 'profoundly melancholic' and socially withdrawn. Although there is no direct reference to his speaking Italian, it is fair to assume he used his native tongue.[73] Other Italian inmates also seem to have experienced severe reactions to their confinement, such as John M. in 1900. A farm labourer aged thirty, John was diagnosed as melancholic, was always 'crying and whining as if in pain', and attempted suicide.[74] Among the cases at Yarra Bend are a small number of Jewish inmates who, as Broome writes, constituted a distinct cultural group in colonial Victoria. In 1891, for example, one Jewish inmate at Yarra Bend lived in inner-city Carlton and worked as tailor.[75] Another worked as a 'dealer' in Carlton in 1900 before his committal.[76] These men perhaps faced the loneliness described by Broome, who points out that their lives were marked by homosocial religious society, a lack of kosher butchery practices, and little attention to Jewish custom.[77] By examining such individuals and their responses to institutional confinement, this chapter shows that social identity could also shape the emotional worlds of patients.

SOUND, LANGUAGE, GESTURES, AND EXPRESSIONS

Colonial mental hospitals were places which housed people from many different countries, implying great 'sonic diversity' among inmates in both language and culture, as Dolly MacKinnon suggests; she argues for an analysis of the 'sonic demographic' of the institution.[78] McCarthy also considers traces of 'place, language and accent' in the Auckland and Dunedin patient records.[79] Using these very suggestive models, we can locate ethnicity in the sounds, language, gestures, and expressions found in the patient case books. So far, several cases in our Victorian data mention poor or broken English and the need for an asylum interpreter. Chinese patients needing the services of Mr. Hodge, interpreter, included forty-four-year-old Ah Fong, a hawker who had been in gaol before he came to Yarra Bend in 1891. In 1894, the superintendent noted that Kooey Y. spoke 'no English'. Charles Lum T. managed to convey to the interpreter that he thought people wanted to kill him in 1891. Although the native place of Robert R. was unknown, he could not speak English in 1888. German man Johan S. spoke only broken English in 1900, and in the same year, Frenchman Leon J. told doctors through an interpreter that he had been starving and vagrant before his admission. The problem of miscommunication and language difference was heightened inside institutional contexts because insanity was itself often incoherent, making other forms of cultural or linguistic diversity challenging for inmates and doctors alike. Although we tend not to reveal them for ethical reasons, the very 'sound' of surnames is provocative for the researcher, and may also have been for contemporaries. Surnames like Pedrotti, Maranto, Abrahaam, Judeman, Spitz, and Sutton all evoke meanings associated with places and with ethnic identities.

Cultural diversity was complex and could produce unhappiness and distress among those confined in colonial institutional settings. In institutions in British India, for instance, some patients evinced religious taboos around food and social contact with others of different cultural or caste backgrounds and status.[80] In colonial Victoria, some European patients verbalised their distaste at having to share their space with the Chinese. But what did the Chinese make of their surroundings and companions? They too were most likely irritated by the diet, the dominant customs and religious practices of the institution, and reacted accordingly. A Chinese inmate who committed suicide at Yarra Bend in 1878, as reported by the official inspector, hung himself from a window using a strip of blanket.[81] The behaviours of depressed Italian inmates who were overtly distressed inside the asylum are noted above. Such ethnic divisions and tensions present in the records will shed more light on categories of ethnicity itself, as well as issues surrounding diagnoses and treatments including attitudes towards non-English-speaking inmates. The institutional practice of photographing inmates, more prominent by 1900, also suggests avenues of analysis.[82] There is no photograph of the former barman Joseph V., who in 1885 was confined at the age of twenty-three and described as being 'dull and stupid in appearance with a dusky type of face'.[83] His skin tone probably resembled that of many patients who came to Yarra Bend unwashed and unkempt, sometimes having been living rough. But the physical assessments of patients, such as the interest shown in their appearance, sometimes provide coded commentaries on assumptions about ethnicity.

THE CONTENT OF DELUSIONS

The delusions present in the records of Yarra Bend also reveal potential ways of understanding social identities. This research set out to establish the many kinds of relationships between mental illness and migration, from patterns of ill health and heredity to social dislocation and trouble settling among migrant communities. In this sense, a colonial set of case studies provides a potentially rich site for the analysis of social tension and discord, especially perhaps expressed through racial or ethnic difference. Several historians remind us of the importance that could be attached to the content of delusions recorded in patient cases. Elizabeth Malcolm writes that Sander Gilman's work about the representation of disease can assist in this task to try to find out more about the relationship between culture at large and the 'delusional system' evident in patient voices.[84] John Burnham used Tasmania records to interrogate the relationship between delusional content and social context, and David Goodman comments on the way that gold was part of the 'delusional life of Victorian lunatics' in the 1850s.[85]

Among the Yarra Bend cases is the story of Dominico P., originally from Naples, who believed that he owned a gold mine in 1894.[86]

Religious delusions sometimes took the place of or presented anxieties around racial difference inside colonial institutions.[87] Delusions also reflected social tensions, such as expressions of fear of Malay (Muslims) among white patients in Cape Town.[88] McCarthy notes some differences between the delusions of Irish, Scottish, and English migrants at Auckland, and Labrum produces evidence for Auckland which highlights the inappropriateness of Pakeha patients whose delusions indicated forms of sympathy with Māori.[89] At Yarra Bend in 1894, Henry O. imagined his own fortunes to be closely tied to a Chinese patient when he said that they would both be hung.[90]

An array of delusions of grandeur could be analysed for their meanings in relation to ethnicity, such as the Englishwoman named Elizabeth who believed herself to be Queen Elizabeth in 1888, or Alice who in 1885 mentioned that her marriage certificate linked her to royalty, or the Chinese man who believed himself to be Emperor of China in 1873.[91] Ethnic tension colours the account by a German woman Ernestine R. in 1888 who feared she had been bewitched by an Egyptian woman who had tried to 'unroof her house'. In the same year Catherine P. from London was afraid that the Fenians would kill her or burn down the building. Transferred from the Immigrants' Home, she had perhaps been vocal there about her unease.[92] Sectarian conflict persisted in colonial contexts.[93] Several delusions relate to place, with inmates confused about where they were or where they had come from, including Robert W. who in 1891 believed he was back in Manchester.[94] Indeed, getting out of the colony might have been one fantasy that many patients shared, given that it had become their prison. In her delusion, Linda M.'s 'saviour' had 'given up the colony', whereas another patient believed herself to be on the boat to Ireland.[95]

CONCLUSIONS

In an effort to locate ethnicity inside colonial institutions, with a specific focus on colonial Victoria, this chapter has positioned this research within the field of study of 'colonial psychiatry'. It implicitly references Richard Keller's argument that colonial psychiatry must consider the function and operation of 'race' as it explores the relationship between knowledge and power in colonial settings, including white settler colonies, also addressing Waltraud Ernst's notion of the 'colonial idioms' of madness, and Leckie's explorations of the embodiment of ethnicity.[96] Medical constructions of gender, class, and ethnicity have much to reveal about colonial identity making because institutional sites, such as mental hospitals, designed for those deemed most marginal to the successful workings of colonialism, perhaps paradoxically demonstrate its failures and its flawed self-conception. In the process of interrogating the production of social identities in the colonial context, we might specifically examine gender, with a twin focus on both masculinities and femininities. Examples of the usefulness of a gendered approach include further examination of the distinct social concerns about broken and diseased men; and medical anxieties around female imbecility, sexuality, and reproduction. Although this chapter touches on all of these themes, it has privileged questions about ethnicity as a category of analysis.

Traces of ethnicity in the patient case records tell us much about the social and cultural differences in colonial populations, as well as reactions to these. Colonial institutions, this chapter has suggested, tended to capture a wider array of ethnicities than institutions in the home countries of European origin, in part because of migration patterns, as Angela McCarthy's chapter in this volume shows. Yet in seeking these historical traces, we too, like our colonial forebears, produce new forms of knowledge. Ann Laura Stoler writes that the 'making of colonial categories shares [an] ambiguous epistemic space. New social objects were the archives' product as much as subjects of them'.[97] This statement sits at the heart of this approach to the study of insanity and ethnicity in colonial Victoria. The research database contains the details of thousands of cases of individual inmates and it both reproduces the information contained in the patient case books, and constructs new fields for the interpretation of these. Moving from the archive to the database in this way highlights how ethnicity might be found and perceived, but also how it might be characterised and represented. Ian Hacking argues that nineteenth-century statistical processes of what he calls 'making up people' by counting them is another form of inventing and classifying groups which limit the individual.[98]

Having noted this, the data provides a more detailed account of these traces of ethnicity for future researchers and will allow researchers to compare across colonial sites. In particular, we might witness changing patterns of confinement over time, with concentrations of some groups in earlier periods and not at all in later decades. In this way, the very counting of peoples might allow us to shed some light on the asylum's own processes with regard to ethnicity and committal.

NOTES

1. For a discussion about this aspect of colonial Victoria, see R. Broome, *Aboriginal Australians: Black Reponses to White Dominance 1788–2001*, 3rd ed. (Crows Nest: Allen and Unwin, 2001), pp. 56–72, 74–90.
2. D. Goodman, *Gold Seeking: Victoria and California in the 1850s* (Sydney: Allen and Unwin, 1994), p. 198.
3. Ibid., p. 194.
4. Histories of migrants to the colonies reinforce this idea of 'shared cultures': see, for instance, R. Broome, *Arriving* (Sydney: Fairfax, Syme and Weldon, 1984), p. 107.
5. The phrase is from P. Russell (ed.), *For Richer, For Poorer: Early Colonial Marriages* (Melbourne: Melbourne University Press, 1994), p. 6. See also

C. Coleborne, *Reading 'Madness': Gender and Difference in the Colonial Asylum in Victoria, Australia, 1848–1888* (Perth: Network, 2007).

6. Institutions might also be sites for the exploration of colonial mobility; see also A. Hawk, 'Going "mad" in gold country: Migrant populations and the problem of containment in Pacific mining boom regions', *Pacific Historical Review*, 80:1 (2011), pp. 64–96.

7. 'Social identity' is a term used by social psychologists including Henri Tajfel to describe the way that group consciousness determines self-identification into categories. I use the concept to show how identity 'labels' are applied to individuals who occupy specific social groupings and are used in often disabling ways, rather than assuming self-identification, although this process may also have been occurring in the past.

8. See the journal *Social Identity* and its self-description, available at: http://www.tandf.co.uk/journals/carfax/13504630.html (accessed 27 May 2011).

9. M. Sutphen and B. Andrews, *Medicine and Colonial Identity* (London: Routledge, 2003), p. 2.

10. J. Leckie, 'The embodiment of gender and madness in colonial Fiji', *Fijian Studies*, 3:2 (2005), p. 331.

11. W. I. U. Ahmad and H. Bradby, 'Locating ethnicity and health: Exploring concepts and contexts', *Sociology of Health and Illness* 29:6 (2007), p. 796.

12. J. Carey and C. McLiskey (eds.), *Creating White Australia* (Sydney: Sydney University Press, 2009), pp. ix–xxiii.

13. W. Anderson, *The Cultivation of Whiteness: Science, Health and Racial Destiny in Australia* (Melbourne: Melbourne University Press, 2002).

14. C. Coleborne, *Madness in the Family: Insanity and Institutions in the Australasian Colonial World, 1860–1914* (Basingstoke: Palgrave Macmillan, 2010), ch. 1 and 2, pp. 15–64. See also B. Labrum, 'The boundaries of femininity: Madness and gender in New Zealand, 1870–1910', in W. Chan, D. E. Chunn, and R. Menzies (eds.), *Women, Madness and the Law: A Feminist Reader* (London: Glasshouse, 2005), p. 61.

15. A. Curthoys, 'White, British, and European: Historicising identity in settler societies', in Carey and McLisky (eds.), *Creating White Australia*, p. 23.

16. A. Perry, 'Reproducing colonialism in British Columbia, 1849–1871', in T. Ballantyne and A. Burton (eds.), *Bodies in Contact: Rethinking Colonial Encounters in World History* (Durham, NC: Duke University Press, 2005), p. 143; J. Comaroff, 'Reflections on the colonial state, in South Africa and elsewhere: Factions, fragments, facts and fictions', *Social Identities*, 4:3 (1998), pp. 321–61.

17. A. McCarthy, 'Ethnicity, migration and the lunatic asylum in early twentieth-century Auckland, New Zealand', *Social History of Medicine*, 21:1 (2008), p. 63.

18. Stephen Garton presents a similar finding about the patterns of admission for the inmates of the hospitals for the insane in Sydney; see S. Garton, *Medicine and Madness: A Social History of Insanity in New South Wales, 1880–1940* (Kensington: University of New South Wales Press, 1988), p. 121.

19. See Coleborne, *Madness in the Family*, pp. 152–53.

20. J. Andrews and A. Digby (eds.) *Sex and Seclusion, Class and Custody: Perspectives on Gender and Class in the History of British and Irish Psychiatry* (Amsterdam: Rodopi, 2004), p. 27.

21. E. Malcolm, '"A most miserable looking object": The Irish in English asylums, 1851–1901: Migration, poverty and prejudice', in J. Belchem and K. Tenfeld (eds.), *Irish and Polish Migration in Comparative Perspective* (Essen: Klartext Verlag, 2003), pp. 121–32.

22. W. Ernst, 'Idioms of madness and colonial boundaries: The case of the European and "native" mentally ill in early nineteenth-century British India', *Comparative Studies in Society and History*, 39:1 (1997), pp. 153–81.

23. J. Mills, *Madness, Cannabis and Colonialism: The 'Native-Only' Lunatic Asylums of British India, 1857–1900* (London: Macmillan / St. Martins, 2000).
24. H. Deacon, 'Insanity, institutions and society: The Case of the Robben Island Lunatic Asylum, 1846–1910', in R. Porter and D. Wright (eds.), *The Confinement of the Insane: International Perspectives, 1800–1965* (Cambridge: Cambridge University Press, 2003), p. 27.
25. P. McCandless, 'Curative asylum, custodial hospital: The South Carolina lunatic asylum and state hospital, 1828–1920', in Porter and Wright (eds.), *The Confinement of the Insane*, p. 190.
26. Leckie, 'The embodiment of gender and madness in colonial Fiji', pp. 319–20.
27. L. Barry and C. Coleborne, 'Insanity and ethnicity in New Zealand: Māori encounters with the Auckland Mental Hospital, 1860–1900', *History of Psychiatry*, 22:3 (2011), pp. 285–301.
28. R. Menzies and T. Palys, 'Turbulent spirits: Aboriginal patients in the British Columbia psychiatry system, 1879–1950', in J. Moran and D. Wright (eds.), *Mental Health and Canadian Society: Historical Perspectives* (Montreal: McGill-Queens University Press, 2006), p. 162.
29. B. Attwood, 'Tarra Bobby, a Brataualung man', *Aboriginal History*, 11:1, pp. 41–57.
30. Public Record Office of Victoria, VPRS 7399/P1, Male Patient Casebooks, 1873, unit 2, fo.158.
31. D. Wright, J. Moran, and S. Gouglas, 'The confinement of the insane in Victorian Canada: The Hamilton and Toronto asylums, c. 1861–1891', in Porter and Wright (eds.), *The Confinement of the Insane*, p. 120; J. D. Abelard, 'The limits of psychiatric reform in Argentina, 1890–1946', in Porter and Wright (eds.), *The Confinement of the Insane*, p. 231.
32. Broome, *Arriving*, p. 126.
33. See Coleborne, *Madness in the Family*, p. 59.
34. The reports of official asylum inspectors were collated and presented annually to parliament. See 'Report of the Inspector of Lunatic Asylums on the Hospitals for the Insane, 1887', table X, Showing the Nationalities and Religious Persuasions of those Admitted for the First Time in 1887 (Melbourne: Government Printer, 1888), p. 10; 'Hospitals for the Insane: Report of the Inspector of Lunatic Asylums, 1890', table 1X, Showing the Nationalities and Religious Persuasions of Those Admitted for the First Time in 1890 (Melbourne: Robert S. Bain, Government Printer, 1891), p. 10; and 'Hospitals for the Insane: Report of the Inspector–General of Lunatic Asylums, 1890', table XVIII, Showing the Nationalities and Religious Persuasions of those Admitted for the First Time During 1909 (Melbourne: J. Kemp, Government Printer, 1910), p. 15.
35. C. Ross, 'Race and insanity in New South Wales, 1878–1887', in *Transactions of the Intercolonial Medical Congress of Australasia* (1889), p. 850.
36. Ibid., p. 852.
37. Ross, 'Race and insanity', pp. 852–53. Although the records of the colonial-born patients might be assumed to be more detailed, given the presence of extended families in the colonies by the late nineteenth century, they often are not. In addition, Dr. Ross asserted his confidence in the mental health of the 'hybrid' born, or those with colonial birth but immigrant parentage, but the numbers of patients with colonial backgrounds began to increase over time, shaking confidence in the view that immigrants brought mental instability with them to the colonies.
38. M. Lewis, *Managing Madness: Psychiatry and Society in Australia, 1788–1980* (Canberra: Australian Government Publishing Service, 1988), p. 30.

39. I. Hacking, 'Making up people', in T. Heller et al. (eds.), *Reconstructing Individualism* (Stanford, CA: Stanford University Press, 1986); see also I. Hacking, *The Taming of Chance* (Cambridge: Cambridge University Press, 1991).
40. For example, in the 1850s migrants to Victoria included a range of men seeking their fortunes in gold, such as the Italian-speaking Swiss who arrived in 1854 and 1855. Most of the Chinese gold seekers came from Canton provinces after 1853; see Broome, *Arriving*, pp. 69–70.
41. McCarthy, 'Ethnicity, migration and the lunatic asylum', pp. 54–55.
42. VPRS 7399/P1, 1888, unit 7, fo. 245.
43. VPRS 7399/P1, 1888, unit 7, fo. 261.This patient's ethnicity is unclear; his surname is recorded with an alias.
44. VPRS 7399/P1, 1894, unit10, fo. 102.
45. VPRS 7399/P1, 1873, unit 2, fo. 180.
46. VPRS 7399/P1, 1900, unit 12, fo. 265.
47. Garton, *Medicine and Madness*, pp. 104–5.
48. K. Canning, 'The body as a method? Reflections on the place of the body in gender history', *Gender and History*, 11:3 (1999), pp. 499–513; see also Ballantyne and Burton (eds.), *Bodies in Contact*, p. 406.
49. Broome, *Arriving*, pp. 73–74.
50. See Leckie, 'The embodiment of gender and madness in colonial Fiji', pp. 322–33.
51. Mills, *Madness, Cannabis and Colonialism*; p. 5; Labrum, 'The boundaries of femininity', p. 67.
52. E. J. Teng, 'An island of women: Gender in Qing travel writing about Taiwan', in Ballantyne and Burton (eds.), *Bodies in Contact*, p. 51.
53. See Coleborne, *Reading 'Madness'*.
54. A. Atkinson, *The Europeans in Australia, A History: Volume Two, Democracy*, (Melbourne: Oxford University Press, 2004), p. 269.
55. Ibid., pp. 271, 269.
56. Anderson, *The Cultivation of Whiteness*, p. 43.
57. S. Swain, 'The poor people of Melbourne', in G. Davison, D. Dunstan, and C. McConville (eds.), *The Outcasts of Melbourne: Essays in Social History* (Sydney: Allen and Unwin, 1985), pp. 101–2.
58. Davison, Dunstan, and McConville (eds.), *The Outcasts of Melbourne*, pp. 7–8, 15; A. Brown-May, *Melbourne Street Life* (Melbourne: Australian Scholarly/Arcadia and Museum Victoria, 1998), pp. 121–22 and pp. 163–64.
59. VPRS 7399/P1, 1873, unit 2, fo. 29. See also cases of hawkers: VPRS7399/P1, 1891, unit 9, fo. 56; VPRS 7399/P1, 1891, unit 9, fo. 68.
60. More than 10,000 immigrants had used these homes by mid 1853; Broome, *Arriving*, p. 76.
61. VPRS 7399/P1, 1873, unit 2, fo. 164.
62. VPRS 7399/P1, 1873, unit 2, fo. 198.
63. VPRS 7399/P1, 1891, unit 9, fo. 32.
64. VPRS 7399/P1, 1894, unit 10, fo. 26.
65. VPRS 7399/P1, 1894, unit10, fo. 91.
66. VPRS 7399/P1, 1891, unit 9, fo. 29; VPRS 7399/P1, 1891, unit 9, fo. 32.
67. VPRS 7399/P1, 1891, unit 9, fo. 14.
68. 'Annual Report', Immigrants' Aid Society Home for Houseless and Destitute Persons (AIS) (1874), p. 3
69. 'Annual Report', AIS (1872), p. 2.
70. VPRS 7400/P1, Female patient case books, 1885, unit 8, fo. 134. See Coleborne, *Reading 'Madness'*, on gender and identity inside the colonial asylum, pp. 57–79.

71. 'Report of the Inspector of Lunatic Asylums on the Hospitals for the Insane for 1879' (Melbourne: John Ferres, Government Printer, 1880), p. 26.
72. Broome, *Arriving*, p. 107.
73. VPRS 7399/P1, 1891, unit 9, fo. 58.
74. VPRS 7399/P1, 1900, unit 12, fo. 316.
75. VPRS 7399/P1, 1891, unit 9, fo. 82.
76. VPRS 7399/P1, 1900, unit 12, fo. 275.
77. Broome, *Arriving*, p. 63.
78. D. MacKinnon, '"Hearing madness": The soundscape of the asylum', in C. Coleborne and D. MacKinnon (eds.), *Madness in Australia: Histories, Heritage and the Asylum* (St Lucia: University of Queensland Press, 2003), pp. 77–78.
79. McCarthy, 'Ethnicity, migration and the lunatic asylum', p. 56; Angela McCarthy, 'A difficult voyage', *History Scotland*, 10:4 (2010), esp. pp. 30–31.
80. S. Jain, 'Psychiatry and confinement in India', in Porter and Wright (eds.), *The Confinement of the Insane*, p. 278.
81. 'Report of the Inspector of Lunatic Asylums on the Hospitals for the Insane for 1879', p. 22
82. On asylum photography, see B. Brookes, 'Pictures of parts, people and places: Photography and the asylum', in C. Coleborne and D. MacKinnon (eds.), *Exhibiting Madness in Museums: Remembering Psychiatry through Collections and Display* (New York: Routledge, 2011), pp. 30–47.
83. VPRS 7399/P1, 1885, unit 6, fo. 137.
84. Malcolm, '"A most miserable looking object"', p. 132.
85. J. C. Burnham, 'Psychotic delusions as a key to historical cultures: Tasmania, 1830–1940', *Journal of Social History*, 13:3 (1980), pp. 368–83; Goodman, *Gold Seeking*, p. 201. Yet to his great surprise, Burnham found that for Tasmania, although many of the patients committed to the Royal Derwent Hospital in 1849 were of very recent British extraction, very few delusions related to their places of origin. Only two of these seventy-one 'Imperial' lunatics mentioned 'home' in their delusions.
86. VPRS 7399/P1, 1894, unit 10, fo. 32.
87. Jain, 'Psychiatry and confinement in India', p. 279.
88. Deacon, 'Insanity, institutions and society', p. 35.
89. Labrum, 'The boundaries of femininity', p. 69; McCarthy, 'Ethnicity, migration and the lunatic asylum', pp. 55–56.
90. VPRS 7399/P1, 1894, unit10, fo. 46.
91. VPRS 7400/P1, unit 9, 1888, fo. 84; VPRS 7400/P1, 1888, unit 9, fo. 109; VPRS 7399/P1, 1885, unit 6, fo. 148; VPRS 7399/P1, 1873, unit 2, fo. 71.
92. VPRS 7400/P1, 1888, unit 9, fo. 122; VPRS 7400/P1, 1888, unit 9, fo. 151.
93. Broome, *Arriving*, p. 65, 104.
94. VPRS 7400/P1, 1888, unit 9, fo. 125; VPRS 7399/P1, 1891, unit 9, fo. 97; VPRS 7399/P1, 1891, unit 9, fo. 9.
95. VPRS 7400/P1, 1885, unit 8, fo. 110; VPRS 7400/P1, 1885, unit 8, fo. 61.
96. R. Keller, 'Madness and colonialism: Psychiatry in the British and French empires', *Journal of Social History*, 35:2 (2001), pp. 295–326; Ernst, 'Idioms of madness and colonial boundaries'; Leckie, 'The embodiment of gender and madness in colonial Fiji'.
97. A. L. Stoler, *Along the Archival Grain: Epistemic Anxieties and Colonial Common Sense* (Princeton, NJ: Princeton University Press, 2009), p. 43.
98. Hacking, 'Making up people', p. 223.

6 A Degenerate Residuum?

The Migration of Medical Personnel and Medical Ideas about Congenital Idiocy, Heredity, and Racial Degeneracy between Britain and the Auckland Mental Hospital, c. 1870–1900

Maree Dawson

Congenital idiocy, a condition dominant in popular ideas about asylums, has often been neglected in social histories of the asylum.[1] This chapter explores the migration of ideas in psychiatric medicine about congenital idiocy, a condition 'analogous to intellectual disability'.[2] It focuses on the circulation of ideas relating to heredity and racial degeneracy between the Auckland Mental Hospital in New Zealand, and the 'hubs' of British medicine, London and Edinburgh. This chapter argues that the migration of ideas about congenital idiocy occurred through the migration of key personnel at the Auckland Mental Hospital from Britain, specifically, England and Scotland, to Auckland, as well as the availability of British medical journals in New Zealand. It shows that the prevailing medical concerns about congenital idiocy as expressed in Britain differed slightly from those expressed in New Zealand. This is established through a survey of medical journal articles from the *British Medical Journal* (*BMJ*) and the *New Zealand Medical Journal* (*NZMJ*), reports from the *Appendices to the Journal of the House of Representatives* (*AJHR*), and patient case notes from the Auckland Mental Hospital. In addition, this chapter shows that although British medical discourses were dominant in New Zealand, there were also influences from elsewhere in the British Empire and beyond, extending to continental Europe and the United States.

This chapter is composed of three sections. The first section positions the Auckland Mental Hospital within New Zealand and within the British Empire. The second part explores the history of congenital idiocy as a medical diagnosis, and the relevance of these historical theories to ideas about congenital idiocy deployed at the Auckland Mental Hospital. This section also highlights the connections between causes of congenital idiocy, which centre on heredity and racial degeneracy, and wider social concerns in nineteenth-century New Zealand and Britain. These theories were reflected in the asylum patient case notes and reports in the *AJHR*. Within this second section are explanations of the migration of these medical ideas to New Zealand, particularly through the movement to New Zealand of medical personnel trained in Britain. The third section draws out concerns about family and vice, which were both key components of medical and popular discourses about heredity and racial degeneracy and were commonly cited causes of congenital idiocy in Auckland Mental Hospital patient case notes.

AUCKLAND MENTAL HOSPITAL IN THE BRITISH EMPIRE

In 1889, three brothers, James, George, and William, all aged in their thirties, were admitted to the Auckland Mental Hospital with congenital idiocy. According to their admission notes, these men were the children of a woman who had the appearance of 'one who enjoyed a little too much food' and was 'subject to occasional epileptic fits'.[3] Both parents were described as 'thoroughly respectable and very industrious', with the father of these men described as 'a sensible managing man' who had 'earned by his own industry enough to buy and improve a bad farm and keep the family very comfortably. Very seldom he took two or three glasses of spirits'.[4] But the mother's family included some who were 'eccentric and to some extent dangerous for want of sufficient mental control. Some were addicted to vices, and one was supposed to have suffered a long sentence for a serious crime'.[5] These case notes exemplify how 'evidence' of an imperfect family tree was seized upon in medical discourses and used as an explanation for patients' conditions, and allowed blame for these conditions to be attributed.

The Auckland Mental Hospital was established in 1867, near the centre of Auckland city, located in the northern half of the North Island of New Zealand. This asylum serviced a region of almost 100,000 square kilometres, encompassing both rural and urban areas and comprising a population of roughly 140,000 people in 1889.[6] Auckland was 'an organised settlement, with a more diverse ethnic population' than Otago or Canterbury, which were also organised settlements with mental asylums within their regions.[7] Although each of the larger regions in nineteenth-century New Zealand had specific characteristics, including their own 'class-based identities and organisations', the differences between the larger settlements, and the 'exceptionalism' of Auckland, should not be overstated.[8] Therefore, many of the conclusions reached in this chapter are applicable to other mental hospitals in nineteenth-century New Zealand. New Zealand psychiatry's concerns with heredity and racial degeneracy both had a medical and non-medical context. The non-medical context of these concerns relates to the aspirations and fears of society; the emergence of ideas about national health and efficiency, concepts closely linked to racial degeneration and the role of heredity in mental illness, were critical to the way medicine operated in New Zealand. Ethnicity is a key component of New Zealand history, particularly histories of concerns about racial degeneracy in New

Zealand psychiatry.[9] Emma Spooner argues that in 'white' settler colonies, such as New Zealand, the 'gaze' of official medical records focused more on 'white' members of society.[10] This focus was a consequence of the belief held by New Zealand's white population, particularly those of English descent, that they needed to maintain their position of superiority, particularly in relation to non-European populations, within New Zealand.[11] Compounding this, New Zealand's self-perception as a 'social laboratory' meant that New Zealand was supposed to 'avoid the old world evils' that plagued British society and the consequent anxiety about living up to this promise intensified concerns about the degeneration of the white race.[12] White New Zealand, at this time a population mostly local born but also including immigrants predominantly from England and Scotland, had a self-perception of being like the Britain of old, a place still free from the evils of industrialisation, over-crowding, and vice.[13] But concerns about heredity and racial degeneracy with regard to medical conditions permeated parts of New Zealand society in the nineteenth century. For instance, books about mental and moral science were advertised for sale by an Auckland publisher, along with Charles Darwin's *The Origin of Species*, and works by renowned English psychiatrist, Henry Maudsley.[14]

Despite this migratory 'inheritance' of concerns about heredity and racial degeneracy, medical ideas from Britain—where most doctors at the Auckland Mental Hospital had trained—were not adopted in a wholesale manner at Auckland. Rather, the more conservative ideas were adhered to while the rest were ignored or not acknowledged. The similarities in discourse about congenital idiocy between Auckland and Britain were due to the flow of information between Britain and the rest of the empire, including New Zealand. This flow of information occurred through published addresses and medical journals. Definitions of congenital idiocy are shown in medical journals dating from at least as far back as the 1860s. Medical journals were instrumental in the flows of information and ideas about diagnostic categories, and many of these definitions were employed in New Zealand, as well as overseas. Daniel Pick has already considered the influence of medical journals in the spread of ideas about degeneracy and congenital idiocy, going so far as to credit English-based medical journals with 'reformulating the language surrounding the 'condition of England question' with regard to a medical hypothesis about degeneration.[15] Therefore, medical journals, particularly *BMJ*, form a key body of evidence for this chapter.

This migration also occurred on a personal level, as doctors trained at British medical schools made up a large proportion of doctors at the Auckland Mental Hospital, directly importing ideas from British medicine and psychiatry into New Zealand and into the Auckland Mental Hospital. Although there were differences in practices and definitions of congenital idiocy between the Auckland Mental Hospital and British medical institutions, there were also similarities. In particular, concerns about a 'degenerate residuum' were part of wider discussions of national efficiency, which permeated the British Empire in the nineteenth century, and foregrounded the popularity of eugenics in the early twentieth century.[16]

HISTORIES OF CONGENITAL IDIOCY

The secondary texts *Faces of Degeneration* by Daniel Pick and German Berrios's *The History of Mental Symptoms* relate to both congenital idiocy and concerns about heredity and racial degeneracy. Both texts trace the rise of psychiatry over the eighteenth, nineteenth, and twentieth centuries in western Europe and Britain, places from which most New Zealand medical theory migrated. Berrios argues that although 'behaviours pertaining to "mental retardation"' have probably occurred since the beginning of human existence, the 'medicalisation' of congenital idiocy only occurred in the seventeenth century.[17] This section of the chapter therefore traces the history of congenital idiocy from this time. At this time, terms such as 'amentia, imbecility, morosis, foolishness, stupidity, simplicity, idiocy, dotage and senility' were employed to name 'states of cognitive and behavioural deterioration leading to psychosocial incompetence'.[18] The first medical theorist of interest in the history of congenital idiocy is William Cullen, an eighteenth-century Scottish medical theorist, who explained insanity as being a type of neurosis.[19] Cullen's nosography defined amentia, the category of neuroses related to congenital idiocy, as 'imbecility of the judging facility with inability to perceive or remember'.[20] Following Cullen, Frenchman Philippe Pinel defined *idiotisme* as an 'abolition of the functions of understanding and feeling, either acquired or congenital'.[21] Pinel in his 1801 work extended this definition to include 'total or partial obliteration of the intellectual powers and affections: universal torpor, detached, half-articulated sounds or entire absence of speech from want of ideas'.[22] These characteristics, particularly in descriptions of patients' inabilities to speak, appeared frequently in the congenital idiocy patients' case notes written at the Auckland Mental Hospital. An example of this is the case note for Charles C., a patient in the Auckland Mental Hospital admitted in 1882, which described Charles as 'a strong and healthy patient. Noisy, destructive and filthy. Appears to have some delusions but rarely speaks'.[23]

Slightly later in the nineteenth century, Jean-Etienne Dominique Esquirol described idiocy as a disorder of intellect in which the 'intellectual faculties are never manifested or developed for lack of education'.[24] By the mid-nineteenth century, Esquirol's 'psychiatric approach' was challenged by Edouard Seguin, who suggested that 'colonies of defectives' could be 'disciplined into normalcy' and ultimately rejoin society as 'productive workers'.[25] The idea of 'defectives' becoming 'productive workers' was popular at the Auckland Mental Hospital. For example, Catherine B., a patient admitted to the Auckland Mental Hospital as an imbecile, was recorded up to seventeen years after her admission as 'doing no work'.[26] Catherine was also described as 'dazed and demented. Frequently makes a sound like a locust. Dirty in habits'.[27] The case note suggests that Catherine suffered from a considerable mental impairment, and working was not a reasonable expectation. But the repetitive expression of 'does no work' in her case notes suggests that employment of some nature was very much expected of congenital idiocy patients.

Despite the adoption of ideas of 'productive defectives', other parts of Seguin's 'educative approach' never took hold at the Auckland Mental Hospital. This may have been due to a lack of resources needed to fund the close supervision required in this 'educative approach', or it may be a consequence of the belief in congenital idiocy as an inherited and incurable condition. This belief, that congenital idiocy was inherited and incurable, carried with it the idea of a 'degenerative taint'.[28] The idea of a degenerating group of people, crucial to many of the anxieties around congenital idiocy, was developed by Frenchman Bernard Morel in 1857.[29] Morel suggested that 'melancholia, mania, dementia, and physical stigmata', the last of which often characterised congenital idiocy, may have been due to alcoholism and masturbation, behaviours that were said by Morel to 'alter the human seed'.[30] Congenital idiocy patient case notes from the Auckland Mental Hospital frequently mentioned a history of alcoholism and masturbation in patients' families. This was also often cited in cases of other mental illnesses and deficiency. Francis Galton's ideas about correlation and the 'hereditary origin' or intellectual differences were also important to nineteenth-century ideas about congenital idiocy.[31] But there is evidence that medical writers in New Zealand had some ideas of their own about degeneracy and the 'hereditary origin' of intellectual difference and insanity. In an article published in the *NZMJ* in 1888, E. W. Alexander, who was trained in London and became the medical superintendent of Ashburn Hall, a private mental hospital in Dunedin, wrote that it was the 'inheritance of mental instability brought by emigrants from the old centres of civilisation' which should be regarded as the main source of insanity in New Zealand.[32] This concern with the immigration of the insane, or of those with a hereditary tendency to insanity, is different from the primary British concerns about insanity, which were with the threat which the reproduction of the 'underclasses' in the existing British population presented to the British race as a whole. Among the proponents of these fears in Britain was Henry Maudsley.

Daniel Pick describes Maudsley's work as indicative of a broadening of Victorian-era social commentary, in which the 'confluence of medico-psychiatric theory of degenerescence' and a 'Darwinian theory of evolutionary regression' contributed and merged into larger fears about urbanisation and modernity.[33] Among other Victorian-era social concerns were fears that a degenerate 'relative deterioration' would damage the imperial race, in turn producing a 'degenerative effect' on Britain and its empire.[34] In his 1894 contribution to the *BMJ*, W. Lloyd Andriezen verbalised his fear that some of the neuroses and insanities were increasing due to the 'breeding and intermarriage' of the neurotic and the insane, 'thus intensifying their morbid tendencies'.[35] Andriezen also suggested that 'nature herself stamps out the insanities; they end in sterile idiocy', but he felt that this was insufficient, as a 'vast and intermediate progeny had to be endured' which would 'exhibit all the intermediate phases of the insanities and the criminalities'.[36] Degeneracy theory was promoted most strongly in Britain by Henry Maudsley, who applied the idea to the British debate about habitual criminals.[37] Maudsley promoted degeneracy theory and its basis in the penal system, to lend weight to the idea that mental illness was inherited and that a 'tendency to insanity could not be controlled by the will of the individual'.[38] As Maudsley stated in his *Responsibility in Mental Disease*, published in 1874:

> When the insane temperament has been developed in its most marked form, we must acknowledge that the hereditary predisposition has assumed the character of deterioration of race, and that the individual represents the beginning of a degeneracy, which, if not checked by favourable circumstances, will go on increasing from generation to generation and finally end in the extreme degeneracy of idiocy.[39]

Another influential medical personality associated with congenital idiocy is John Langdon-Down. Although the names Cullen, Pinel, Esquirol, Seguin, and Morel are virtually meaningless to modern understandings of congenital idiocy, Down, after whom the term 'Down syndrome' was named, has a continuing influence on medical discourses of congenital idiocy. Down highlighted the 'curious ethnological resemblances of certain groups of idiots', dividing this cohort into Caucasian, Ethiopian, Malay, and Mongolian types.[40] This classification was adopted in the Auckland Mental Hospital in only a few instances. For example, Emily L., a child-patient described as being 'deficient of mental capacity, evidently congenital', was also said to 'suggest in many ways that she is the subject of imbecility of the Mongolian type—she is small for her age, broad faced, flat nosed, has oblique eye slits, bends very flexibly at all the joints'.[41] However, these divisions were never really embraced at the Auckland Mental Hospital, although skull shape and circumference was recorded in many congenital idiocy cases, a practice in accordance with principles of phrenology.

Phrenology, 'an anthropology, which sought to find the contours of racial difference and social degeneracy in the shape and weight of the skull', was referred to in medical publications as early as the mid-nineteenth century.[42] Bernard Morel cited phrenology, a theory described using clinical, scientific terminology, as a mark of 'severe degenerative cause'.[43] But in some instances references to phrenology were couched in religious terms, as did Samuel G. Howe, the nineteenth-century American author of *The Causes of Idiocy*, describing the 'size and shape of the head and the proportionate development of its different parts' as being the 'fingermarks of the creator'.[44] This discourse diverges considerably from the strong 'heredity and degeneracy' path which those involved in phrenology had otherwise trodden.

The link between phrenology and congenital idiocy was also strong in medical journals. The *BMJ* outlined one case in which the patient was described as having a 'face shaped like an ape's; the facial plane has a decided slope backwards, instead of being vertical as in the normal head'.[45] At the Auckland Mental Hospital, a patient's skull circumference was not uniformly recorded in case notes. In an 1887 article in the *BMJ*, Down described patients with 'narrow palates, bad foreheads and facial exaggeration', characteristics which Down grouped as 'cranial and other signs of racial degeneration', all of which commonly appeared in congenital idiocy patients.[46] Meanwhile, at the Auckland Mental Hospital, patient case notes described patients diagnosed as congenital idiots as 'imbecile with all the typical characteristics', such as 'a very small cranium, quite out of proportion to the facial part of the skull'.[47] This entry shows that the ideas about congenital idiocy popular in late nineteenth-century Britain were adopted into the everyday language of the patient case notes at the Auckland Mental Hospital.

Yet by the end of the nineteenth century, the popularity of cranial shape and capacity as an explanation for congenital idiocy had begun to decline. As a predominant contributor to the *BMJ*, Dr. Shuttleworth wrote in 1894, 'it is a mistake to suppose, as we find laid down even in students' textbooks, that of necessity the brain of an idiot is undersized'.[48] However, dimensions of other physical features were still considered relevant to the diagnosis of congenital idiocy. So-called 'deformations of the mouth', described by Down, among others, are an example of this, and were referred to in Auckland Mental Hospital patient case notes.[49]

CONGENITAL IDIOCY IN NEW ZEALAND

Social conditions and concerns about the future of the white race in New Zealand fuelled fears about congenital idiocy and racial degeneracy in New Zealand society and in New Zealand medicine. Ideas about heredity and racial degeneracy were prevalent in medicine in New Zealand in the nineteenth century, and were even more explicit in congenital idiocy cases. The emergence of ideas about national health and efficiency, concepts closely linked to racial degeneration and the role of heredity in mental illness, were critical to the way medicine operated in New Zealand. This concern with national fitness and efficiency was shared with other parts of the British Empire. As already discussed, British medicine was concerned with the impact of the criminal and low classes of society 'out-breeding' the middle classes, whereas in South Africa, as Harriet Deacon explores, admissions of specific groups of patients was determined by the effect of those patients on the wider white and economically dominant society.[50]

Catharine Coleborne argues that the consciousness of white racial superiority, the need to maintain this, and the consequent 'inward looking
gaze' was shared between New Zealand and Australia.[51] Coleborne cites
Frederic Manning's address given as president of the Intercolonial Medical
Congress of Australasia, in 1889, as evidence of this prevailing concern
with the well-being of the white race and the need to maintain racial superiority in terms of health. In this address, Manning, the Inspector General
for the Insane in New South Wales between 1865 and 1898, compared
'proportions of insanity' in Australia to those of Great Britain, the United
States, Canada, and the 'principal European countries'.[52] This comparison
of statistics which describe a country's insane population was also a reflection of the general movement in many nineteenth-century Western societies
towards science and rationalism. In the case of New Zealand, Erik Olssen
describes this change as 'challenging the moral-religious values of the nineteenth century'.[53]

Despite shared discourses about congenital idiocy between New Zealand and elsewhere in the British World, there was a clear difference in
medical terminology used in discussions of congenital idiocy. This chapter does not differentiate between the terms 'idiocy' and 'imbecility', as
they appear to have been fairly interchangeable in the case notes from the
Auckland Mental Hospital.[54] The *AJHR* annual report on all of New Zealand's publicly funded mental hospitals includes tables showing 'causes of
insanity in admissions'. These reports allow us to trace changes in official classifications of the condition. For example, the *AJHR* report on the
causes of insanity of all patients admitted to New Zealand mental hospitals
in 1880 refers to a condition labelled 'congenital (decay and imbecility)',
whereas the equivalent report from 1881 refers to 'congenital (idiocy and
imbecility)'.[55] By 1890, the only reference to congenital idiocy and imbecility in the 'causes of insanity' table in the *AJHR* was simply a classification labelled 'congenital'.[56] The *AJHR* report into causes of insanity in
New Zealand mental hospitals for 1895 also referred to congenital idiocy
patients under the heading 'congenital and hereditary'.[57] The classification
remained at the end of the nineteenth century. The conservative nature of
these classifications, and the slow pace at which they changed as compared
to ideas in the *BMJ*, may suggest two factors at play. This variation may be
due to differences in medical discourses between New Zealand and Britain; however, a more likely explanation lies in the different media in which
these classifications were expressed. The *AJHR* reports were written by
the medical superintendent, responsible to the government for all publicly
funded New Zealand asylums. These were men with heavy workloads who
were unable or unwilling to focus exclusively on one type of mental condition, such as congenital idiocy. Meanwhile, *BMJ* articles on congenital
idiocy were written by men who often worked in institutions dedicated to
congenital idiocy, or who were seeking to build their reputation as authorities on the condition. In view of this, differences in classifications would

be expected, despite the migration of many other ideas about congenital idiocy.

As already discussed, the foreign origins of New Zealand medicine are reflected in the definitions of congenital idiocy deployed at the Auckland Mental Hospital, as well as the explanations offered for the condition. But there is a caveat to this hypothetical transplanting of medical theories and treatments of congenital idiocy from elsewhere in the Western world. David Wright addresses this in his work on Canadian asylums, particularly their treatment of congenital idiots.[58] A similar warning is given by Peter McCandless in his discussion of women in the South Carolina Lunatic Asylum.[59] Although we do know there were similarities between Europe, North America, Australia, and New Zealand in the treatment of congenital idiots and a degree of assumed similarity underpins the idea of the migration of medical ideas, the extent of these similarities cannot be assumed. But trans-colonial histories provide a compromise of sorts, between historians who favour the idea of a universal, Empire-wide medical model and those who argue for the disparateness of medical practices throughout the British Empire. For example, Coleborne argues that mental hospitals in different colonial settings may have had more in common with each other than they did with the metropolis.[60] However, theories of trans-colonialism are helpful in exploring the relevance of other parts of the empire to the history of mental health in Auckland and New Zealand.[61]

Towards the end of the nineteenth century, medical views on congenital idiocy became more concerned with the separation of congenital idiots into grades, as well as the application of this concept to the 'normal population'.[62] Thomas Clouston, working in the 1880s, classed mental disorders into 'mental depression, mental exhaltation, and mental enfeeblement'.[63] Clouston divided 'mental enfeeblement' into that of childhood and that of old age, and described congenital idiocy as occurring 'if the brain development is arrested before birth or in childhood'.[64] The career of Thomas Clouston shows the highly migratory nature of psychiatric medicine between Britain and New Zealand in the nineteenth century. During his career in Edinburgh, Clouston worked with David Skae, father of Frederick, the first inspector-general of lunatic asylums in New Zealand.[65] Furthermore, numerous articles written by Clouston appeared in the *BMJ*, a highly influential publication on New Zealand medicine.[66]

FAMILIES AND VICE

The stated causes of congenital idiocy provide another way of looking at the influences shaping this diagnostic category. By 1875 idiocy was defined in a *BMJ* article by George Grabham, future inspector-general of lunatic asylums in New Zealand, but at that time medical superintendent to the Asylum for Idiots at Earlswood in England, as 'an absence or arrest of development of the intellectual and moral faculties, either congenital, or occurring in new-born children'.[67] Hereditary, parental, accidental, endemic, or a combination of these factors were cited as the causes of idiocy. However, a hereditary predisposition was identified as the 'chief agent in the production of mental deficiency'.[68] Even where an 'actual mental disease' could not be identified in a patient's family history, a family history of neuroses or even parental eccentricity usually could be found.[69] Analysis of all congenital idiocy cases from the Auckland Mental Hospital shows that degeneration and 'family and vice' were frequently cited causes of congenital idiocy for patients admitted between 1870 and 1900. These causes are also common in medical journals and reference books as causes of congenital idiocy. For example, the case of Emily L., a patient admitted to the hospital at a very young age as a congenital idiot, was cited as an instance of hereditary taint. The synopsis of Emily's medical certificate stated that her mother 'is now in Avondale Asylum and grandmother died there. Father's mental capacity is inferior'.[70] These details show that Emily's family had a history of mental illness and deficiency.

Auckland Mental Hospital patient case notes also show that 'degeneracy' and 'family and vice' were not mutually exclusive. For example, Edward W. was said to have such a condition because of 'drink and heredity', with his father having been in the Yarra Bend Asylum in Australia for twenty-seven years.[71] This case invokes ideas of degeneration and heredity, and family and vice. As Coleborne argues, the family was located as both the site of 'cure' and the site of 'vice' in the asylums of the period.[72] Beyond the Auckland Mental Hospital, heredity was identified by Down as 'one of the great causes' of congenital idiocy, in his address delivered to the Medical Society in London.[73] In order to accurately establish the causes of heredity, Langdon Down recommended 'examining into the physical conformation of parents and grandparents'.[74] Down believed that such an investigation would show that idiocy is frequently 'the culmination in the individual of a gradual degenerative process'.[75] Although such an investigation was impeded at the Auckland Mental Hospital by the relatively short time in which there have been asylums in New Zealand, the paucity of evidence was no deterrent to medical officials citing heredity as a significant cause of mental illness and deficiency. The 'Annual report on lunatic asylums of New Zealand' for 1881 stated, in a paragraph referring to patients admitted with congenital idiocy or puerperal insanity, that 'heredity predisposition was assigned as a cause in only thirty-five cases, but doubtless existed in many more'.[76] Five years later, the 'Annual report on lunatic asylums' applied this idea of understated heredity in the patient records to all patients in mental hospitals across New Zealand.[77] The first of these reports was written by Frederick Skae, who trained at the University of Edinburgh, reinforcing the validity and importance of medical migration of personnel and ideas; and the latter report was penned by Duncan MacGregor, another Edinburgh graduate.[78] The lack of local evidence for the role of heredity as a cause of mental illness and deficiency was likely compensated for by referral to foreign, particularly British, statistics and discourses. There was clear support for the idea of heredity as a key contributor to congenital idiocy, as Down explained in *BMJ*, when he wrote that the causes of congenital idiocy were not always 'operative in a single generation'.[79] However, some cases at the Auckland Mental Hospital which included several members of the same family provide New Zealand examples of the 'physical conformation of parents and grandparents'.[80] The case of Emily L., who was admitted as 'of deficient mental capacity, evidently congenital', was the daughter of Mary L., another patient in the Auckland Mental Hospital. Emily's grandmother is recorded as dying in the Auckland Mental Hospital. Emily's father was also under the gaze of the Auckland Mental Hospital, as he is described in Emily's case notes as being of 'inferior mental capacity'.[81] But cases such as this, which offer such a clear line of descendants, all directly linked to the Auckland Mental Hospital, are rare among admissions from the nineteenth century. Nevertheless, in another example of the significance of migration to histories of colonial asylums, family histories provided in some patient case notes show that admissions of family members to asylums on the other side of the world were related to the diagnosis of patients at the Auckland Mental Hospital. For example, both the mother and grandmother of Betsy J., a 'congenital imbecile', are recorded in Betsy's case note as being admitted to an unnamed Irish asylum.[82] Interestingly, there is evidence to suggest that some parents of congenital idiots admitted to the Auckland Mental Hospital were aware of the significance attached to family history. Charles W.'s mother is quoted in his case note as saying that 'there is no trace of hereditary disease or insanity in the family; the patient's father is a drunkard and has deserted the family, but he did not drink before the birth of the patient'.[83]

Alcohol was especially prevalent in case notes and medical journals in discussions of attribution of congenital idiocy. At the Auckland Mental Hospital, patient Mary B.'s congenital idiocy was attributed to her father's habit of being 'too free with drink'.[84] But in some other cases, 'vice' was an undefined weakness. In the case of William B., one of three brothers admitted to the Auckland Mental Hospital under the diagnosis of congenital idiocy, the explanation presented in the case notes for his condition was that William's mother's relations were 'addicted to vices'.[85] Samuel Howe also discussed the role of parental vice and sin, the 'violation of natural laws', on the congenital idiot progeny.[86] Howe specified that the parents of congenital idiots were often guilty of being 'very unhealthy or scrofulous, intermarrying with blood relatives, being intemperate, or being guilty of sensual excess which impaired their constitutions'.[87] Howe's words show that ideas about vice as a contributing factor in congenital idiocy spread beyond the British Empire, into the wider English-speaking world.

As Howe mentioned, the very composition of families was also a dominant concern in both medical journals and patient case notes. The case notes of Betsy J., a congenital idiocy patient at the Auckland Mental Hospital, state that her father and mother were cousins, a relationship described in medical texts of the time as a 'consanguineous marriage'.[88] Medical texts also linked consanguineous marriage to congenital idiocy, but the views expressed in the medical publications differed. While the *BMJ* published articles in the 1890s concluding that consanguinity accounted for a very small percentage of cases of congenital idiocy in British institutions, discourses in the *BMJ* around congenital idiocy also at times persisted in highlighting the risk of such relationships, including references to 'sad instances of defective children, the offspring of neurotic cousins'.[89] But the expression of ideas about the role of heredity in psychiatric conditions at the Auckland Mental Hospital in the patient case notes is generally more subtle than is the case in medical journals and other medical texts from overseas. However, there are instances where these ideas appear in the case notes. Concerns about poor marriage choices were discussed in the *BMJ*, which bemoaned the 'difficulty of giving advice to persons contemplating marriage in whose family there is insanity', and were also articulated at the Auckland Mental Hospital.[90] For example, the father of patient Luise H., a congenital idiot patient at the Auckland Mental Hospital, was described as being 'very erratic', and a man whom Luise's mother had 'married against people's wishes'.[91]

CONCLUSIONS

While New Zealand–based doctors had their own ideas and concerns about heredity and degeneracy in relation to congenital idiocy, evidence from the Auckland Mental Hospital demonstrates the transfer and migration of ideas about congenital idiocy from Great Britain. This shows that medical personnel employed at the Auckland Mental Asylum between 1870 and 1900 were strongly influenced by British medical ideas. This transfer of medical ideas about congenital idiocy occurred through the physical migration of British-trained doctors to New Zealand, where they became inspectors-general of lunatic asylums and medical superintendents of individual mental hospitals, including the Auckland Mental Hospital. Another important conduit for the migration of medical ideas to New Zealand was through the New Zealand readership of British medical journals. Contained within these medical theories were ideas about the role of heredity and the spectre of racial degeneracy. Whereas Bernard Morel and other 'doctors of degeneration' from across Western Europe and Great Britain constructed the threat of degeneration of European society in terms of an 'empirically demonstrable medical biological or physical anthropological fact',[92] the stated link between degeneration, heredity, and congenital idiocy ensured that the condition captured a position of concern and at times fear, in public consciousness throughout Europe, the Empire, and New Zealand.

At times, this threat centred on the perceived threats of which migration presented to the national fitness and efficiency of the country, particularly in relation to non-white migrants. In New Zealand, these fears, imported from elsewhere, were adapted to the context of nineteenth-century New Zealand and its identity as a white settler colony, interacting with and undermining the country's identity as free of 'old-world evils'.

NOTES

1. J. Saunders, 'Quarantining the weak-minded: Psychiatric definitions of degeneracy and the late-Victorian asylum', in W. F. Bynum, R. Porter, and M. Shepherd (eds.), *The Anatomy of Madness: Essays in the History of Psychiatry* (London: Routledge, 1988), p. 274.
2. P. Wickham, 'Idiocy in Virginia, 1616–1860', *Bulletin of History of Medicine*, 80:4 (2006), p. 677.
3. Archives New Zealand, Auckland Regional Office (hereafter ANZ ARO), YCAA, 1048/5, 378.
4. ANZ ARO, YCAA, 1048/5, 378.
5. Ibid.
6. *Statistics for the Colony of New Zealand 1890 & 91* (Wellington: Office of the Registrar-General, 1891), p. 18.
7. A. McCarthy, 'Ethnicity, migration and the lunatic asylum in early twentieth century Auckland, New Zealand', *Social History of Medicine*, 21:1 (2008), p. 50.
8. T. Ballantyne, 'The State, politics and power, 1769–1893', in G. Byrnes (ed.), *The New Oxford History of New Zealand* (Melbourne: Oxford University Press, 2009), p. 119.
9. Sally Swartz argues that Britain 'exported her psychiatric philosophy and practices in which class and race were linked, to the colonies'. See S. Swartz, 'The black insane in the Cape, 1891–1920', *Journal of South African Studies*, 1:3 (1995), p. 406.
10. E. Spooner, 'Digging for the families of the "mad": Locating the family in the Auckland Asylum archives, 1870–1911' (MA thesis, University of Waikato, 2006), p. 28. This is also supported by C. Coleborne, 'Health and illness, 1840s-1990s', in Byrnes (ed.), *The New Oxford History of New Zealand*, p. 501.
11. The preference for white immigrants in New Zealand is shown in *New Zealand Parliamentary Debates* (*NZPD*) from the nineteenth century. In particular, see Hon. W. Fitzgerald, 'Immigration', *NZPD*, 19 (1875), pp. 464–82. Fitzgerald stated that immigration 'derived from the Continental Countries in Europe has turned out eminently satisfactory'. This contrasts with views put forward about Chinese immigration and the so-called 'yellow agony'. R. Reeves, member for Grey Valley, argued that it was the 'duty of the Government to take immediate steps to prevent what may become a very great evil in this colony'. See 'Chinese importation', *NZPD*, 28 (26 July-2 September 1878), p. 417.
12. Spooner, 'Digging for the families of the mad', p. 33.
13. 'Birthplaces of the People—Census 1886', *Report on the Statistics of New Zealand 1890*, (Wellington: Government Printer, 1891), p. 25. For a discussion of the fragmented nature of 'Britain' in the mid-nineteenth century, see J. Belich, *Making Peoples: A History of the New Zealanders* (Auckland: Penguin, 1996), pp. 287–312. Irish migration was much less of an articulated concern in nineteenth-century New Zealand than was the case in Britain. See

A. McClintock, *Imperial Leather, Race, Gender and Sexuality in the Colonial Contest* (London: Routledge, 1995), p. 5. There is very little evidence in Auckland Mental Hospital patient case notes of Irish admissions being of particular concern.

14. *Daily Southern Cross* (18 April 1870), p. 5.
15. D. Pick, *Faces of Degeneration: A European Disorder c. 1848–1918* (Cambridge: Cambridge University Press, 1993), p. 178.
16. A. Digby, 'Contexts and perspectives', in D. Wright and A. Digby (eds.), *From Idiocy to Mental Deficiency: Historical Perspectives on People with Learning Disabilities* (London: Routledge, 1996), p. 6.
17. G. Berrios, *The History of Mental Symptoms: Descriptive Pathology Since the Nineteenth Century* (Cambridge: Cambridge University Press, 1996), p. 159.
18. Ibid., p. 172.
19. R. Porter, *The Greatest Benefit to Mankind* (London: Fontana, 1999), p. 260.
20. Berrios, *The History of Mental Symptoms*, p. 159.
21. Porter, *The Greatest Benefit to Mankind*, p. 495; Berrios, *The History of Mental Symptoms*, p. 160.
22. Porter, *The Greatest Benefit to Mankind*, p. 495; Berrios, *The History of Mental Symptoms*, p. 160.
23. ANZ ARO, YCAA, 1048/5, 165.
24. Berrios, *The History of Mental Symptoms*, p. 160.
25. Porter, *The Greatest Benefit to Mankind*, p. 506.
26. ANZ ARO, YCAA, 1048/5, 695.
27. Ibid.
28. Berrios, *The History of Mental Symptoms*, p. 162.
29. Ibid., p. 428; P. Prestwich, 'Morel, Benedict-Augustin', in W. F. Bynum and H. Bynum (eds.), *Dictionary of Medical Biography Volume M-R* (Westport, CT: Greenwood, 2007), p. 896.
30. Berrios, *The History of Mental Symptoms*, p. 428.
31. Ibid., p. 423.
32. E. W. Alexander, 'Insanity in New Zealand, with suggestions for the disposal of the chronic Insane', *New Zealand Medical Journal (NZMJ)*, (March 1888), p. 159.
33. Pick, *Faces of Degeneration*, p. 203.
34. Ibid., p. 184.
35. W. Andriezen, 'Discussion on the prevention of insanity', *British Medical Journal (BMJ)* (8 September 1894), p. 520.
36. Ibid., p. 520.
37. Saunders, 'Quarantining the weak-minded', p. 277.
38. Ibid., p. 277.
39. H. Maudsley, *Responsibility in Mental Disease* (London, 1874), pp. 46–48, as quoted in Saunders, 'Quarantining the weak-minded', p. 277.
40. J. Langdon Down, quoted in G. Shuttleworth, 'Clinical lecture on idiocy and imbecility—delivered to students of Owens College, Manchester', *BMJ* (30 January 1886), p. 184.
41. ANZ ARO, YCAA, 1048/353. One of the two doctors who signed Emily's admission certificate was Dr. William Close-Erson, a doctor licensed in Glasgow and London. See R. Wright-St. Clair, *Medical Practitioners in New Zealand from 1840–1930* (Hamilton: R. Wright-St. Clair, 2003), p. 128. Close-Erson's British training and subsequent New Zealand career suggests that medical theories about congenital idiocy and mental illness were brought from Great Britain in the form of trained medical personnel, as well as written texts.

42. Pick, *Faces of Degeneration*, p. 51.
43. R. C. Olby, 'Constitutional and hereditary disorders', in W. F. Bynum and R. Porter (eds.), *Companion Encyclopedia of the History of Medicine*, vol. 1 (London: Routledge, 1997), p. 416.
44. S. G. Howe, *On the Causes of Idiocy* (Manchester, NH: Ayer, 1858), p. ix.
45. 'Reports of medical and surgical practice in the hospital and asylums of Great Britain and Ireland', *BMJ* (6 April 1878), p. 482.
46. J. Langdon Down, 'Lettsomian lectures on some of the mental afflictions of childhood and youth', *BMJ* (22 January 1887), p. 149.
47. ANZ ARO, YCAA, 1048/5, 751.
48. Shuttleworth, 'Clinical lecture', *BMJ* (30 January 1886), p. 184.
49. J. Langdon Down, 'Abstracts of the Lettsomian lectures on some of the mental afflictions of childhood and youth', *BMJ* (8 January 1887), p. 50.
50. H. Deacon, 'Insanity, institutions and society: The case of the Robben Island Lunatic Asylum, 1846–1910', in R. Porter and D. Wright (eds.), *The Confinement of the Insane: International Perspectives, 1800–1965* (Cambridge: Cambridge University Press, 2003), pp. 20–53.
51. C. Coleborne, *'Madness' in the Family: Insanity and Institutions in the Australasian Colonial World, 1860–1914* (Houndmills: Palgrave Macmillan, 2010).
52. F. N. Manning, 'President's address', in *Transactions of the Intercolonial Medical Congress of Australasia* (Melbourne, 1889), pp. 817–20.
53. E. Olssen, 'Towards a new society', in G. Rice (ed.), *The Oxford History of New Zealand*, 2nd ed. (Auckland: Oxford University Press, 1992), p. 267.
54. For further discussion on different terminology used in labeling congenital idiocy, see Digby, 'Contexts and perspectives'.
55. *Appendices to the Journal of the House of Representatives (AJHR)*, (1880), 3, G; *AJHR* (1881), 2, H-13.
56. *AJHR* (1890), 3, H-12.
57. *AJHR* (1895), 3, H-16.
58. D. Wright, J. Moran and S. Gouglas, 'The confinement of the insane in Victorian Canada: The Hamilton and Toronto asylums, c. 1861–1891', in R. Porter and D. Wright (eds.), *The Confinement of the Insane: International Perspectives, 1800–1965*, p. 112.
59. P. McCandless, 'A female malady? Women at the South Carolina lunatic asylum, 1828–1915', *Journal of the History of Medicine*, 54 (1999), p. 551.
60. C. Coleborne, 'Making 'mad' populations in settler colonies: The work of law and medicine in the creation of the colonial system', in D. Kirkby and C. Coleborne (eds.), *Law, History and Colonialism: The Reach of Empire* (Manchester: Manchester University Press, 2001), p. 108.
61. K. Pickles, 'Colonisation, empire and gender', in Byrnes (ed.), *The New Oxford History of New Zealand*, p. 223.
62. Berrios, *The History of Mental Symptoms*, p. 164.
63. Ibid., p. 172.
64. Ibid., p. 183.
65. 'Obituary. Sir Thomas Smith Clouston', *BMJ* (24 April 1915), pp. 744–46.
66. L. E. Barnett, 'Editorial: Amalgamation of Australasian medical journals', *NZMJ*, 1:7 (1894), pp. 170–2. Barnett argued that 'the most successful intercolonial journal would not take the place of the *Lancet* or the *BMJ*'.
67. G. W. Grabham, 'Remarks on the origin, varieties and termination of idiocy', *BMJ* (16 January 1875), p. 73.
68. Ibid., 'Remarks on the origin', p. 74.
69. Ibid., p. 74.
70. ANZ ARO, YCAA, 1048/8, 353.

71. ANZ ARO, YCAA, 1048/5, 333.
72. Coleborne, *Madness in the Family.*
73. J. Langdon Down, 'Lettsomian Lectures', *BMJ* (22 January 1887), p. 149.
74. Ibid.
75. Ibid.
76. 'Annual report on lunatic asylums of New Zealand', *AJHR* (1881), H-13, p. 2.
77. 'Annual report on lunatic asylums of New Zealand', *AJHR* (1886), H-6, p. 4.
78. Wright-St. Clair, *Medical Practitioners in New Zealand,* pp. 241, 346.
79. Down, 'Lettsomian Lectures', p. 149.
80. Ibid., p. 149.
81. ANZ ARO, YCAA, 1048/8, 353.
82. ANZ ARO, YCAA, 1048/6, 221.
83. ANZ ARO, YCAA, 1048/5, 753.
84. ANZ ARO, YCAA, 1048/9, 35.
85. ANZ ARO, YCAA, 1048/5, 378.
86. Howe, *The Causes of Idiocy,* p. ix.
87. Ibid., p. 3.
88. ANZ ARO, YCAA, 1048/6, 221.
89. G. E. Shuttleworth, 'Discussions on the prevention of insanity, Part III', *BMJ* (8 September 1894), p. 520.
90. H. Tuke, 'The prevention of insanity, Part III', *BMJ* (8 September 1894), p. 521.
91. ANZ ARO, YCAA, 1048/4, 107.
92. Pick, *Faces of Degeneration,* pp. 11–20.

7 Medical Migration and the Treatment of Insanity in New Zealand

The Doctors of Ashburn Hall, Dunedin, 1882–1910

Elspeth Knewstubb

Ashburn Hall in Dunedin, New Zealand's first and only private lunatic asylum, was established in October 1882 by James Hume, who had been the lay superintendent at the public Dunedin Lunatic Asylum, and Dr. Edward William Alexander. Like other British colonial asylums in the late nineteenth century, Ashburn Hall was run by men who had received their medical educations in Britain.[1] The very existence of lunatic asylums in colonial settings marked the colonies as self-consciously 'British', showing that colonial management of social and political life compared favourably with that in the metropole.[2] This chapter examines three medical superintendents at Ashburn Hall between 1882 and 1910, Edward William Alexander, Frank Hay, and Edward Henry Alexander, who were all influenced by British medical thought. They were, however, subject to many influences, both 'intellectual' and 'cultural', which shaped their treatment of patients and their interpretations of patient behaviour. The picture offered here shows some of the complexity and variety of influences at play in their medical practices at Ashburn Hall. The doctors' intellectual worlds were not made of a simple flow from Britain to New Zealand. Travel to other countries for study, reading of international medical writings, and correspondence with other medical practitioners all played a part in forming doctors' practices at Ashburn Hall.

As well as keeping up to date with medical science, the three doctors were members of the colonial bourgeoisie and, in their writings about patient behaviour, the cultural influences on the doctors' practices become evident. The doctors measured patient behaviour against bourgeois respectable mores. Patient case notes were characterised by 'difference' within the asylum, with gender, ethnic, or religious deviations from bourgeois respectable norms in particular being treated as symptomatic of insanity. The combination of intellectual and cultural influences on doctors' practices, although unique to individual medical practitioners, was common among New Zealand psychiatrists. The experiences of these three doctors are representative of patterns in New Zealand psychiatry more generally. A closer examination of the three medical superintendents of Ashburn Hall, therefore, highlights the complexity of the influences on New Zealand psychiatry.

This chapter employs a biographical approach, which has been used effectively by some historians to demonstrate developments in the history of psychiatry.[3] The Ashburn Hall doctors' biographies, particularly their education and employment histories, reveal some of the intellectual influences on New Zealand psychiatry. The histories of medical professionals shaped practices of treatment in the colonies they migrated to. The first of the three doctors trained in England and France, whereas the other two trained in Scottish universities and were employed in Scottish asylums. British institutions commonly trained medical professionals for the colonies.[4] British medicine, however, was not a homogenous entity in the nineteenth century. Medical courses differed between universities.[5] Employment in asylums, post-graduate study, travel to observe practices in Europe or America, and the reading of medical journals all played a part in the formation of medical knowledge. An examination of the doctors' practices also reveals an ongoing engagement with international networks of medical thought. The doctors' practices at Ashburn were more complex than a simple adoption of the English, French, or Scottish practices. Medical 'webs of empire', like other intellectual networks, wove back and forth around the world.[6]

The second section of this chapter deals with the influence of bourgeois cultural standards on the doctors' judgements of patients. The three doctors were all white middle-class Anglican men, and as such it is unsurprising that bourgeois values informed their conceptions of normality and abnormality. These conceptions were at times linked to medical science, such as in the association of a woman's insanity with her reproductive cycle. The doctors often judged patient behaviour against middle-class norms without direct reference to medicine, however. They explained some patients' departures from normality through reference to gender, ethnic, or religious differences as they perceived them.

MEDICAL BIOGRAPHIES, INTELLECTUAL NETWORKS, AND ASYLUM MEDICINE

The first of the three medical superintendents of Ashburn Hall between 1882 and 1910, Edward William Alexander, was co-founder of Ashburn Hall and its medical officer until March 1897. Alexander was born in 1828 in the British colony of St. Helena in the South Atlantic Ocean. He travelled to England to receive his medical education at King's College Hospital in London, also undertaking training in Paris at the Hôpital-du-Midi before qualifying as a Member of the Royal College of Surgeons in England in 1853. Edward William's first professional appointment was as colonial surgeon to St. Helena. In 1861 he returned to London and became a licentiate of the Royal College of Physicians. He then travelled through Europe visiting French, Austrian, Swiss, and Italian hospitals, including the famous Paris asylums the Salpêtrière and Bicêtre. In 1863, Alexander migrated to

Dunedin. He served as the medical officer for the Dunedin Asylum in 1870 and 1876 and was a member of the Commission of Enquiry into the Constitution and Management of the Dunedin Hospital and Lunatic Asylum in 1863/64.[7]

There was no formal instruction on the treatment of mental disease available at any educational institution in Britain until later in the nineteenth century.[8] Alexander may have received some instruction on insanity through attendance at public lectures. Alexander Morison, for example, delivered a series of lectures in London on the treatment of mental disease several years before Alexander's medical education took place.[9] However, the main educational influence on Edward William Alexander's knowledge of the treatment of the insane was French. French psychiatry was fairly static in the early 1860s, when Alexander visited Parisian asylums. The major breakthrough of 'moral treatment' had come several decades earlier. By mid-century this method of treating the insane through kindness, good nutrition, occupational therapy, and entertainment in a domestic milieu with limited medical intervention had become the generally accepted practice for treating the insane throughout the Western world. Research into mental diseases continued, however. At the Salpêtrière, Moreau de Tours, for example, published several articles in the 1860s suggesting that the baffling 'protean' quality of nervous diseases such as hysteria was due to their hereditary nature.[10] An emphasis on heredity was also on the rise in Britain, influenced by social-Darwinist ideas.[11] It is therefore difficult to trace any definitively French or English influence on Edward William's practice, although he clearly felt an intellectual debt to the French tradition. He and Hume named the wing for female patients at Ashburn Hall 'Pinel', after the French founder of moral treatment, Philippe Pinel.[12]

The educational influences of Frank Hay, Edward William's successor as medical superintendent, are easier to trace. His medical education and early employment both took place in Scotland. Hay was born in Lucknow, India, in 1867. He studied medicine at the University of Aberdeen, and graduated in 1890 with the qualification of bachelor of medicine, master of surgery. Like Alexander, Hay's medical degree probably included little instruction on the treatment of mental illness. His main source of knowledge on the treatment of insanity before his arrival in New Zealand was through his employment from 1890 to 1896 at the James Murray Royal Asylum in Perth, Scotland.[13] Duncan MacGregor, inspector-general of lunatic asylums in New Zealand, when considering Hay's appointment to Ashburn, thought Hay's training under the superintendent of James Murray Asylum, Dr. Urquhart, to be a considerable point in his favour.[14]

Urquhart's influence can be seen in Hay's preoccupation with improving the asylum buildings and grounds at Ashburn, particularly the plumbing and drainage. Urquhart was the author of the article about asylum construction in Daniel Hack Tuke's 1892 *Dictionary of Psychological Medicine*.[15] Asylum architecture was an important aspect of moral treatment and included 'maximum security, ample ventilation, efficient drainage, optimal visibility . . . and, not least, efficient classification of the different grades of lunatics'.[16] Architecture was a uniform preoccupation of nineteenth-century alienists, and Urquhart would have imbued his trainee Hay with his ideas on the importance of asylum layout.

The move from Edward William Alexander's superintendence to Frank Hay's was marked by other changes as well. Hay's note taking at Ashburn is considerably more detailed, especially with regard to the physical condition of patients. A comparison between the entries for each doctor's first patient demonstrates this. The first patient admitted by Alexander, William M., had a very brief admission note, comprising only four sentences to describe his entire condition.[17] Hay's first admission note, on the other hand, was modelled on the pro forma case book used at the James Murray Asylum. It contained three sections with several subheadings in each describing the patient's physical condition, her history, and her current mental condition.[18] The higher level of detail of Hay's record keeping reflects the increasing emphasis during the last decades of the nineteenth century on 'scientific' approaches to mental medicine.[19] In 1900 Hay introduced a pro forma case book at Ashburn, which contained similar categories to that at James Murray's Asylum.

Hay left Ashburn Hall in 1904 to become deputy inspector-general of asylums and Edward Henry Alexander, the son of Edward William, became medical superintendent, remaining at Ashburn Hall until 1911. He was born in Dunedin in 1867, the same year as Hay, and his medical education took place at the same time as Hay's. Edward Henry began study at the University of Otago's new medical school and completed his degree at the University of Edinburgh. A medical education from the University of Edinburgh carried a high degree of prestige. Students from all over the world, especially Britain and the Empire, travelled there to study.[20] Unlike Alexander senior and Hay, Edward Henry's medical education included a component of instruction on the treatment of insanity. At the medical school at Edinburgh Thomas Clouston, the superintendent of Edinburgh Royal Asylum at Morningside, held the post of lecturer in insanity from 1879 to 1910. He taught a summer course which included clinical instruction at Morningside and demonstrations on the pathology of insanity using specimens and diagrams. Edward Henry, after graduating a bachelor of medicine, master of surgery in 1890, served as an assistant in the Morningside and then Fife Asylums in Scotland before returning to New Zealand in mid-1892.[21]

E. H. Alexander's case book entries from 1904 to 1910 are less detailed in some respects than Hay's. In 1908 he introduced a new pro forma case book, which contained fewer categories. One particular change was the reversion to only a small section on bodily condition. Hugh L., for example, was simply described as 'very stout'.[22] Despite Alexander's less detailed note taking, the inspector-general's reports about the treatment and level of care provided at Ashburn Hall remained positive. In 1907, Hay, then the inspector-general, observed that 'the entries in the case-book disclose a thoroughness and a scientific appreciation of the facts observed which is highly creditable', going on to praise Edward Henry's personal knowledge of his patients.[23] Contemporary officials, therefore, approved Edward Henry's management. There were also several changes in the premises during his tenure as superintendent. Electric light was installed by 1908, in keeping with the aim to improve the premises, and a new cottage built for male patients requiring separate treatment.[24]

The changes the Ashburn Hall doctors instituted during their tenures were aimed at improving patient classification, diagnosis, treatment, comfort, and care at the private asylum. They did not simply institute changes when they took up their positions, however, remaining engaged throughout their careers with wider intellectual networks, reading, publishing, and corresponding. This kept their practices evolving. In 1888, more than twenty years after his migration to New Zealand, Edward William Alexander published an article in the *New Zealand Medical Journal* which engaged with a wide range of contemporary international methods of treatment of mental illness. He argued that some features of the Scottish system of caring for the insane, notably the practise of boarding-out harmless lunatics to private families, should be used in New Zealand, and pointed to a similar practise in Belgium. He also made reference to the practise in Wisconsin of providing 'county asylums' with fewer than 100 patients, arguing that this would be more suitable in New Zealand than the large asylums already established.[25]

Edward William also corresponded with other doctors. He wrote to ask Thomas Clouston, for example, to recommend a suitable doctor as medical superintendent, showing a continuing respect for British, particularly Scottish, psychiatry.[26] Even after his retirement, the elder Alexander undertook to keep Ashburn Hall abreast of developments in psychiatric care. As late as February 1907, three months before his death, Edward William discussed with Inspector-General Hay the 'various projects he had for continuing to maintain [Ashburn Hall] in the van by anticipating up-to-date requirements'.[27]

Hay also engaged with international medical networks throughout his career.[28] His reports as inspector general show that he kept abreast of developments in the field and encouraged opportunities for New Zealand scholarship to contribute. He supported an initiative of Edward Henry Alexander's to establish a neuropathology laboratory at Ashburn Hall to perform research autopsies on mental patients.[29] Hay also remained a member of the Medico-Psychological Association of Great Britain and Ireland, which he had joined in 1890. In 1910 he recommended the establishment of a diploma in psychological medicine governed by Medico-Psychological Association guidelines.[30] Hay showed an active interest in keeping New Zealand psychiatry up to date and in increasing specialisation in New Zealand.

Edward Henry Alexander's practice also shows a continuing engagement with British and European medical scholarship. 'Hebephrenia', 'paranoia', and 'dementia praecox' all appeared as diagnoses in Ashburn cases during his tenure.[31] These diagnostic labels were popularised by German psychiatrist Emil Kraepelin in the mid-1890s. As British doctors continued to favour 'delusional insanity' as the diagnostic category for these conditions, Edward Henry's use of these terms in his practice shows that he was familiar with and influenced by developments in European scholarship.[32]

The younger Alexander also sought to contribute to the scientific study of insanity. In 1907 he planned to employ a British doctor 'engaged in scientific clinical research in psychiatry to be associated with him in his work'. This man, Bernard Sampson of the City of Birmingham Asylum, did not take up the appointment.[33] In 1909, the inspector-general's report again shows Alexander's intention to add a research element into the running of Ashburn Hall, through his plan to build a neuropathology laboratory to perform research autopsies.[34] Edward Henry, like his predecessors at Ashburn Hall, was influenced by and sought to contribute to a wide international network of psychiatric medicine.

BOURGEOIS CULTURE AND MEDICAL PRACTICE: DOCTORS, PATIENTS, AND DIFFERENCE

Intellectual influences were not the only ones at play in the doctors' practices. Doctors' writings about patients in their case notes reveal the influence of bourgeois culture and standards of respectability in their definitions of normality and abnormality. All three doctors were born and spent much of their lives in British colonies. Medicine was a common choice of career among the nineteenth-century middle class, particularly for those who lacked the social connections and capital needed to make their way in other socially acceptable professions like the military or the church.[35] The three doctors, like other middle-class colonial inhabitants, felt the value attached to maintaining and enforcing a respectable standard of behaviour in New Zealand. Kirsten McKenzie, in her study of scandal and colonial society, explains that respectability in colonial settings was even more precarious and contested than in Britain, and was constructed under the imagined gaze of 'home'. Respectability was a weapon in colonial situations where social mobility was more rapid than in Britain.[36]

The Ashburn doctors commented on a number of patient behaviours showing deviation from bourgeois respectable ideals. Where patients were markedly different from the bourgeois norm as perceived by the doctors, these differences became part of the pathology of their mental illness. This is especially evident in the Ashburn doctors' comments relating to gender and sexual propriety, but also occasionally to ethnicity, religion, and class.

The primary classification of patients in Ashburn Hall was through gender; men and women were separated in the space of the asylum and held to gendered standards of behaviour. Female behaviour in particular was closely scrutinised, and even slight variation from the bourgeois feminine ideal received comment. Amy S. had a 'tendency to be "forward" & occasionally [indulged] in meaningless sarcasm'.[37] Catharine Coleborne, in her study of the asylum in colonial Victoria, Australia, considers two factors particularly significant in assessing women's experience of insanity: 'the perceived weakness of the female body, and the dangerousness of the woman outside the family/community'.[38] As Ashburn Hall was a private asylum, patients were usually admitted from within their positions in the family or community. The medical perception of the weakness of the female body, however, can easily be traced through the case records. Thirty women, approximately 14 per cent of all female cases admitted between 1882 and 1910, had the cause of their insanity listed in the 'Register of Admissions' assigned to some form of their biological function, for example, childbirth. Nine women were admitted to Ashburn Hall with some kind of puerperal insanity between 1882 and 1910.[39] This diagnosis could cover many types of mental illness both acute and chronic. Hilary Marland attributes the rise of the puerperal insanity diagnosis in nineteenth-century Britain to increasing medicalisation of childbirth. Although reproduction was a natural function, women's bodies and minds were defined as unstable, full of risk, and in need of medical intervention.[40]

The doctors also believed that other stages of women's biological cycle caused or contributed to mental instability. Lactation appeared as the cause of insanity for seven women admitted, and the climacteric (menopause) as the cause of insanity for a further fourteen women.[41] Bronwyn Labrum, in her study of women in the Auckland Asylum in New Zealand, points out that 'doctors saw in menopause further signs of woman's subjection to her biology'.[42] Women's biological cycles were heavily pathologised by the male medical elite and the link of women's madness to her reproductive cycle was made not only in establishing a cause but in charting the progress of a case. In November 1886, for example, Edward William Alexander noted of forty-two-year-old, 'mania' patient Janet B. that her 'menstrual periods are always times of excitement'.[43]

As well as the medical attribution of insanity to biological function, many female patients transgressed the bounds of 'normal' feminine behaviour. Female sanity was equated with proper bourgeois femininity.[44] Insane symptoms included destructiveness and violence, or indifference to husbands or children. Departures from the demure pious and maternal feminine ideal were considered symptomatic of illness. This link was occasionally explicit. Hay recorded in 1903 that the thirty-year-old Australian patient Felicia G.'s 'self-assertive manner & a tendency to show a want of respect for others', were 'either morbid or the result of ill-breeding'.[45] It is in these judgements passed by the doctors about a patient's condition that we can unpick some of the attributes of 'normal' femininity in the doctors' eyes. When female patients were quiet and well behaved, working at feminine tasks such as sewing or knitting, and showing the proper deference to the medical super-intendent, this showed an improvement in their condition.

Edward William Alexander's notes about the thirty-seven-year-old single Josephine R. of Christchurch reveal his prejudices regarding a women's proper place and behaviour. She was admitted in 1888, diagnosed with 'acute mania' caused by 'over-excitement'. Part of the original entry on admission reads as follows:

> Fond of studying phrenology and read books on physiology & psy-chology which *she says* enlightened her. She came to Dunedin 3 weeks back . . . she advocated the case of a girl sentenced for theft who had pleaded impulse to steal. She visited the Gaol to see her and had inter-view with the Industrial School Keeper. She also was much interested in a deranged lady living at home.[46]

There is an implication that Alexander did not believe Josephine's study could have 'enlightened her'. Education and advocacy on behalf of others seem here to be unhealthy and exciting, not the appropriate pursuits for a respectable woman. Elaine Showalter, in her groundbreaking feminist history of madness, asserts that doctors influenced by social Darwinism linked the increase in nervous disorder in the late nineteenth century to women's ambition. Men and women had their natural spheres, and men-tal breakdown might be the consequence of women defying their nature.[47] As Josephine's case note reveals, Edward William Alexander shared this uneasiness about a woman stepping outside her natural sphere.

It was not merely women, however, whose behaviour was judged by bourgeois standards of appropriate gendered and sexual behaviour. One form of behaviour which caused concern in both male and female cases was masturbation. Ann Goldberg in her study of the Eberbach Asylum in Germany in the early to mid-nineteenth century shows that masturba-tion was seen as a cause of a wide range of illnesses, both physical and mental. This association gave a secular scientific rationale to the prohibi-tion of masturbation. It was a fear specific to the bourgeoisie, considered particularly insidious as it could be undertaken in secret and violated ideals of respectable behaviour such as self-restraint and female purity.[48] At Ash-burn, twenty-four-year-old married woman Mary M. was one of several female patients who masturbated. She was diagnosed as delusional, and her recorded symptoms included incoherent rambling and destructiveness. She cut off all her own hair and raked ashes out of the fire into the room with her hands.[49] The nineteenth-century medical profession, according to Goldberg, linked female masturbation to energetic forms of mental illness such as mania and violence. By contrast, male masturbation was linked to degeneration, effeminacy, and enfeeblement.[50] Herbert P.'s admission note bears this out. He was described as 'a weak-minded young man & evidently a bad masturbator. Glance arrested, hands in pockets, not much to say for himself'.[51] His diagnosis was dementia.

As well as being the cause of certain types of insane symptoms, the presence of masturbation could disrupt improvements to patients' mental states. Edward Henry Alexander recorded in September 1904 that Herbert P. 'continues to have periods corresponding probably with masturbational excess in which he dresses himself up & refuses to work'.[52] Working was an important part of moral therapy. Anne Digby, studying moral treatment at the York Retreat, draws a link between the work therapy offered as part of moral treatment and the nineteenth-century bourgeois work ethic.[53] Men were encouraged to work at gardening or farm work, while women were limited to the more traditionally feminine tasks of sewing and knitting, or helping in the kitchen and laundry. A gendered division of labour was common in moral treatment regimes and shows that doctors were concerned with behaviour befitting gender norms. New Zealand masculinity has had a long association with hard work. This began with the idea of the rough, hard-working, often itinerant frontier male, and was tempered in the last third of the nineteenth century with bourgeois respectable values. The growth of urban centres witnessed the rise of a class of self-made men who believed in the bourgeois ethic of hard work, savings, and disciplined self-help.[54] Gender historian Chris Brickell observes that 'masturbation posed a clear threat to one's manliness in part because it demonstrated the failure of masculine self-control'.[55] Herbert's refusal to work and the link of this to masturbation shows masturbation as disrupting improvement and causing a breakdown of the bourgeois work ethic in an individual.

Although the bourgeois ethic formed the basis for judgements about male patients at the private asylum, the comments which male behaviour received in different cases did show varying standards of masculinity, particularly in relation to class. William L., a barrister admitted after a suicide attempt, was described as 'pale and soft'. He had attempted suicide to save his fiancée from the 'dishonour' of marrying a man who would drag her to misery.[56] Edward William Alexander recorded in William's case a deep level of introspection, high notion of honour, and emotional delicacy reminiscent of the romantic hero as described by Ruth Harris in her exploration of male crimes of passion in late nineteenth-century France.[57] These characteristics and his profession as a barrister separated William from other male patients. Whereas most men were expected to work as part of their recovery, an improvement was noted in William's case when he started coming out to watch others work and driving himself about.[58] Perhaps there was something to the idea expressed by Herbert P. on his refusal to work in the garden that 'gentlemen do not work'.[59] Herbert's claim to be a gentleman was ignored. He was a farmer. William L., on the other hand, was a barrister. The masculine ideal might vary depending on the social position of the patient.

Although gender was the most obvious marker of difference within Ashburn Hall, the doctors sometimes explained patient behaviour with reference to a patient's ethnicity. As Angela McCarthy highlights in relation to the Auckland Asylum, the migration experience and ethnic background of doctors helped shape their perceptions and labelling of patients.[60] All three Ashburn doctors were born in British colonies to British parents, and educated in England or Scotland. Their descriptions of patients of British or western-European descent are seldom framed in ethnic terms. Other patients' ethnicity, however, received comment, and was sometimes pathologised. When half-caste Māori farmer John G. was admitted in 1900 as a 'voluntary boarder', his case was heavily racialised by Hay who linked John's Māori ethnicity to his insane symptoms. In the admission note Hay recorded that 'his gestures suggest the prepotency of the Maori parent. Very dirty, unwashed appearance'.[61] The juxtaposition of the two sentences implies that Hay thought John's dirtiness as well as his gestures were due to the influence of his Māori mother.[62]

Later Hay commented that John G.'s gestures suggested a haka.[63] He also mentioned John talking about 'big feasts of Pig & bean & potatoes—rubbing his stomach & going on like a Maori'.[64] The recording of these behaviours suggests Hay considered them symptoms as surely as John's violence and obscene language. John's father was Irish, but Hay identified John's insane symptoms with Māori rather than Irish ethnicity. This is interesting given the contemporary concern of asylum doctors around the world with the high numbers of Irish committed to asylums.[65] John's Māori descent cast him as 'uncivilised'. The medical profession, in attempting to treat John and render him 'sane', was complicit in the colonial civilising process.[66]

Māori were in general under-represented in asylums, particularly in Dunedin where the Māori population was small. The Auckland Asylum in the North Island had the highest concentration of Māori patients, admitting seventy-two between 1860 and 1900.[67] John G.'s presence in Ashburn Hall was unique in Hay's experience. He was the only Māori or part-Māori admitted between 1882 and 1910. Indeed, as Hay arrived in Dunedin to practise at Ashburn Hall only three years before John's admission, he had likely had little contact with Māori at all. This may be why John's case was discussed in more obviously 'racialised' terms than any other in Ashburn Hall between 1882 and 1910.

There were other cases where a patient's ethnicity became significant in how their behaviour was analysed by the doctors. Wing K., a Chinese shopkeeper, was admitted in 1885 with delusional mania. The notes about his case are brief, and most of the information contained in them seems to come from his brother.[68] Coleborne, examining Chinese asylum patients in colonial Victoria, reveals that the medical discourse used about Chinese male patients reflected wider fears about Chinese.[69] Wing K., by contrast, was almost ignored by Edward William Alexander. He spent four months in the asylum, during which Alexander made very few entries about his case. The following quote is one example: 'Seems to be quite delusional. Takes food well. Told his brother he wanted to kill a countryman whom he said had done something to him'.[70] There were no notes about whether Wing K. was working in the asylum, what he did for leisure, or whether he interacted with any other patients. This may have been due to language difficulties as Wing K. may not have spoken English. Whether the cause was Alexander's inability to communicate with his patient, or simply that he did not think Wing's behaviour worth recording, the medical discourse about this particular Chinese patient casts him as a non-entity with little agency or personality, rather than reflecting white settler fears about the Chinese.

The third ethnicity which the doctors considered inherently deviant from the bourgeois respectable norm was Jewish. Jewish patients were physically described by 'racial' markers; they were of the 'Semitic type' as well as of a different religion from the Christian doctors.[71] Jewishness was at times an explanation for parts of patient behaviour while in the asylum. Hay paraphrased conversations with an elderly Jewish patient Hannah L. in December 1900: 'The repetition of a few Hebrew words is sure to elicit confidences, in which, if asked what she thinks of the guyem, (?) Christian, she will try to be very just but generally end by giving [*illegible*] the conversation jewish character'.[72] The ostensible purpose of this note was to establish Hannah's state of mental confusion. Her senility, it would seem, led her to give the conversation a 'Jewish character'. A sane woman would not do so.

Amy S. was also judged with some reference to her Jewish ethnicity, although her religion was Catholic. Hay attributed thirty-four-year-old Amy's interest in the elderly Hannah L. to the fact that both were Hebrew.[73] This was perhaps the only similarity Hay could see between these two patients, but it was also one of the things which marked them as different from the Anglo-European bourgeois norm. When non-Jewish patients interacted or took an interest in each other, a shared Scottish or English ethnicity or shared Protestantism was never mentioned as the reason, although these patients might well share such ties. Ethnicity, like gender and religion, was used by the Ashburn Hall doctors as a marker of patient difference and to explain oddities of patient behaviour. The prejudice most evident in Hay's case notes about Amy S., however, was about the irrationality of Catholicism.

Patient religion was only recorded in about 35 per cent of all cases admitted between 1882 and 1910.[74] From the information available it becomes clear that the majority of patients were Protestant, particularly Anglican or Presbyterian, in keeping with the make-up of the wider Dunedin and Otago society in the late nineteenth century from which the Ashburn population was mostly drawn.[75] Only fourteen patients, about 10 per cent of those for whom religion was recorded, were listed as Catholic. There were also a handful of Jews and freethinkers.[76] The three doctors were Anglican, and Hay especially seems to have considered Catholic patients more inherently irrational than Protestants. Amy S. provides the prime example. In December 1900, Hay recorded, 'There is no bible reading or epileptic religiosity (she is a Roman Catholic)'.[77] In the cases notes for Protestant epileptic patients the absence of religiosity is not commented upon, suggesting that Hay expected religiosity in Catholic patients more than in Protestant ones. Oonagh Walsh in her study of the Ballinasloe Asylum in Galway, Ireland, in the late nineteenth century highlights a presumption among Protestant ministers that Catholicism inclined its followers more towards insanity, especially religious excitement, than Protestantism.[78] Hay's comments in Amy's case imply that this presumption was not confined to the clergy.

Another Catholic patient's behaviour was explained by a reference to religion. Hay recorded that Ellen B. 'feels that she cannot say her prayers, on one occasion knelt down & counted to 99 (She is a Roman Catholic)'.[79] This parenthetic note about her religion seems intended to explain the oddity of counting to ninety-nine. Non-Catholic patients who exhibited religiosity or odd religious behaviour within the asylum do not have their religious denomination parenthetically inserted to account for it. William S., for example, read the Bible, made somersaults to amuse the devil, and argued with another patient about religion, but his specific religion was never recorded.[80]

Although all patient religious delusions were recorded as irrational, the doctors' own perception of religious difference seems to lend an extra degree of irrationality to Catholicism. Religion, however, was not simply dismissed in favour of medical 'science' in attempting to bring about a cure of insanity. Proper and appropriate religious worship was part of the ideal of bourgeois respectability, especially in women. A Presbyterian weekly service took place at Ashburn, and some of the more well-behaved patients were allowed to attend churches in Dunedin. Nineteenth-century asylum doctors believed that while excess religiosity and undue pondering over questions of salvation was likely to impede recovery, the proper degree of piety and rational worship was a sign of improvement.[81] Patient experience of religion within Ashburn Hall was allowed and even encouraged as long as it did not exacerbate insane symptoms. Religion, along with ethnicity, gender, and class, was a marker of patient difference at Ashburn Hall.

CONCLUSION

The Ashburn Hall doctors' backgrounds reveal that the translation of medical knowledge and practice from the metropole to the colonies involved a complex range of influences both intellectual and cultural. Medical influences were more nuanced than a direct translation of English or Scottish medicine to the colonial setting. British medicine was not homogeneous. There were differences between teaching at different universities and practices at different institutions. The doctors' educations in England and Scotland and their employment prior to migration or return to New Zealand formed the basis for their knowledge of the treatment of the insane. Scottish influences especially played a part as two of the three doctors trained at Scottish universities and asylums. Scottish training was common among New Zealand medical practitioners, and its impact on New Zealand medicine deserves further attention.[82] Nor were English and Scottish medicine the only influences on the three doctors' practices at Ashburn Hall. The translation of medical knowledge to the New Zealand setting continued after the doctors arrived, through their ongoing engagement with international medical scholarship. Other intellectual influences identified in this chapter were French, Belgian, North American, and German. These intellectual influences combined with complex cultural factors in the definition of patient pathology in the private asylum.

The Ashburn Hall doctors' case notes provide a window through which to view the operation of bourgeois norms in defining sane and insane behaviours, revealing some of the cultural influences at play. These doctors were all born in British colonies and educated in British institutions, and migrated to New Zealand with conceptions of respectability as well as medical knowledge. They, like other members of the colonial bourgeoisie, constructed respectable behaviour through reference to British norms, imagining themselves under the gaze of the metropole. Patient behaviour was measured against standards of bourgeois respectability, with patients expected to perform gender-appropriate tasks and act according to appropriate social mores. Gendered standards were combined with class standards leading to a variation in the standards of masculinity to which different patients were expected to conform. Doctors also made judgements about patients along ethnic and religious lines, especially those of non-European ethnicity and Catholic patients. The relationship between bourgeois norms and medical science was at times direct, as in the prohibition of masturbation or the link of female reproductive cycles to insanity. Often, however, the doctors' views on sanity and insanity were constructed through reference to patients' deviations from the male white Protestant norm as the doctors perceived it. Women, those of non-European descent, and Catholic patients were inherently set apart from this norm, and these differences at times became symptoms of insanity.

NOTES

1. W. Brunton, 'Out of the shadows: Some historical underpinnings of mental health policy', in B. Dalley and M. Tennant (eds.), *Past Judgement: Social Policy in New Zealand History* (Dunedin: University of Otago Press, 2004), p. 77; C. Coleborne, *Madness in the Family: Insanity and Institutions in the Australasian Colonial World, 1860–1914* (Basingstoke: Palgrave Macmillan, 2010), pp. 32–36.
2. A. Bashford, 'Medicine, gender, and empire', in P. Levine (ed.), *Gender and Empire* (Oxford: Oxford University Press, 2004), pp. 117–21; W. Ernst, 'Out of sight and out of mind: Insanity in early nineteenth-century British

India', in J. Melling and B. Forsythe (eds.), *Insanity, Institutions and Society, 1800–1914* (London: Routledge, 1999), pp. 245–46.

3. See for example A. Scull, C. MacKenzie, and N. Hervey, *Masters of Bedlam: The Transformation of the Mad-Doctoring Trade* (Princeton, NJ: Princeton University Press, 1996); M. MacDonald, *Mystical Bedlam: Madness, Anxiety, and Healing in Seventeenth-Century England* (Cambridge: Cambridge University Press, 1981), ch. two.

4. M. A. Crowther and M. W. Dupree, *Medical Lives in the Age of Surgical Revolution* (Cambridge: Cambridge University Press, 2007), p. 5.

5. C. Pennington, *The Modernisation of Medical Teaching at Aberdeen in the Nineteenth Century* (Aberdeen: Aberdeen University Press, 1994), pp. 16–17.

6. Tony Ballantyne considers the 'web' to be a more accurate metaphor for how knowledge was transmitted around the British Empire than the previously traditional spoked wheel metaphor which places the metropole at the hub, with all knowledge flowing through it. The web accounts for knowledge travelling from colony to colony without being mediated through Britain. See T. Ballantyne, *Orientalism and Race: Aryanism in the British Empire* (Houndmills: Palgrave, 2002).

7. R. E. Wright-St. Clair, *Medical Practitioners in New Zealand, 1840–1930* (Hamilton: R. E. Wright-St. Clair, 2003), p. 33; *The Cyclopedia of New Zealand*, vol. 4, *Otago and Southland* (Christchurch: Horace J. Weeks, 1905), p. 245; R. V. Fulton, *Medical Practice in Otago and Southland in the Early Days: A Description of the Manner of Life, Trials and Difficulties of Some of the Pioneer Doctors, of the Places in Which, and of the People Among Whom, they Laboured* (Wellington: Colonial Associates, 1983), pp. 290–91; J. C. Medlicott, 'The History of Ashburn Hall, 1882–1947' (MA thesis, University of Otago, 1972), p. 9.

8. The course of lectures on insanity available at the Edinburgh University from 1859 was the first. See Crowther and Dupree, *Medical Lives in the Age of Surgical Revolution*, p. 213.

9. Scull et al., *Masters of Bedlam*, pp. 135–40.

10. J. Goldstein, *Console and Classify: The French Psychiatric Profession in the Nineteenth Century* (Cambridge: Cambridge University Press, 1987), p. 328.

11. R. Harris, *Murders and Madness: Medicine, Law, and Society in the Fin de Siècle* (Oxford: Clarendon, 1989), p. 64.

12. The male ward was named 'Mitchell', most likely after American neurologist Silas Weir Mitchell, who pioneered the 'rest cure' for nervous disease. Another two wards opened in 1891 and 1896 were called 'Conolly', after John Conolly, English asylum doctor and pioneer of non-restraint; and 'Tuke', after the Tuke family who instituted moral treatment in England. See C. Duder, *The Ashburn Clinic: The Place and the People* (Dunedin: Ashburn Clinic, 2007), pp. 17–18.

13. 'Obituary: Dr Frank Hay', *New Zealand Medical Journal*, 24:123 (October 1925), pp. 265–67.

14. *Appendices to the Journal of the House of Representatives* (*AJHR*), 1904, H-7, 12.

15. Obituary, 'Alex Reid Urquhart', *British Medical Journal*, 2:2955 (18 August 1917), p. 237

16. R. Porter, 'Madness and its institutions', in A. Wear (ed.), *Medicine in Society: Historical Essays* (Cambridge: Cambridge University Press, 1992), p. 297.

17. Hocken Collections (HC), University of Otago, AG-447–6/04, Ashburn Hall (AH), 'Report Book—Intermediate Case Book, Vol. 1', p. 2.

18. HC, AG-447–6/05, AH, 'Report Book—Intermediate Case Book, Vol. 3', pp. 110–11. University of Dundee Archive, Dundee, THB 29/8/6/7, Murray's Royal Asylum, extract of patient case book, fo. 90, 1890.

19. J. Andrews, 'Case notes, case histories, and the patient's experience of insanity at Gartnavel Royal Asylum, Glasgow, in the nineteenth century', *Social History of Medicine*, 11:2 (1998), p. 260.
20. Crowther and Dupree, *Medical Lives in the Age of Surgical Revolution*, pp. 213, 22–26.
21. *AJHR*, 1900, H-7, 11; Wright-St. Clair, *Medical Practitioners in New Zealand*, p. 33.
22. HC, AG-447–6/02, AH, 'Case Book, 1908–1927', fo. 140.
23. *AJHR*, 1907, H-7, 32.
24. *AJHR*, 1908, H-7, 21.
25. E. W. Alexander, 'Insanity in New Zealand, with suggestions for the disposal of the chronic insane', *New Zealand Medical Journal*, 1:3 (March 1888), pp. 162–64.
26. A. Somerville, 'Ashburn Hall and Its Place in Society, 1882–1904' (MA thesis, University of Otago, 1996), p. 36.
27. *AJHR*, 1907, H-7, p. 32.
28. While employed at the James Murray Asylum Hay published 'Notes of a case of epilepsy with aphasia', *Journal of Mental Science*, 41:173 (1895), pp. 307–19.
29. Hay's support for the proposed laboratory is discussed in 'Report on mental hospitals', *AJHR*, 1910, H-7, p. 5.
30. *AJHR*, 1910, H-7, p. 6.
31. HC, AG-447–5/01, AH, 'Register of Admissions, 1882–1948'.
32. W. F. Bynum, 'Tuke's *Dictionary* and Psychiatry at the Turn of the Century', in G. E. Berrios and H. Freeman (eds.), *150 Years of British Psychiatry, 1841–1991* (London: Gaskell, 1991), p. 173.
33. *AJHR*, 1907, H-7, p. 32; Medlicott, 'The history of Ashburn Hall', p. 42.
34. *AJHR*, 1910, H-7, p. 5.
35. Scull et al., *Masters of Bedlam*, p. 85.
36. K. McKenzie, *Scandal in the Colonies: Sydney and Cape Town, 1820–1850* (Melbourne: Melbourne University Press, 2004), pp. 12–13.
37. HC, AG-447–6/05, AH, 'Report Book, Vol. 3', p. 182.
38. Coleborne, *Reading 'Madness'*, pp. 58–62, quote at pp. 61–62.
39. HC, AG-447–5/01, AH, 'Register of Admissions'.
40. H. Marland, *Dangerous Motherhood: Insanity and Childbirth in Victorian Britain* (Houndmills: Palgrave Macmillan, 2004), p. 20.
41. HC, AG-447–5/01, AH, 'Register of Admissions'.
42. B. Labrum, 'Gender and lunacy: A study of women patients at the Auckland Lunatic Asylum, 1870–1910' (MA thesis, Massey University, 1990), p. 169.
43. HC, AG-447–6/04, AH, 'Report Book, Vol. 1', p. 71.
44. Coleborne, *Reading 'Madness'*, p. 88.
45. HC, AG-447–6/01, AH, 'Case Book 1882–1907', fo. 93.
46. HC, AG-447–6/04, AH, 'Report Book, Vol. 1', p. 155. Italics added.
47. E. Showalter, *The Female Malady: Women, Madness and English Culture, 1830–1980* (New York: Pantheon, 1985), pp. 121–23.
48. A. Goldberg, *Sex, Religion and the Making of Modern Madness: The Eberbach Asylum and German Society, 1815–1849* (New York: Oxford University Press, 1999), pp. 88–91.
49. HC, AG-447–6/04, AH, 'Report Book, Vol. 1', p. 29.
50. Goldberg, *Sex, Religion and the Making of Modern Madness*, p. 90.
51. HC, AG-447–6/01, AH, 'Case Book 1882–1907', fo. 100.
52. Ibid.
53. A. Digby, *Madness, Morality and Medicine: A Study of the York Retreat, 1796–1914* (Cambridge: Cambridge University Press, 1985), p. 48.
54. J. Phillips, *A Man's Country? The Image of the Pakeha Male: A History* (Auckland: Penguin, 1987), pp. 47–50.

55. C. Brickell, 'Same-sex desire and the asylum: A colonial experience', *New Zealand Journal of History*, 39:2 (2005), p. 166.
56. HC, AG-447–6/04, AH, 'Report Book, Vol. 1', p. 7.
57. Harris, *Murders and Madness*, p. 304.
58. HC, AG-447–6/04, AH, 'Report Book, Vol. 1', p. 7.
59. HC, AG-447–6/01, AH, 'Case Book 1882–1907', fo. 100.
60. A. McCarthy, 'Ethnicity, migration and the lunatic asylum in early twentieth-century Auckland, New Zealand', *Social History of Medicine*, 21:1 (2008), p. 48.
61. HC, AG-447–6/01, AH, 'Case Book 1882–1907', fo. 37.
62. L. Burke, '"The Voices Caused Him to Become Porangi": Maori Patients in the Auckland Lunatic Asylum, 1860–1900' (MA thesis, University of Waikato, 2006), p. 35.
63. A Māori war dance.
64. HC, AG-447–6/01, AH, 'Case Book 1882–1907', fo. 37.
65. See E. Malcolm, '"A most miserable looking object": The Irish in English asylums, 1850–1901', in J. Belchem and K. Tenfelde (eds.), *Irish and Polish Migration in Comparative Perspective* (Essen: Klartext, 2003), pp. 121–32; E. Malcolm '"Ireland's crowded madhouses": The institutional confinement of the insane in nineteenth- and twentieth-century Ireland', in R. Porter and D. Wright (eds.), *The Confinement of the Insane: International Perspectives, 1800–1965* (Cambridge: Cambridge University Press, 2003), pp. 315–33.
66. Burke, '"The Voices Caused Him to Become Porangi"', pp. 35–36.
67. Ibid., pp. 10–11.
68. HC, AG-447–6/04, AH, 'Report Book, Vol. 1', p. 77.
69. C. Coleborne, 'Making "mad" populations in settler colonies: The work of law and medicine in the creation of the colonial asylum', in D. Kirkby and C. Coleborne (eds.), *Law, History, Colonialism: The Reach of Empire* (Manchester: Manchester University Press, 2001), p. 116.
70. HC, AG-447–6/04, AH, 'Report Book, Vol. 1', p. 77.
71. HC, AG-447–6/01, AH, 'Case Book 1882–1907', fo. 52.
72. Ibid., fo. 29.
73. Ibid., fo. 30.
74. About 410 patients were treated at Ashburn Hall during this time period.
75. 'Religions of the people', table VI, *New Zealand Census, 1896* (Wellington: Government Printer, 1897), p. 90.
76. The Ashburn Hall statistics come from an analysis of the patient case books, HC, AG-447–6/01–6/06.
77. HC, AG-447–6/01, AH, 'Case Book 1882 -1907', fo. 30.
78. O. Walsh, '"The designs of providence": Race, religion and Irish insanity', in Melling and Forsythe (eds.), *Insanity, Institutions and Society*, pp. 230–31.
79. HC, AG-447–6/05, AH, 'Report Book, Vol. 3', p. 187.
80. HC, AG-447–6/01, AH, 'Case Book 1882-1907', fo. 25.
81. Walsh, p. 229, citing W. A. F Browne, 'What asylums were, are, and ought to be', in A. Scull (ed.), *The Asylum as Utopia: W. A. F. Browne and the Mid-Nineteenth Century Consolidation of Psychiatry* (London: Routledge, 1991), pp. 208–12.
82. W. Ernst, 'The social history of Pakeha psychiatry in nineteenth-century New Zealand: Main themes', in L. Bryder (ed.), *A Healthy Country: Essay on the Social History of Medicine in New Zealand* (Wellington: Bridget Williams, 1991), p. 75.

8 'Lost Souls'

Madness, Suicide, and Migration in Colonial Fiji until 1920

Jacqueline Leckie

In 1884 Fiji's colonial secretary Dr. William MacGregor lamented, 'Fiji is a great sufferer from the arrival here of insane and incurable persons'.[1] He was well placed to say this as Fiji's chief medical officer and as a former surgeon at Aberdeen's Royal Lunatic Asylum and superintendent of the Lunatic Asylum in Mauritius. Like many colonial administrators MacGregor traversed colonial networks from Aberdeen to the Seychelles, Mauritius, Fiji, British New Guinea, Lagos, Newfoundland, and Queensland before retiring to Scotland.[2]

During the same year as MacGregor's gloomy assessment of Fiji as a destination of mad migrants, he bravely took charge of the rescue operation when the Indian immigrant ship *Syria* was wrecked on Nasilai Reef. In 1884 he recalled 'people falling, fainting, drowning all around one, the cries for instant help, uttered in an unknown tongue, but emphasised by looks of agony'.[3] MacGregor's intervention parallels his efforts to rescue 'wrecked minds' as during the same year he was pivotal in introducing lunacy legislation into Fiji and the opening of the Public Lunatic Asylum in Suva. This still functions as one of the Pacific Islands' oldest psychiatric facilities and since 1960 has been known as St. Giles Hospital.

When MacGregor referred to Fiji as a great sufferer from the arrival of insane persons he was pointing to Fiji as a hub within the colonial Pacific. Fiji was a nexus of indentured migrants, not only from India, but also from other Pacific Islands, such as the Solomon Islands, New Hebrides (Vanuatu), Tokelau, and Gilbert and Ellice Islands (Kiribati and Tuvalu). This chapter traces how some immigrants in Fiji between 1879 and 1920 became legally certified as insane or of 'unsound mind'.[4] It also considers the link between migration, mental illness, and suicide through focusing on *Girmitiyas*, Indian indentured immigrants, because of their prominence within early asylum records and debates about suicide in Fiji. This chapter follows the archival flows of their journey to Fiji, disembarkment and indenture in Fiji, and the surfacing of madness[5] and self-harm. Fiji also attracted many European travellers and settlers, so this chapter also addresses their journeys into lunacy or suicide in early colonial Fiji.

Although *Girmitiyas* and Europeans shared Suva's lunatic asylum, they were worlds apart.[6] All indentured labourers and European settlers were displaced in Fiji, not only due to physical dislocation from migration, but also because of the profound shifts in their cultural worlds. The impact and length of this varied, and for a minority of immigrants in Fiji, migration exacerbated or caused behaviour that contemporaries designated as evidence of insanity.[7] Some 'lost souls', already anguished by their physical and social dislocation, were also tormented by their mental condition and sought release. The most extreme consequence was suicide, but institutional confinement or repatriation could also be a form of death. In exploring these issues, it is acknowledged that connections between the broader spectrum of madness (today termed mental illness or mental disorder), self-harm and suicide are highly problematic—more so within different cultures.[8] Detailed historical evidence beyond official reports relevant to this in Fiji is sketchy, and like Ann Laura Stoler, I navigate along the archival grain. Stoler advocates that we read archives as condensed sites of epistemological and political anxiety rather than as skewed and biased sources.[9]

GIRMITIYAS AND MADNESS

The arrival of the *Leonidas* off Levuka on 14 May 1879 represented more than the first indentured labourers coming to Fiji from India.[10] It opened a defining trajectory in Fiji's development that would bring approximately 60,965 Indian labourers recruited mainly for the sugar industry, which became the foundation of Fiji's modern economy. Two of the immigrants on the *Leonidas* were declared to be of unsound mind upon arrival and so were not indentured. They were women: Ozeeari, a Muslim aged twenty-eight; and Sukudaia, a Hindu Bania, aged twenty-four.[11] Ozeeari had a daughter in India whereas Sukudaia's daughter accompanied her on the ship. Ozeeari died on 2 June 1880,[12] but Sukudaia survived. By 1884 Sukudaia had made her way to Suva where she roamed the streets, 'with no restraint'.[13] She was the first woman and second patient to be committed to Fiji's newly established Public Lunatic Asylum. The chief warden, Mr. Ferris, observed that Sukudaia was sometimes extremely violent and 'gave great trouble to the male patients who refused to have anything to do with her'. Two years later, she died in the asylum from tuberculosis.[14]

By 1916, with the abolishment of indenture in Fiji, an increasing number of Indians admitted to the asylum had served their indentures. Contracts were for five years, but most *Girmitiyas* re-indentured for another five years because they were not entitled to a free return passage until they had spent ten years' residence in Fiji, unless they were declared rejects or incapables.[15] Consequently, during the early twentieth century many former *Girmitiya* patients could not be repatriated and were instead admitted into the asylum as destitute. Physical destitution or poverty exacerbated mental illness, but mental illness also precipitated some migrants into destitution. The mentally fragile were less able to secure employment and accommodation after their contracts finished.

Sami was twelve years old when he left his father in India to be indentured in Fiji.[16] Nine years later, in 1919, he tried to drown in the Navua River and refused to eat, speak, or move, and was then committed as insane to the asylum with a diagnosis of severe melancholia. He died there in 1940 with no property or known relatives. This reflects how by 1920 an increasing number of Indian immigrants spent longer periods in the asylum because they could not be repatriated to India and did not have family to support them in Fiji. Sami was young when he left India, so it is unlikely that he would have been identified as suffering from severe melancholia. Was this induced by his experience as a *Girmitiya*? At what stage during migration and resettlement did mental illness become evident? Although the recruitment process was subject to various checks, including medical inspections, there were clearly loopholes through which mentally ill *Girmitiyas* were recruited.

DISPLACED MINDS AND RECRUITMENT

After Fiji's asylum opened until around 1914, similar proportions of indigenous Fijians and Indo Fijians were admitted there. Europeans and other ethnic groups each accounted for around 15 per cent of admissions before 1900, but thereafter this proportion declined. The rate of Indo Fijian admissions after 1914 was higher than other ethnicities until the 1960s.[17] Before 1920 almost all of the Indo Fijian patients in the asylum were *Girmitiyas*. Some were mentally ill before recruitment to Fiji; others found their mental state deteriorated during the voyage or was induced by the severe conditions on Fiji's plantations. The latter included the harsh realities of the labour process (especially long working days and physically demanding work, compounded by extremely low pay at 'task rates'), cramped living conditions on 'labour lines', and also the authoritarian and violent culture of the plantation.[18] This was endorsed by the colonial state.[19]

Historians Kenneth Gillion and Brij Lal have documented the 'filtering process' through which prospective labourers were accepted or rejected for indenture to Fiji.[20] Recruiters might find a mentally insecure person easy 'prey', but recruits underwent medical inspection at ports in Calcutta and Madras. When Fiji became a destination for indentured labour the process of medical inspection was, on paper, more regulated than that to earlier destinations such as in the Caribbean. Emigration passes had to be completed at the port of embarkation,[21] with emigrants' details, including certification from the surgeons-superintendent,[22] the depot surgeon, the protector of emigrants, and the colonial emigration agent at the port that the emigrant 'is free from all bodily and mental diseases'.[23]

Despite these checks, mentally and physically impaired workers were recruited. This speaks to the rapacious demand for plantation labour, although it was in the interest of the surgeons-superintendent to reject those who presented with obvious illness because surgeons-superintendents were paid a gratuity for each *Girmitiya* who disembarked alive.[24] However, mental illness is not necessarily overt, so labourers with previous episodes of insanity could have passed through the recruitment process. Thakur, for example, was certified as free of mental disease when he was accepted as a *Girmitiya* for Fiji.[25] At the Calcutta depot he probably would have presented as an ideal labourer because he had completed six years indenture in Mauritius. In Fiji his history of mental illness emerged, after he tried to kill his wife and children, along with attempting to assault others. He spent six days in gaol but five days later, another 'attack', which lasted fourteen days, precipitated confinement in the lunatic asylum. Thakur's admission papers record several 'attacks' during a period of sixteen years, including frequent hospital admissions while in Mauritius. It is unlikely that this was raised when he was examined in Calcutta. This reiterates the episodic and changing nature of mental illness and how a person could have a productive life despite suffering from severe mental illness. Thakur was aged forty when he was admitted to Fiji's asylum. Two weeks later he was repatriated to India, along with his wife and a child.

It is also conceivable that emigration officials, including surgeons-superintendents, were oblivious to existing mental distress because of cultural and language differences. For example, Gajadhar's peers said he had 'manifested signs of mental alienation in India' before indenture in Fiji in 1885. Two years later Koronivia's manager signed Gajadhar's admission papers to the asylum. Gajadhar spent two years there and was diagnosed with acute mania. His delusions reflected both his emigration experience and his cultural background. Gajadhar claimed that he was the manager of the Koronivia Sugar Estate and the inspector of immigration. He also insisted he was a 'great Brahmin' who desired to be worshipped.[26]

INTO THE KALA PANI

Cultural and religious taboos for some South Asian migrants venturing abroad, as well as the uncertainty of the journey, is encapsulated in the phrase *kala pani* (black waters). Colonial officials also recognised the trauma and despondency that could set in on a long voyage[27] that also entailed, for many, a severing of kin and community ties. James Laing, surgeons-superintendent, advised as follows:

> I *know* that many people die from Nostalgia . . . can it be wondered at with all their caste prejudices, their leaving their native land, perhaps never to see it again, and being thrown among people strange in habits,

language and even colour? The excitement of the newness of everything keeps them up for a time, but soon dies away, and is followed by depression when they realise what they have done; and to prevent this I would urge their being employed as much as possible while on board, and encouraged in every available means of entertainment.[28]

Despite efforts to keep *Girmitiyas* occupied during the voyage, serious mental distress was evident. The tragedies were those who committed or attempted suicide, or harmed others. Less clear was the despair that set in during the long voyage to Fiji. Hubraji, aged twenty-two years, jumped from the *Avon* in 1899. She also defecated in and destroyed her clothing and was violent towards other passengers, as well as singing, crying, or laughing. When examined in Suva she refused to answer questions and was briefly committed to the asylum before being returned to Calcutta.[29]

Jahaji bhai or *jahaji bhen* (men and women together on a ship) might have considered a *Girmitiya*'s behaviour as bizarre, but this did not necessarily convince medical authorities in Fiji that an immigrant was insane. Rajani was so disruptive that the ship's surgeon had to confine her in handcuffs many times during her voyage to Fiji in 1892, and her shipmates called her a *pugali* (mad person). The asylum's medical superintendent did not accept this as evidence of insanity, but rather 'violence of character, or rather deportment . . . disorderly and not insane'. He considered reports of her shipboard behaviour as 'riotous conduct . . . but . . . insufficiently weighty proof of insanity to turn the scale'.[30] Rajani was still discharged from her indenture and repatriated to India along with another patient Lalmokur (discussed below). Other migrants were severely disturbed on the ship, but this ceased after disembarkment and they worked for many years before being certified as insane. One *Girmitiya* had an 'attack' aboard the *Iman* in 1885 but lived in Fiji for twenty-three years before being admitted to the asylum from Suva prison.[31]

DISEMBARKATION AND PHYSICAL AND MENTAL DISPLACEMENT

Indentured migrants were again medically examined after disembarkation. This might be when madness induced on the voyage became evident, such as in 1892 when Lalmokur 'acted foolishly', absconded from the Immigration Depot, and was then briefly committed to the asylum.[32] Migrants who were rejected for work had to be repatriated, but there might be a delay of several months before a passage and adequate supervision could be guaranteed on a ship to India. This created problems concerning where insane immigrants could be securely detained while waiting for repatriation. Prisons were not deemed humane, but mentally disturbed migrants might be too disruptive to be confined in a hospital or at the immigration depot.

This dilemma had been a reason for establishing a lunatic asylum in Suva.[33] Another motivation was that the asylum could be a place of observation to ascertain if a migrant was genuinely insane, although there is no evidence of feigned madness among *Girmitiyas* admitted to the asylum. Colonial authorities were guided by both humane and economic imperatives. Fiji's governor, Sir William Des Voeux, advised the secretary to the government of India that it would better to return lunatics to India rather than maintain them indefinitely in Fiji, because 'for India the cost of taking proper care of such patients would probably be much less than here, while residence in their own country would in such cases increase the probability of a restoration to health'.[34] The secretary of the government of India accepted this but assured Fiji's colonial secretary that enquiries would be made into why such coolie immigrants were permitted to emigrate from India.[35]

Once the asylum had opened, a rejected *Girmitiya* who was certified as insane could be admitted as a private patient. In 1900 the agent general of immigration signed admission papers for a *Girmitiya*, aged twenty-four years, who had been highly disruptive in hospital, 'vociferous and raving', smearing his body with boiled rice, exposing his genitals in public, and experiencing hallucinations.[36] After two months in the asylum he was repatriated to Calcutta, along with his wife and family. A female *Girmitiya* classified as a 'reject immigrant' had suffered a 'continuing attack since arrival in colony' in 1913. She had been noisy and quarrelsome or morose and hurting herself during three months as a patient at the colonial hospital.[37] After four months at the asylum, she was repatriated to India.

NARAK AND MENTAL BREAKDOWN

The biggest environmental factor in mental breakdown for the Indian immigrants was the physical and mental stress they endured as indentured labourers. The *Girmitiyas* in Fiji referred to the exploitative and miserable experience of plantation work as *narak*, or hell. Although the majority of *Girmitiyas* developed coping strategies, high suicide rates among Indo Fijians were indicative of the extreme solution to which many resorted to finish their mental, social, and physical distress.[38] Other labourers did not end their lives but exhibited crazy behaviour on the plantations. At Naleba estate in 1915 a *Girmitiya* leaped naked on to his employer's horse and 'rode madly around'. This was three years after he had arrived in Fiji. He spent about six months in the asylum but seven years later was readmitted for twenty-one months with the diagnosis of dementia.[39] His later admission papers stated that he was 'not violent and on several days "quite normal", but without reason breaks out again'.[40]

Indian nationalist supporters C. F. Andrews and Reverend W. W. Pearson, along with Florence Garnham of the London Missionary Society, Calcutta, campaigned about the high rates of suicide among male

Indo-Fijian indentured migrants in Fiji, compared to India and other colonies where there was indenture.[41] The *Register of Deaths of Indian Immigrants* recorded 291 suicides, of which 259 were male and 32 female,[42] a discrepancy attributed by state officials to sexual jealousy determined by the disproportionate number of women to men on the plantations.[43] The agent general of immigration explicitly articulated this in a 1909 report.[44] According to historian Brij Lal, such observers assumed that indentured men were 'unable to obtain or, worse still, keep their women, who supposedly exploited their sexuality to promote their own material interests, the men—so the argument ran—descended into despondency and melancholia and committed suicide. Or, alternatively, they murdered their women first and then took their own lives'.[45]

One such probable case was Venkatewa Reddi, who complained of illness to the overseer on the plantation where he worked and was ordered to hospital. Instead he walked nineteen miles to the sugar mill at Lautoka, where he threw himself into the shredder. The mill was stopped, but his remains were unrecognisable. The death inquiry could not find any reason for Reddi's suicide but implicated the cause was a woman he had been cohabiting with had left him for another man.[46]

Historians have critiqued the attention to high suicide rates among *Girmitiyas* and also the correlation with sexual jealousy. Julie Parle argues that the settler state in Natal and Zululand blamed the epidemic of suicides among Indians on their 'nature', that is, Indian culture.[47] Similar assumptions about cultural dispositions to suicide can be found in the Fiji records. Parle contrasts the emphasis on Indian suicide rates with a lack of comparable evidence of suicide among whites and Africans. She also suggests that suicide within the latter categories may have been under-reported. Likewise, data concerning suicide among those who were not *Girmitiyas* in early colonial Fiji is incomplete, but there is evidence of suicide among indigenous Fijians and Europeans. This excludes attempts at self-destruction that are often under-reported, especially among women.

Historians in Fiji have contextualised suicide and mental breakdown within the context of indenture. Lal identified that indenture disrupted the networks of kinship, marriage, caste, and religion,[48] significantly contributing to suicide among *Girmitiyas*. He asserted that suicide was both a cry of despair and an act of protest directed at the indenture system: 'suicide was a rational and understandable response to a terrible and alienating situation'.[49]

The relentless and repetitive labour process that *Girmitiyas* in Fiji endured was another source of physical and mental stress. Lal reiterated that most Indian immigrants were used to hard physical labour, but in India this would have been punctuated with breaks such as the wedding season, monsoons, and religious festivals: 'the sudden realization that an intended sojourn in Fiji would in all likelihood become permanent exile could have been unbearable for some immigrants'.[50] Contemporaries drew similar conclusions, as when the manager at a colonial sugar refinery (CSR) plantation in Lautoka reported the death of Subbarayan: 'Deceased probably despaired at what confronted him in the shape of work. He only arrived at the estate from the depot on the 4th and suicided on the 11th'.[51] Lal also suggests that the small number of migrants of higher caste may have perhaps 'more keenly felt' displacement and the harsh realities of unaccustomed physical work:

> Outnumbered in an alien environment, socially and economically impotent, deprived of the support of the paraphernalia of culture and religion that had buttressed their traditional position in village India, they suffered more from the cultural upheaval and change that emigration brought about. The ritual prescriptions regarding endogamy, untouchability and commensality were irrelevant or impossible to maintain in the new context.[52]

Such tensions were revealed at the inquiry into Manesa's death by hanging from a tree on Navuso plantation. Manesa was a Rajput (warrior caste) and was remembered by a workmate as a 'great reader and writer and a high caste man'. A hospital servant testified that Manesa had been in a melancholy mood before the suicide and had said, 'I do not feel inclined to work any longer at Navuso as the work was hard. . . . He said he was unaccustomed to hard [work] . . . here a man with a small amount of knowledge is made a Sirdar [overseer] while another with good education has to do hard manual labour, like myself'.[53]

Suicide represents an extreme of responses to the labour process, but a greater unspecified number of *Girmitiyas* reacted with chronic sadness or severe depression. Although some labour historians have regarded suicide in the workplace as a form of resistance or agency,[54] there has been less attention to the more hidden signs of depression in work contexts. Refusal to work could reflect workplace resistance but might also indicate depression or a mental or physical inability to perform tasks. Colonial authorities who sometimes dismissed this as malingering also acknowledged the impact of displacement. An estate manager sought Dhurma's repatriation in 1884 stating, 'this woman in not right in her mind, and only works when she chooses'.[55] Dhurma had undergone profound upheaval; aged thirty-six, she was comparatively mature when she emigrated from Calcutta; and contrary to gender norms within her Brahman caste, she was unmarried, had left her son in her village, and enlisted as a labourer for faraway Fiji. Some asylum admission records cited an inability or refusal to work. In 1882 Chuni was indentured to a Taveuni copra estate in 1882, but four years later was certified as a lunatic. According to the plantation overseer, for nearly eighteen months Chuni 'refuses to obey all orders and answer any questions put to him; talks to himself, wants to wander away and if stopped resists the person in charge of him and on several occasions attacked him with stones. Has wandered away from estate on several occasions'.[56]

Three years later Chuni was repatriated to India along with four other 'incapable' migrants from the asylum. Among these were two *Girmitiyas*, described by chief medical officer Dr. Bolton Corney as 'quiet and orderly men though in a condition which renders them quite incapable of earning a living in this colony or of properly conducting their own affairs'. Although not violent to others, one of these patients had 'hammered his head on the floor to propitiate goddess Kali who he had offended in Calcutta'.[57]

THE VIOLENCE OF MADNESS AND INDENTURE

Most cases of mentally distressed *Girmitiyas* are replete with violence to self and others, or from others. Contemporary experts presented sexual jealousy as the cause of suicide among *Girmitiyas*, but officials also recognised that Fiji's plantations could be enclaves of violence where vulnerable migrants might be driven to suicide: 'several suicides were reported during 1905 of indentured immigrants, in most cases they were recent arrivals, and it appeared that in more than one case, ill-usage by a Sardar [overseer] was alleged as the cause of suicide'.[58] The correlation between institutional violence and suicide or mental illness remained ambiguous, with the victim's testimony usually questioned. In 1909 a *Girmitiya*, working on a CSR plantation near Labasa, made a 'very determined attempt at suicide; cut his throat very severely completely severing windpipe. Will never be able to speak above a whisper and will always have to keep tube in throat to breathe through'. He accused his employer of assaulting him before he died, but Macuata's stipendary magistrate dismissed this.[59] A later inquiry in 1919 into the suicide of Soman suggested that this had been precipitated by an attack from five men. Although a medical examination had confirmed he was in 'great pain all over the body wherever touched', an overseer denied the attack.[60]

Soman's story points to the intersection of the plantation system, violence, and displacement. Constable Khan stated that Soman spoke in unintelligible Madrassi to Calcuttans and Fijians. It is unclear from the records if this communication breakdown was indicative of Soman's madness or of linguistic barriers. Soman was also diagnosed as melancholic and, like several Indians admitted to the asylum, along with those of other ethnicities, appeared to be severely depressed.[61] Displacement through migration can be considered a dominant factor. Depression possibly compounded among *Girmitiyas* who left close family in India, such as a married woman admitted in 1887 with mania and 'thoughts of her children in India'. She died in the asylum six months later.[62] The loneliness and longing for family left behind, so common among migrants,[63] could lead to self-harm. Nizar was admitted to the asylum on 25 December 1921 after attempting to slit his throat in the cane fields. His testimony was translated by a police officer from Hindi into English and then transcribed by a doctor. This revealed that Nizar had been plagued by dreams and hallucinations during which his parents asked, 'What did you leave your house for and go to another country?' He answered, 'Because it is God's wish'. Nizar said that his father had been crying every day since he left and wanted him to return to India.[64]

OTHER LOST SOULS

Some other migrants responded to their displacement in similar ways to the *Girmitiyas*, through 'malingering', absconding, and violence, to exhibiting severe mental distress. Between 1884 and 1916, approximately twenty-nine patients in the lunatic asylum had migrated to Fiji as labourers from other Pacific Islands. Jimi, originally from the Solomon Islands, was first indentured as a plantation labourer in Samoa. In 1894 he sailed to Fiji, but during the voyage twice tried to jump overboard. At the Immigration Depot on Nukulau Island he tried to swim to nearby Makaluva Island and when rescued said he did not know what he was doing. Upon admission to the asylum, the immigration agent observed Jimi as 'dull, depressed and melancholy'. After six months in the asylum, Jimi was repatriated to his home island in the Solomon Islands.[65]

Fiji attracted independent migrants, with European settlers dominating before 1920. Several purchased or leased land to develop plantations and businesses. From the early twentieth century Indians (mainly Gujaratis and Punjabis) and Chinese also independently migrated to Fiji. Although Fiji's colonial hierarchy had clear racial categorisation between Europeans, Fijians, Indians, and others, class and traditional status could disrupt these boundaries. Europeans accounted for around 15 per cent of admissions to the asylum before 1900, but then this proportion substantially declined.

European lunatics were a minority both within Fiji and the asylum, but the archives have left more detail of their migration into madness than the *Girmitiyas*. This was partly because of language but also because of their position at the apex of the colonial hierarchy. Richard Keller suggests that insane Europeans may have compromised colonial hegemony and the construction of the rational European.[66] Mad European women threatened colonial order and bourgeois identity with their violation of sexuality and other gendered norms.[67]

TRANSIENT LOST SOULS

Since the late eighteenth century, the Pacific Islands have attracted European travellers, some in search of 'paradise' or to mend a 'broken soul'. This has ranged from artists such as Paul Gauguin to the fictional Sadie Thompson (of Somerset Maugham's novel *Rain*) to contemporary backpackers. Such travellers included the mentally unwell, and this condition could precipitate continual or periodic movement. These travellers often chose to not put down roots, or they were rejected by local European communities because of public transgressions that extended beyond colonial eccentricities and conventions. Transient Europeans who stepped outside the public norms expected of Europeans in Fiji could be especially threatening to local colonial sensibilities.

Some travellers were able to pay the costs of the impact of their outrageous behaviour. Others became dependent on local communities as both a moral and a financial liability. As with *Girmitiyas*, the colony was reluctant to provide financial support for mad Europeans. A prison doctor recommended in 1884 that European lunatics be 'kept in a neighbouring colony with a temperate climate', as 'the pecuniary cost to us would be less'.[68] The acting superintendent of police warned that Fiji could become a destination for 'neighbouring colonies . . . to rid themselves at the expense of this colony of inconvenient and troublesome burdens'. Allen's admission to Suva Gaol for vagrancy and lunacy in 1883 had sparked this concern, after he sailed to Fiji from Port Chalmers, New Zealand. Allen had been assured of work in Rewa District but could not find his employer.[69]

European itinerants in the Pacific before 1920 were either travellers or workers on ships.[70] Fiji was not always a destination but often where they were removed from a ship if they had seriously 'broken down'. Suva was convenient for this once an asylum operated there. This also became a space to dry out mania induced by alcohol that gripped some travellers either on board ship or within Pacific ports. Sean was one of the asylum's first itinerant European patients. Originally from Ireland, he was a sailor en route to New Caledonia. There he married and had two children, but after his wife died his mental deterioration and alcoholism escalated. In 1882 he stowed away in the coalbunkers of the PS *Thistle* that sailed from Noumea to Fiji, where he was discovered and declared insane. Fiji did not have the legislation or infrastructure to commit him as a lunatic, so Sean was temporarily incarcerated, but later returned to prison as a vagrant. He was committed to the asylum as soon as it opened, but when discharged eight years later authorities despaired that he could avoid the temptations of alcohol in Suva. The colonial secretary recommended he be sent to 'a more civilised and larger port'. A relief fund (for destitutes) paid his passage to Noumea.[71]

THE BREAKDOWN OF SETTLEMENT

Many Europeans committed to the asylum were poor. Before 1920 several European men had migrated to Fiji with dreams of amassing fortunes as planters, or to take advantage of economic and occupational opportunities in the colony. These ambitions were shattered for many due to factors including environment, economic slumps, and colonial restrictions on access to land and labour. By the 1880s the CSR had a monopoly over sugar production while the state limited further access to indigenous controlled land. After 1920 the plantation system devolved to production by small-scale Indian leaseholders. Many settlers did not have the temperament, health, or resources to cope with these changes. This would have been compounded by pre-existing mental illness before migration to Fiji and exacerbated by the challenges of settlement. Governor Gordon declared, 'It should always be remembered that this is emphatically not a white man's colony'.[72]

Claudia Knapman also documented that neither was Fiji a white woman's colony. She describes the impact Arthur Carr's madness and economic failure had on his family.[73] Following treatment for mental illness in Sydney he emigrated to Fiji where his brothers were sugar planters. Carr's venture into banana and pineapple farming failed. During 1897 he was a patient for ten months in the asylum and was re-admitted four more times until his death in 1907, aged forty-four. His depressive and manic outbreaks in Fiji were attributed to 'sun' and worry about land transactions. His wife, Lillie, took responsibility for herself and their four daughters by converting the banana plantation into a dairy and poultry farm. Knapman interviewed a daughter: 'My father wasn't a very well man and Mother had quite a lot to do'. Lillie also faced the burden of paying his maintenance of ten shillings a day as a private patient, but the colonial secretary ruled that Carr's fees would be remitted pending his recovery.[74]

Carr's story is indicative of how the breakdown of settlement compounded with mental breakdown for some Europeans. The impact of the physical and cultural environment, loneliness, and economic failure precipitated some to turn to alcohol and others to religious extremism, or they tyrannised their staff and families. Some were discretely repatriated to Australia, New Zealand, or the United Kingdom but a minority became destitute. When bizarre behaviour was exhibited in ways outside community tolerance, or when destitution became public, they came to the attention of the police, doctors, and other colonial authorities. Similar to the *Girmitiyas*, the conundrum was whether this constituted insanity and where such 'unfortunates' could be cared for in a secure environment.

As with Indian immigrants, European immigrants in Fiji also committed suicide. Data concerning suicide among non-*Girmitiyas* was under-reported, but there is some evidence of suicide and attempted suicide among European migrants. Contemporaries did not problematize suicide rates among Europeans in Fiji, along similar lines to that of the *Girmitiyas*.[75] Neither was there the simplistic correlation of suicide with the disproportion of the sexes or sexual jealousy that dominated discourse concerning *Girmitiyas* and suicide.

Between 1884 and 1 January 1920 approximately forty-six Europeans were admitted to the asylum.[76] Only eight of these patients were reported as suicidal before commitment or while in care there. One of the asylum's first patients, Annie, a European waitress, was admitted by her husband in 1884 as a private patient after suffering from 'puerperal insanity'. Aged only twenty-one, the medical superintendent reported that she had undergone two attacks of chorea and had a generally hard life. According to the district medical officer, 'she should be certified on the basis of [being] hurried and agitated, great irritability, obscenity of language and husband said she was outrageous and had strong dislike of him'. Reports described her as suicidal, paranoid that violence was being inflicted upon her, and threatening violence towards her husband.

The full extent of suicide and self-harm among Europeans in Fiji was probably undisclosed by family, so is not evident within the public record. One exception was when John Miller attempted to slit his throat in 1883 because of 'pecuniary difficulties', aggravated by chronic dysentery. In a letter to A. Taylor, Taveuni's stipendary magistrate, Miller appealed against being prosecuted for attempted suicide on compassionate grounds:

> For some time back I have been suffering from great depression of spirits.
> Which upon Friday morning last got so unbearable, that in an evil moment, I rashly drew that Razor which your Officer has,—across my throat—I have no excuse to appear for this rash act, an act which I will regret the longest day I live.
> Thank God the wound inflicted was only a very slight one.
> I am aware I am guilty of a very serious offence.
> May God forgive my madness.[77]

At least two CSR officers also killed themselves. One sent half his salary home to support his mother and sisters before shooting himself, and another placed a dynamite cap in his mouth.[78]

CONCLUSION

Fiji has long been a centre of migrants and travellers in the Pacific. The mentally fragile have also been caught up in this, but for them displacement has been many edged, not only that of place, work, culture, and family, but also of the mind and mental stability. Suva's asylum and lunacy legislation was introduced to cope with the extreme consequences of displacement—the 'insane and incurable persons' to whom MacGregor referred.

Despite regulations for indentured labour to Fiji, some severely mentally ill migrants were recruited. This is indicative of colonial labour demands and economic pressures within India. Conditions on the voyage out and on the plantations were restrictive and often violent, where migrants from divergent backgrounds cohabited confined spaces with limited relief from repetitive and arduous work. Some mentally ill *Girmitiyas* were repatriated before completing indentures, but others endured *narak*. A minority of *Girmitiyas* responded to this through self-harm and suicide. Contemporaries regarded numerical gender disparity and resultant sexual jealousy as explanations of this. Hindsight indicates that this overlooked the wider context and the progression of mental illness.

Migration and madness studies have concentrated on settlement in new lands. This chapter has addressed mentally ill Indian and European migrants in Fiji, but it also raises the question of the outcome of insane migrants who were repatriated from Fiji. Although colonial authorities justified the repatriation of 'incurable' *Girmitiyas* to India because they would receive better care there, there is no evidence of this outcome. What happened to families such as Thakur's? The family of a returned *Girmitiya* with no earnings would have been unlikely to be welcomed into a village and family environment. Other *Girmitiya* marriages were hastily arranged 'depot marriages' before emigration. If the wife was from a different region or caste than her husband, she would not be accepted into either her natal village or within her husband's kin in India.

'Madness' migrated to Fiji, but the environment and working conditions there exacerbated and in some cases may have caused mental illness. The lunatics who found their way to the asylum were from all ethnicities, but this chapter has focused on *Girmitiyas*, indentured labourers who comprised the largest group of migrants in Fiji before 1920. It has also considered European migrants, many assuming they would slot into the top of the racial hierarchy in Fiji. But mentally disturbed Europeans were not always so easily placed or welcomed there. Also addressed were 'displaced minds' who never made it to the asylum because they either killed themselves or were deported from Fiji.

Fiji was one of the many smaller colonies that tried to find a solution to madness and displacement. During the late nineteenth century this was through the establishment of a lunatic asylum for all migrants. Although meagre in resources, funding, and staff, it continued to be one refuge for 'lost souls' during the twentieth century. In the twenty-first century it is still a major psychiatric institution within the Pacific Islands.

NOTES

1. Colonial Secretariat Office (CSO) Minute Paper (MP) 84/86, 21 April 1886. See R. B. Joyce, *Sir William MacGregor* (Melbourne: Oxford University Press, 1971).
2. For collections on colonial networks of psychiatry, see W. Ernst and T. Mueller (eds.), *Transnational Psychiatries: Social and Cultural Histories of Psychiatry in Comparative Perspective, c. 1800–2000* (Cambridge: Cambridge Scholars Publishing, 2010); and S. Mahone and M. Vaughan (eds.), *Psychiatry and Empire* (Houndmills: Palgrave MacMillan, 2007).
3. Macgregor cited in B. V. Lal, *Chalo Jahaji: On a Journey Through Indenture in Fiji* (Suva: Fiji Museum / Division of Pacific and Asian History, Australian National University: Prashant Pacific, 2000), p. 153.

4. 'An Ordinance to Provide for the Care and Maintenance of Lunatics and Idiots', *Fiji Royal Gazette*, 3/1884.
5. The concept of surfacing is taken from L. Jackson, *Surfacing Up: Psychiatry and Social Order in Colonial Zimbabwe, 1908–1968* (Ithaca, NY: Cornell University Press, 2005).
6. The asylum also catered to indigenous Fijians, as during the asylum's early years they comprised a significant proportion of patients. This is beyond the scope of this chapter but is addressed in J. Leckie, 'Modernity and the management of madness in colonial Fiji', *Paideuma*, 50 (2004), pp. 251–74; J. Leckie, 'Unsettled minds: Colonialism, gender and settling madness in Fiji', in S. Mahone and M. Vaughan (eds.), *Psychiatry and Empire*, pp. 99–123; J. Leckie, 'Islands, asylums and communities: Fiji and the colonial Pacific', in Ernst and Mueller (eds.), *Transnational Psychiatries*, pp. 24–50.
7. For details of historical constructions of insanity in Fiji, see Leckie, 'Modernity and the management of madness', pp. 260–66; Leckie, 'Unsettled minds'.
8. See, for example, G. Berrios, *The History of Mental Symptoms: Descriptive Psychopathology Since the Nineteenth Century* (Cambridge: Cambridge University Press, 1996); J. Weaver and D. Wright (eds.), *Histories of Suicide: International Perspectives on Self-destruction in the Modern World* (Toronto: University of Toronto Press, 2009).
9. A. L Stoler, *Along the Archival Grain: Epistemic Anxieties and Colonial Common Sense* (Princeton, NJ: Princeton University Press, 2010), p. 21.
10. Lal, *Chalo Jahaji,* pp. 143-51.
11. CSO 241/84. Sukudaia is the name on admission papers to the Public Lunatic Asylum. She is recorded as Sudaia on CSO MP 82/2287 and as Sookdaie on CSO 241/84. Her emigration pass is no. 79 and Ozeeari's is no. 406. Unless stated, personal information is from admission papers (cited as patient number [PN] and case notes, located at St. Giles Hospital) or from CSO files, Fiji National Archives.
12. General register of Indian immigrants, 1879–1916 (microform) (Fiji: Dept. of Immigration and Central Archives of Fiji and the Western Pacific High Commission).
13. CSO 241/84.
14. PN 2.
15. K. L. Gillion, *Fiji's Indian Migrants: A History to the End of Indenture in 1920* (1962; reprint, Melbourne: Oxford University Press, 1973), pp. 190–97. Families had to accompany rejected *Girmitiyas* to India.
16. PN 580. Sami is a pseudonym. For ethical reasons and because of Fiji's small population, pseudonyms are used unless referring to individuals within the public domain. Where possible, emigration passes of insane *Girmitiyas* have been checked, but these numbers are not cited unless publicly known.
17. These are approximations based on annual reports of St. Giles Hospital and admission certificates. I am revising a database covering 3,129 admissions between 1884 and 1964, which is why precise figures are unavailable.
18. *Girmitiyas* were paid according to time rates or by task, but employers in Fiji increasingly adopted task payments. This led to over-tasking—squeezing as much labour as possible from workers within a set timeframe. See Gillion, *Fiji's Indian Migrants*, pp. 82–90. On the culture of violence on Fiji's plantations, see V. Naidu, *The Violence of Indenture* (Suva: World University Service/School of Social and Economic Development, University of the South Pacific, 1980).
19. The power imbalance in workers' upholding complaints against employers through legal processes and the futility of other overt forms of workers'

resistance is outlined in B. V. Lal, 'Murmurs of dissent: Non-resistance on Fiji plantations', *Hawaiian Journal of History*, 20 (1986), pp. 188–214.

20. Gillion, *Fiji's Indian Migrants*, pp. 29–36; B. V. Lal, *Girmitiyas: The Origins of the Fiji Indians* (Canberra: Journal of Pacific History, 1983), pp. 28–33.
21. For legislation, see B. V. Lal, *Crossing the Kala Pani: A Documentary History of Indian Indenture in Fiji* (Division of Pacific and Asian History, ANU, Canberra / Fiji Museum, Suva: Prashant Pacific Book, 1998) pp. 49–94.
22. The surgeons-superintendent was responsible for the welfare of *Girmitiyas* on the ship. See Gillion, *Fiji's Indian Migrants,* pp. 60–63.
23. Wording from emigration passes.
24. Gillion, *Fiji's Indian Migrants*, p. 61.
25. PN 70.
26. PN 38. Brahmins (or Brahmans) are the highest ritual caste in India. Many were priests or teachers, but several were also poor. Some Brahmans became *Girmitiyas*, probably because of economic or other reasons, such as to evade religious and cultural strictures and expectations in India.
27. The passage from Calcutta to Fiji could take between eleven to eighteen weeks. Lal, *Crossing the Kala Pani*, p. 9.
28. J. M. Laing, *Hand Book for Surgeons Superintendent of the Coolie Emigration Service* (Colonial Office, March 1889), reprinted in Lal, *Crossing the Kala Pani*, p. 39.
29. PN 152.
30. PN 72.
31. PN 286.
32. PN 71.
33. Leckie, 'Modernity and the management of madness in colonial Fiji', pp. 251-56.
34. CSO 2886/85, despatch no. 119, 27 September 1883.
35. CSO 2886/85, 25 January 1884.
36. PN 161.
37. PN 391.
38. Lal, *Chao Jahaji*, p. 216, cites that the Fiji Indian suicide rate during the first decade and a half of the twentieth century was the highest among all Indian labour importing colonies in Africa and the West Indies and much higher than in India. The rates for Indo Fijians were 0.780 per thousand in 1900 and 0.831 per thousand in 1910.
39. PN 429.
40. PN 720.
41. C. F. Andrews and W. W. Pearson, *Indian Indentured Labour in Fiji: An Independent Enquiry* (Calcutta: Star Printing Works, 1916); F. Garnham, *A Report on the Social and Moral Conditions of Indians in Fiji* (Sydney: Kingston, 1918). Garnham's investigation was on behalf of forty-six women's groups in Australia and New Zealand.
42. B. V. Lal, 'Veil of dishonour: Sexual jealousy and suicide on Fiji plantations', *Journal of Pacific History*, 20:3 (1985), p. 136.
43. Lal, 'Veil of dishonour', p. 137, cites that in 1912 there were 43.17 Indian females to 100 males.
44. CP 28/10, 1 June 1910.
45. Lal, 'Veil of dishonour', p. 137.
46. CP 21/08, 14 May 1908.
47. J. Parle, '"This painful subject": Racial politics and suicide in colonial Natal and Zululand', in Weaver and Wright (eds.), *Histories of Suicide*, p. 157.

48. Lal, 'Veil of dishonour', p. 138. He did not use the term network but integrative institutions, following E. Durkheim, *Suicide: A Study in Sociology*, translated by J.A. Spaulding and G. Simpson (London: Routledge and Kegan, 1952). Lal, 'Veil of dishonour', p. 147, also drew on H. Kushner's 'Immigrant suicide in the United States: Towards a psycho-social history', *Journal of Social History*, 18:1 (1984), pp. 3–24. Kushner later critiqued that social integration provided protection against self-harm and suicide, in 'Suicide, gender and the fear of modernity', in Weaver and Wright (eds.), *Histories of Suicide*, pp. 19-51.

49. Lal, 'Veil of dishonour', pp. 154-55

50. Lal, 'Veil of dishonour', p. 148. As noted, *Girmitiyas* were not entitled to a return passage until completing two five-year indentures. A return passage cost between five to ten pounds and likely was not financially viable, especially as many *Girmitiyas* accumulated debts or fines. It was also shameful and not practical to return to India without earnings.

51. CSO MP 2281/1905, 23 May 1905.

52. Lal, 'Veil of dishonour', pp. 150-51.

53. CSO MP 1346/90.

54. For example, R. Cohen, 'Resistance and hidden forms of consciousness among African workers', *Review of African Political Economy*, 19 (1980), pp. 8–22; K. Saunders, '"Troublesome Servants": The strategies of resistance employed by Melanesian indentured labourers on plantations in colonial Queensland', *Journal of Pacific History*, 14:3 (1979), p. 181—although she qualifies suicide as not so much a positive response, but the 'effects of defeat'. Also, A. Wells and J. Gilbert, 'Structure of domination and forms of resistance on Yucatecan estates during the late Pofiriato, ca. 1880–1915', in B. V. Lal, D. Munro, and E. D. Beechert (eds.), *Plantation Workers: Resistance and Accommodation* (Honolulu: University of Hawaii Press, 1993), pp. 273–75, 293. For a nuanced discussion of labour resistance and labour accommodation, see D. Munro, 'Patterns of resistance and accommodation', in Lal, Munro, and Beechert, *Plantation Workers*, pp. 1–32.

55. CSO 2886/85.

56. PN 27.

57. PN 51 and PN 49.

58. CSO MP 1045/1916.

59. CSO MP 8312/1909.

60. PN 570.

61. Berrios, *The History of Mental Symptoms*, pp. 298–300, outlines the shifting historical discourse of affective disorders and the transformation of melancholia into today's classification as depression. In colonial Fiji classifications of mental diseases varied between admission papers and official reports. Between 1884 and 1922 'melancholy and suicidal' constituted a major category of published statistics for insanity, but admission papers and suicide reports used the term melancholic or described conditions associated with this such as 'low in spirits'. A Solomon Islands indentured labourer admitted to the asylum in 1909 (PN 303) exhibited 'marked mental depression'. He had also tried to commit suicide.

62. PN 37.

63. Noted by C. Coleborne, *Madness in the Family: Insanity and Institutions in the Australasian Colonial World, 1860–1914* (Houndmills: Palgrave MacMillan, 2010), pp. 47–51.

64. PN 680. This case is outside the chapter's time period but illustrates the anguish of migration.

65. PN 144.
66. R. C. Keller, 'Madness and colonization: Psychiatry in the British and French empires 1800–1962', *Journal of Social History*, 35:2 (2001), pp. 298–99.
67. See A. Stoler, *Race and the Education of Desire: Foucault's History of Sexuality and the Colonial Order of Things* (Durham, NC: Duke University Press, 1995), p. 8. For details in Fiji, see Leckie, 'Unsettled minds', pp. 99–123.
68. CSO 1340/84, 4 July 1884, extract prison medical journal.
69. CSO 968/83, 9 April 1883.
70. Mental stress on island trading ships is discussed in F. Steel, 'Oceania under steam: Maritime cultures, colonial histories 1870s-1910s' (PhD dissertation, Australian National University, 2007).
71. PN 7. I was unable to find any further documentation on relief funds in Fiji during this period.
72. Cited in L. Veracini, 'Emphatically not a white man's colony', *Journal of Pacific History*, 43:2 (2008), pp. 189–205.
73. C. Knapman, *White Women in Fiji, 1835–1930: The Ruin of Empire?* (Sydney: Allen and Unwin, 1986), p. 63, 69. Carr's asylum records are from admission papers.
74. Knapman, *White Women in Fiji, 1835–1930*, p. 69; CSO 540/1897. Daily rates for first class patients were 10/- for the first three months, then 6/- 8d, and for second class patients, 2/- followed by 1/- 6d (CP 4/1887).
75. See also Parle, 'This painful subject', p. 157.
76. Complete details including ethnicity, cause of disorder and other details are not available for all admission papers either because these were not supplied at admission or because some records have been damaged by infestation.
77. CSO 3172/83, 1 Dec 1883.
78. Knapman, *White Women in Fiji, 1835–1930*, p. 94.

9 Between Two Psychiatric Regimes
Migration and Psychiatry in Early Twentieth-Century Japan

Akihito Suzuki

In the now extensive historiography of the Victorian rise of the asylum, urban-rural migration has attracted the attention of some historians. Andrew Scull argues that the rise of custodial care of the insane was a consequence of the arrival of a mature capitalist economy and the 'commercialization of existence'.[1] Although Scull cautions against a simple view of seeing the asylum as an answer to the problems of migrants to cities, whose original family and kinship ties had weakened and who had become insane, his idea of understanding the rise of the asylum in the context of the development of the capitalist system and accompanying social change has inspired historians to examine whether migration had an impact on committal to psychiatric institutions. Works by John Walton, Mark Finnane, David Wright, Joseph Melling, Bill Forsythe, and Richard Adair all explore the influence of 'interdependence between economic change, migration flows, and family support structures' on the committal to asylums in Anglo-American and European contexts.[2]

Migration provides a promising research perspective for the history of psychiatric care in Japan, too. Indeed, the history of migration was intertwined with the development and the transformation of Japanese psychiatric provision. A long-term perspective will be helpful here. Under the semi-feudal system of government of Tokugawa Shogunate (1603–1867), migration within the country was limited and emigration to foreign countries was strictly forbidden. The population remained roughly stable at around 30 million from the late seventeenth century until the early nineteenth century.[3] Under this regime of limited migration and stable population, Japan had not developed collective psychiatric provisions known in European countries from the early modern period, such as general hospitals in France or private madhouses in England. The home of the patient was a normal and normative site of psychiatric confinement or care. When in the nineteenth century people started to move around more extensively and the population started to grow steadily, psychiatric provision in collective forms began to emerge. Two psychiatric hospitals were established in Edo and Osaka in the early nineteenth century. After the Meiji Revolution in 1868, which set Japan for modernisation and Westernisation and removed a legal barrier for migration, psychiatric hospitals multiplied. On the surface, the Japanese rise of institutions for confinement from the late nineteenth- and early twentieth-century appears to have been caused by the state policy and the Westernisation of medicine. At a deeper level, however, the societal change and more mobile population acted as a background of the new institutional confinement of the insane.

With this large picture in mind, this chapter attempts to examine the question of migration and psychiatric care in early twentieth-century Japan. The period offers an interesting case because it was characterised by the stark contrast between the psychiatric provision in the city and that in the countryside. Large cities had acquired both public and private hospitals for the insane, whereas in rural areas care for the insane was largely given in patients' own homes. This contrast was due to the lack of a national system of psychiatric provision realised in England in 1845 and in many European countries in the nineteenth century.[4] As such, the situation has long been understood as the disparity between the progressive urban Japan which was catching up with the West and the more 'backward' rural Japan: the benefit of modernity and Westernisation in the form of psychiatric hospital had reached only in the city, while the countryside had been denied the gift of 'civilisation'. Although there is some truth in this typically Whiggish view, this chapter is more interested in examining urban-rural connections than in emphasising the contrast. When migrants who had moved to the city from the countryside became insane and could not be treated at their homes, they had several options: entering a hospital in the city or returning to their original home in the country to be cared for there. The decision was not just that of places of the city or the country; it was also about the types of care, namely, in the hospital or in the home. Many patients combined the two in their long trajectory of care and treatment. Psychiatric hospitals in early twentieth-century Japanese cities were thus a node in this complex flow of urban-rural migration in two ways, rather than a warehouse of unwanted people. The social history of psychiatry in Japan should be understood in the context of the migration of people between two regimes of urban and rural psychiatric provision.

This 'nodal' view of the asylum connects the history of psychiatric provision in Japan with other important aspects in the making of modern Japan. Migration has been one of the major issues in the historiography of Japanese modernity in general. In both cultural and economic terms, urban-rural migration was fundamental in the making of modern Japan and has been a subject of extensive arguments and debates. Culturally, the modern Japanese were (and still are) expected to feel special emotional bonds with the place of one's birth, typically imagined as a small rural village with rice paddies and small mountains. Countless novels were written on the subject of homecoming and nostalgia, and dozens of songs expressed the sentiment of leaving one's rural hometown. The fact that many such songs were set to the tunes of Scottish folksongs (for example, 'Auld Lang Syne') reveals that this sentiment of a rural home was a relatively new addition to Japanese culture or even an invented tradition.[5] The tradition has continued to the present age, and a contemporary Japanese anime film director Hayao Miyazaki has been making shrewd use of the collective memory of a rural home-village in mega-hit works such as *My Neighbor Totoro* (1988) and *Spirited Away* (2001). Economically, the supply of migrant labourers from rural areas was vital to the growth of the Japanese economy in the early phase of its industrialisation in the early twentieth century. Since the proto-industrialisation in the eighteenth- and nineteenth-centuries was centred in rural villages and towns, the economic development in this phase did not result in urbanisation.[6] In contrast, the twentieth century witnessed rapid growth of the influx of population in cities, whose populations grew by 15 per cent to 20 per cent every five years.[7] The rapid urbanisation supported the hectic industrialisation of Japan, as well as created manifold problems familiar to historians of industrialising cities around the world.

The following part of this chapter attempts to examine psychiatry from the migrants' point of view, setting it in the larger context of the modernisation of Japanese society. It first provides a broad sketch of early modern provision for the insane in Japan. In both urban and rural areas in early modern Japan, institutional provision was limited, and care at home was the dominant style. The second section will show that from the beginning of the twentieth century, urban and rural areas developed very different systems of psychiatric care: cities started to have psychiatric hospitals, whereas the countryside continued to rely on confinement at home. The contrast was due to two acts of legislation, namely, the Mental Patients' Custody Act (1900) and the Mental Hospitals Act (1919). These two acts shaped Japanese psychiatric provision into two different regimes for the cities and the country through social and economic forces. The third section will examine how the patients or patients' families combined the dual regimes.

A few words are necessary about the sources of the case studies used in this chapter. The sources for this examination of the network of psychiatric care are taken from the archive of Ōji Brain Hospital (hereafter OBH), one of the most successful private psychiatric hospitals in Tokyo.[8] OBH can be considered a microcosm of Japanese psychiatry. In about thirty years from its establishment around 1900, OBH transformed itself from a custodial institution often lacking any medical pretension to a centre of new therapies and innovative development in psychiatry. The figure behind the rapid rise of OBH was Komine Shigeyuki (1883–1942), its medical superintendent, manager, and owner. Komine first studied medicine at a lowly private medical school but subsequently studied abroad at the Wistar Institute in Philadelphia in 1919 and 1920. At Wistar he studied neurophysiology and biochemical analysis of the central nervous system based on animal experimentation under Henry Donaldson. The research resulted in his MD dissertation submitted to Tohoku Imperial University in 1923. The Wistar Institute also provided him with the model to follow, and Komine later established the Komine Research Institute on the premises of the hospital around 1925, where animal and human experiments were conducted.[9] The scientific and experimental orientation provided an important background to the introduction of new therapies to OBH. Komine was also quick to incorporate Freudian psychiatry to the hospital, which had at least two doctors trained in psychoanalysis.[10] Despite its progressive outlook, OBH was deeply integrated into the network of migration between the rural and urban areas in modern Japan, as the chapter goes on to show.

EARLY MODERN HOME CONFINEMENT

The early modern period, which started around the mid-sixteenth century and lasted for about three centuries until the Meiji Revolution in 1868, was a formative period which provided the basis of the modern Japanese psychiatry in many ways.[11] Four types of psychiatric care developed during the early modern period: accommodation in and around religious establishments, psychiatric hospitals, confinement in a non-medical institution, and confinement in the patients' own house.

Religious establishments in Japan took care of insane people during the early modern period as in medieval and early modern Europe.[12] Cure was attempted through religious means such as reading sutras and purifying patients with water from waterfalls.[13] Geographically, they were located in various types of places: remote mountains (where one could find waterfalls), villages, towns, or even suburbs. On the eve of the Meiji Revolution, at least thirty such institutions existed around the country. Interestingly, more than half of the establishments survived and became proper psychiatric hospitals headed by a qualified medical practitioner in the modern period, suggesting certain elements of continuity between the early modern and modern period.

The second and third types, namely, psychiatric hospitals and confinement within non-medical institutions, were restricted to urban areas. In the early nineteenth century, two psychiatric hospitals were established, one in Osaka in 1818 and the other in Edo in 1843, both founded by doctors practising Chinese medicine. Both these early modern medical institution continued in the modern era and became psychiatric hospitals with doctors trained in Western medicine.[14] These psychiatric hospitals were intended for those who paid for the service. On the other hand, the non-medical institutions were for the poor, the Japanese counterpart of general hospitals in early modern France. Two such facilities existed in Edo, one in Asakusa established in 1689 and the other in Shinagawa in 1700. They were for sick prisoners, vagrants, and homeless people, as well as for minor offenders, alcoholics, and lunatics. In 1789 a female ward was erected, and it had four special cages for lunatics. These institutions were managed by the members of the lowest caste under the governors of Edo.[15]

Those institutions in Edo were remarkable for their small size compared with their European counterparts. The only public medical hospital for poor patients in Edo had the capacity for about 100.[16] The combined capacity of two institutions for the poor and the destitute in general, as mentioned above, was about 1,000. These are astonishingly small for a city that had a population of 1 million throughout the early modern period. Paris on the eve of the French Revolution had a smaller population than Edo, but the French capital held about thirty times the number of inmates within its institutions for the poor. Several hundreds were lunatics taken care of at the famous hospitals of Bicêtre and Salpêtrière.[17] Nothing comparable could be observed in Edo, both in terms of the institutionalisation of the indigent and that of the insane.

The lack of institutional provision for the insane suggests the importance of the domestic care and confinement of the insane. The social background of this practice was the establishment of the new rules of household formation for the peasants in early modern Japan: independent peasants replaced serfs that worked for landowners during the medieval period. The new small peasants worked on a small parcel of land which they often owned and passed on to their offspring.[18] The inheritance of the household property encouraged the sense of family solidarity, which was strengthened by the ideology of Confucianism. Reflecting the new importance given to the family, both by the elite and the common people, family now became an important locus for the care of the sick. The care of the infirm, chronically sick, or disabled members within the family was normal and normative.[19] Taking care of a lunatic family member at home was something highly commended by the public authority, and it was consistent with the ethics of family solidarity. An analysis of the collection of 564 cases from Sendai domain between 1677 and 1848 included the stories of domestic care of one lunatic, as well as fifty blind people, forty-nine post-apoplexy paralytics, and eight patients suffering from leprosy. During the early modern period, domestic care of the insane was tightly woven into the economics, ethics, and ideology of a society made up of an independent household responsible for the maintenance of its dependent members.

The use of the family and the domestic space for the confinement of the insane applied also to criminal lunatics. During the Tokugawa Period, the insanity of an offender could reduce the severity of the punishment. Authorities gave a less severe sentence to offenders found to be suffering from mental illness or mental disability. The death penalty or banishment to a remote island could be reduced to imprisonment for life. When a criminal lunatic was imprisoned, his or her family was ordered to confine the person in a secure place in the house.[20] The confinement of a criminal lunatic at home was, however, not always strictly enforced. A prostitute in Edo committed arson in 1829. Because she was found mentally deficient (*gumai*, or stupid), she was exempted from the death penalty and banishment and sentenced to life imprisonment at her father's house in Kōfu, a city about sixty miles west of Edo. Three years later, however, she was found to be out of the father's home and to have visited a nearby spa for treatment. Although this was a glaring breach of the rule, the authorities were lenient and did not punish her, prioritising instead the security of the household confinement.[21] Note also that this case involved the migration of the patient from Edo to a rural area for care at the patient's original home.

The domestic care of the insane was practiced both in large cities and rural areas. Diaries kept by a samurai family in Edo for about thirty years in the mid-eighteenth century mentioned about 250 deaths of their friends and acquaintances, 5 of whom were noted as 'having died within confinement due to insanity'. Two had been confined for two to three years, one for five years, one for nineteen years, and one had been confined for forty years.[22] Confinement at home was regularly practiced in rural areas, too. Documents in a small Moriyama domain between 1746 and 1850 show that about twenty lunatics were confined in a cage built at their own homes during the period in total.[23] Both in urban and rural settings, confinement at home needed the authorisation of the public authority. When an insane person was judged not so dangerous, he or she was put under vigilance. When it was feared the subject would commit a violent act or had actually committed one, he or she was confined in a high-security cage in his or her own house. It was customary to submit a plan of confinement, specifying where the patient should be put. Danger was the standard to calibrate the strength of restraint and confinement.

The psychiatric provision in early modern Japan is thus characterised by two things. The first is that the institutional provision for lunatics was so small that it was almost negligible both in cities and the country. In early modern Europe, such institutions were not very large, but they still acted as the kernel or model upon which people could conceive more large-scale provision for the insane. Early modern Japan had no such kernel for the growth of public asylums. The second is that the lack of such institutions made the urban and rural regimes of psychiatric provision very similar: both regimes almost entirely consisted of care and confinement at home.

MODERN LEGISLATION AND THE DIFFERENTIATION OF URBAN AND RURAL FACILITIES

This early modern structure of the care of the insane developed and transformed in the modern period. Although historians of medicine in Japan tend to emphasise a sharp break resulting from the Westernisation of academic medicine after the Meiji Revolution, continuity and gradual transformation were much more evident in the realm of the care of the insane. Two acts of Parliament played a critical role: the Mental Patients' Confinement Act (1900) and the Mental Hospitals Act (1919).[24] The Confinement Act has often been misrepresented as the beginning of the practice of psychiatric confinement, but such interpretation is deeply flawed; it *regulated* the confinement of lunatics mainly within their own houses. It was prompted by a scandal of wrongful confinement and motivated by the desire to show the modernity of the Japanese legal system to the Western countries. The law required that the confinement of lunatics be done under the authorisation of local government (cities, towns, and villages). Confinement without permission was illegal. A responsible person, usually a family member of the lunatic in question, was required to submit an application for psychiatric confinement to a local authority, accompanied by a doctor's certificate, specifying the place and facility for the special room where the lunatic was to be confined. The spirit behind the Confinement Act was exactly the same as home confinement during the early modern period. The act confirmed a long-standing custom or the local rule and made it into a national law.

The Mental Hospitals Act was conceived in a very different spirit. It was the brainchild of Kure Shuzo, a professor of psychiatry at University of Tokyo and the founding father of modern psychiatry in Japan.[25] Kure was a staunch critic of home confinement and maintained that patients should be treated and cared for by doctors and qualified nurses at hospitals. He was also antagonistic to the treatment and care of patients at religious establishments, maintaining that these places offered only ineffective, unenlightened, and often barbaric treatment. In short, Kure followed a classic path of the medicalisation of the care of the insane, attacking the two traditional loci of care of home and religious establishments, and promoting psychiatric hospitals. As such, Kure has been at the centre of the historiography of Japanese psychiatry; he has been praised by the Whiggish historians and attacked by those leaning towards anti-psychiatry.[26]

These two acts in effect prompted the modern Japanese society to develop two very different patterns of psychiatric care in the urban and rural areas. First, the Confinement Act was clearly intended for a household living in a rural area. One should note that the act required the family to set up a special room to confine an insane member, which presumed that the family owned the house and could make changes to the building. This arrangement was virtually impossible for those who lived in apartment houses, which was a much more common way of living in urban areas, particularly in Edo/Tokyo. In early modern Edo, about 80 per cent of non-samurai people lived in row houses (*nagaya*), whereas in rural towns and villages it was common that more than 80 per cent of residents held their own houses. The situation was roughly the same in Tokyo around 1900. The Confinement Act thus did not work in its original format of home confinement for tenants in Tokyo. For tenants in the city, the answer was recourse to a hospital whose security was made to meet the requirements of the act. The addresses of ten patients admitted to OBH under the Confinement Act have been checked, and none owned the land/house where they lived.

The Confinement Act thus had different impacts on rural and urban areas. For rural areas, it confirmed the traditional way of confinement. It cost virtually nothing for the public authorities because the family bore the cost of maintaining the patient and the building of the special facility. The act was thus a strong disincentive for the public authority in rural areas to pay for the public hospital facility because it confirmed a much cheaper alternative of home confinement. In urban areas, on the other hand, the act effectively pushed lunatics out of their tenements and into hospitals. Within Tokyo, the contrast between the urban and rural areas was stark: the overwhelming majority of home-confined lunatics resided in rural areas, whereas all the hospitals were situated in the urban or suburban parts.

One can gauge the act's impact in the chronological pattern of the establishment of psychiatric hospitals in Tokyo. The public psychiatric hospital in Tokyo was first established in 1879. Around that time, two private psychiatric hospitals were built. For the next twenty years, no psychiatric hospital, either public or private, was built in the city. Around the time of the Confinement Act, however, a sudden boom of building private asylums started; from 1899 to 1910, nine psychiatric hospitals were built, four among them built between 1899 and 1901. They were all privately owned but accepted the patients whose cost was paid by public authorities, that is, the wards of the city of Tokyo. These private hospitals were the response of medical entrepreneurs to the new situation created by the Confinement Act which pushed lunatics out of their home and created a large demand for hospital facility. This was met by the collaboration between the public authority and medical entrepreneurs. The Confinement Act favoured the development of privately owned psychiatric institutions through creating a market for institutional psychiatric service, whereas it opposed rural public authorities having institutional facilities by authorising traditional cheap ways of dealing with the insane. By 1921, 3,894 patients were confined in psychiatric hospitals, and 4,512 were confined at home. Among the hospitalised patients, 2,074 (53 per cent) were in Tokyo, 507 (13 per cent) were in Osaka, and 355 (9 per cent) were in Kyoto. Three prefectures with three major cities together had 75 per cent of the entire hospitalised patients, while these three prefectures had only 17.7 per cent of the national population.[27]

The Mental Hospitals Act in 1919 added another twist to the contrast rather than narrowing the gap between urban and rural prefectures. It created public psychiatric hospitals in places other than Tokyo. In 1918, on the eve of the Hospitals Act, there was only one public asylum, which was in Tokyo and housed 450 patients. By 1940 seven public asylums held 2,500 patients. However, the real agent of the growth of the hospitalisation of the insane was privately owned psychiatric hospitals, some of which accepted public patients as well as fee-paying patients. By 1940, there were 77 such private hospitals which had 14,000 beds, five times as many as that of the seven public hospitals combined. These privately owned hospitals received a fixed number of patients whose cost was paid by the respective public authorities, whereas the private hospitals bought land, built facilities, and hired doctors and nurses at their own cost. For public authorities, this was a great saving of the cost for psychiatric provision; for private hospitals, the acceptance of public patients meant public recognition as well as a form of subsidy.[28]

In short, the Hospitals Act created a paradoxical situation in which public psychiatric provision relied upon the private sector. Whether a prefecture could have public psychiatric beds depended directly on the feasibility of running a private hospital there. One needed a substantial number of relatively wealthy families who would pay for psychiatric services in order to build psychiatric provision for poor lunatics. Because the concentration of well-off clients existed mainly in the cities, the Mental Hospitals Act worked only in prefectures which were urbanised. In 1935, only 22 out of 47 prefectures had public psychiatric beds under the Hospital Act. Tokyo and Osaka succeeded (so to speak) in putting about half of the registered lunatics in hospitals, while the three urbanised prefectures of Kanagawa, Hyogo, and Kyoto institutionalised around 20 per cent. In many rural areas, on the other hand, the rates of hospitalised patients per registered lunatics were below 1 per cent. The Mental Hospitals Act achieved virtually nothing in rural areas.

The urban concentration of psychiatric hospitals did not mean that rural areas lacked any psychiatric facilities apart from the patients' own homes. Indeed, new facilities were emerging in the countryside of late nineteenth- and early twentieth-century Japan. In 1907, Kure Shuzô's survey counted twenty-one religious institutions for the insane around the country, about half of which started the business of taking care of the insane in the late nineteenth and early twentieth century.[29] Many were known to have offered religious healings as well as boarding the patients. Some combined Western medicine and religious healing. The cost of boarding was substantially lower than one at the hospital.

Overall, however, one should emphasise that these rural sites of religious healings were businesses small in scale and were dispersed widely in the country. The number of patients was generally small, housing two to thirty patients; trained attendants were lacking, and the patients were mostly taken care of by their family members. These facilities were not so much psychiatric institutions as places of extended domestic care. It seems unlikely that those places provided a stable and long-term place of care and confinement outside the family in rural areas.

The two acts thus developed and transformed the early modern provision for lunatics: these created very different regimes of psychiatric provision in cities and the countryside. In rural areas, home confinement and vigilance at home was the norm and often the only means both for the rich and the poor, whereas people living in urban areas used psychiatric hospitals.

MIGRANT PATIENTS AND THE NETWORK OF CARE

During the early twentieth century, Japan thus had two regimes of psychiatric care in the city and the country. Seen from the view of a migrant who
had moved from rural areas to the city, this situation meant that he or she
had a choice of the two systems—hospitalisation in the city or care in the
original family home in the countryside from which the patient had come.
Many patients combined both measures. Case notes from OBH reveal that
the hospital was often used as a mediator between the urban regime and the
rural regime. It was often the case that the family of the patient and his or
her relatives formed a network that stretched over urban and rural areas and
provided an informal system of psychiatric care for migrants. A hospital in
the city was one of the nodes in this network. Four cases illustrate the working of the network and the dynamics of the psychiatric migration patterns.

In case 1, the patient's life had been an embodiment of the aspiration of
rural youth in pre-war Japan.[30] He was born in Gunma Prefecture, about
sixty miles north-west of Tokyo, and moved to Tokyo to work as a clerk
in a large department store, a very fashionable job at a stylish place at that
time. He was married with two children. At the time of admission, his
father had been dead due to a stroke, but his mother was still alive and well.
He had four living siblings, two elders and two juniors. He was said to be a
sober, honest, and gentle man. His disease started around ten years earlier,
in 1928. At that time, the diagnosis was neurasthenia. He was treated at
several charitable clinics but did not get well. Towards the end of 1930,
when he was thirty years of age, the patient's own family was intention-
ally broken up and divided into two households. His wife and children
were sent to the wife's original family. The patient's elder brother, who had
also moved from Gunma to Tokyo, started to take care of the patient at
the brother's house. This new arrangement was followed by a formal legal
divorce three years later, and the patient was completely integrated into
the brother's household as a dependent member. It turned out that he was
too troublesome: he did not eat the food prepared by the brother's wife; he
asked for pocket money and became violent if refused; and he wandered
about the city almost every day and occasionally was caught by the police.
After seven years' care at home, the brother asked for his hospitalisation.

Case 2 is a woman who was thirty-one years old and married with two
children.[31] She was born in Shizuoka, about eighty miles south-west of
Tokyo. Her disease started around 1940, three years before her admission.
It took the form of a series of delusional jealousies. She shouted in the street
that a woman had an affair with the husband. She did not take care of her
children, and she told the police that her husband was a spy who had set
a bomb in a bridge. Upon learning this, the husband was summoned to
the police and probably told to be vigilant of his wife. In April 1943, the
patient was sent to her original family in Shizuoka. It was expected that
she would be taken care of there. Soon after her return home, however, she

poured gasoline at the base of her house. Deemed to be too dangerous to be taken care of at home without confinement, she was again returned to the husband's house in Tokyo. She gave further trouble to the husband, selling all the furniture while the husband was away at work in a factory. She was then moved to her brother's house, which was in Tokyo, perhaps as a temporary measure until she was admitted to the hospital.

In case 3, the patient had moved to Tokyo from Iwate Prefecture, about 300 miles north of Tokyo. He stayed at OBH for about seven months in 1937 as a public patient.[32] His diagnosis was GPI, and he was discharged cured. During his stay, he wrote a long and detailed memoir of his life, experience of mental hospitals, and an account of religious cosmology with plenty of illustrations of his dreams and delusions. The memoir tells that he was a taxi driver in Tokyo, married with two children. He quarrelled with another driver over a traffic signal while working and was caught by the police and detained for a few days at the police station. When discharged he was still excited, and he and his wife decided to go to the place where his original family lived. It was in a small island of Iwate Prefecture, and the village was a poor fishing village. His father was deceased, and he stayed at his sister's house. While staying there, his excitement increased, and he was violent against his sister's family and other relatives. For his relatives in the village, this meant he was too much trouble for them to bear. They arranged his admission to a private mental hospital in Tokyo and sent him back to Tokyo without letting him know the plan. He was admitted to Negishi Hospital as a type of emergency and transferred to OBH in a few weeks as a public patient.

Case 4 is a female patient who had come from Mie Prefecture, 200 miles west of Tokyo. She lived with her husband and his parents.[33] In 1911 she first exhibited symptoms of mental illness, the causes of which were traced by the husband to mental exhaustion from nursing her father-in-law at their home. The young couple decided to live by themselves in another part of Tokyo, and the new arrangement temporarily brought her peace. The situation soon worsened, however. She claimed to be an empress or prince and tried to hang herself. The spell of two stays in two psychiatric hospitals and two stays in her birthplaces (in the countryside of Mie Prefecture) continued until November 1913, when she was admitted to OBH for about three weeks' stay.

These cases are taken from a sample of about 150 cases from the archive of OBH. Note well that all cases involved loops between the countryside and the city. They had come to Tokyo, but when they developed mental disease, the patients were sent from Tokyo to their original families in the countryside (except for case 1, whose original family had also moved to Tokyo). When care at their original families was given up, they were again sent back to Tokyo for hospitalisation at OBH or other mental hospitals. Given that the sample is from the case records of a hospital in Tokyo, one can assume that many mental patients were sent to their families residing at their birthplace and received long-term care, or even care for the rest of their life, at their original homes.

The cases show that the incidence of mental disease was deeply unsettling to the family of the patient in terms of the household formation. Even when one had formed his or her own family through marriage in the city, mental illness made the patient go to one's original home in the country-side.[34] All four patients had been settled in Tokyo either through employ-ment and/or marriage. When they developed or started to show symptoms of mental disease, their families were broken up for the purpose of care—temporarily in cases 2 and 3, and decisively with legal action in case 1—and the patients were sent to the household of their original family. As for case 4, the extended family to which she belonged was broken up to form a nuclear family, which was again broken up to send her to her family at her birthplace. In case 1, the patient had been cared for seven years by his 'new' family. Other cases of OBH demonstrate that this long-term care was not unique or exceptional: for example, a patient had been cared for in a village in rural Tokyo for twenty years by an elderly mother, and the death of the mother prompted his hospitalisation. On the other hand, for cases 2, 3, and 4, long-term care at the household in a rural area was given up only after a short trial, and patients were rather quickly sent back to the city.

Most interesting is the negotiation between the patient's family in the city and his or her original family in the countryside over the question of who would assume the responsibility of care. The negotiation depended on the state of city-dwelling patient and that of the family dwelling in the countryside. It obviously depended on the symptoms or the severity of the disease, but these were not the only factors. The issue of the familial sta-tus of the patient was vital in settling the place of care and confinement. There are several reasons to believe that unmarried men or women who had moved to the city from the countryside developed mental disease were routinely sent back to their parents' family in the countryside. There is no such case in my sample of public patients. Admission accounts routinely show that young and single patients who became insane were expelled from their jobs or service and sent to their parents' house. We can safely assume that unmarried migrant patients were routinely sent back to their parents' household in the countryside. Because they had not formed their own household in the city, their parents in the country took care of them as responsible heads of the household.

When the patient had formed his or her own household through mar-riage, the situation became complex. The dissolution of marriage for the purpose of psychiatric care at home was one option, as we have seen in case 1. Even this radical rearrangement of the patient's household could not maintain him for life. Cases 2, 3, and 4 suggest that the helping hands of the former family members were rather lukewarm and limited. One telling case was the mental disease of a Tokyo-born woman who had married without her parents' approval. When she became insane, her husband went to his parents-in-law and sought help. The parents refused, saying that the young couple had married by their own will, and they were not going to help: the implication was that because the daughter had married without the parents' approval, she was now out of the realm of their responsibility. In the end, however, when she was repeatedly caught by the police for disturbing behaviour, the parents assumed at least part of the responsibility, and they, not the husband, asked for her hospitalisation as a public patient.

The migration of psychiatric patients in twentieth-century Japan was thus part of the complex business of negotiating over the space and resources of the psychiatric care within the modernising Japanese society. The contrast in urban and rural facilities for psychiatric provision created the background for the shuttlecocking of the patients between the city and the country. At stake was not only the severity of the disease or the nature of symptoms but setting a boundary of the household's responsibility for its disruptive member. Whereas unmarried mental patients coming from the countryside were directed to their birthplace, patients who had already formed households in Tokyo seem to have pressured the city to expand its psychiatric facilities. A psychiatric hospital was a node in the two-way flow of the people from the countryside to the city and the other way round, with several households negotiating the questions about where and how to take care of the patients and who was responsible to do so. The influx of patients into this node changed through numerous factors: the volume of migration, migrants' behaviour, their choice of where to spend difficult times, and the household's sense of the bounds of its responsibility. This was the microcosm of the transformation of Japan into a modern society.

CONCLUSIONS

The picture emerging from this research shows a mixed economy of psychiatric care which stretched over urban areas and rural ones. Migrant patients' families combined formal and informal types of psychiatric care, the former in the forms of public and private hospitals in cities and the latter provided at the home of the original family or relatives in the countryside. Families and relatives in the countryside were drawn into this system of the mixed economy, partly because of the under-development of the hospital facility in rural areas. In rural areas, psychiatric care was supported neither by public policy nor by market economy, but in the non-market transaction which economic historian Avner Offer calls 'the economy of regard'.[35] The numerical underdevelopment of public psychiatric beds and the prohibitive prices of private beds left room for the involvement of the family, extended family, and relatives of the patient. Perhaps most interesting is that this mixed economy of care had a spatial extension.

This chapter has only scratched the surface of the complex trajectory of migrant patients within the spatially uneven system of psychiatric provision in Japan. During the time of industrialisation, urbanisation, and mass migration to cities, the Japanese government adopted a series of policy decisions that created two radically different psychiatric regimes for cities and the countryside: institutional care for cities and extra-institutional care (confinement or vigilance) for the countryside. Many migrants to large cities, which helped to transform Japan into a modern society, were caught in this complex, difficult, and essentially unsatisfactory system of psychiatric provision.

NOTES

1. A. Scull, *The Most Solitary of Afflictions: Madness and Society in Britain, 1700–1900* (New Haven, CT: Yale University Press, 1993), pp. 26–34.
2. J. K. Walton, 'Lunacy in the Industrial Revolution: A study of asylum admissions in Lancashire, 1845–50', *Journal of Social History*, 13 (1979), pp. 1–21; M. Finnane, 'Asylums, families and the state', *History Workshop Journal*, 20 (1985), pp. 134–48; D. Wright, 'Getting out of the asylum: Understanding the confinement of the insane in the nineteenth century', *Social History of Medicine*, 10 (1997), pp. 137–55; R. Adair, J. Melling, and W. Forsythe, 'Migration, family structure and pauper lunacy in Victorian England: Admissions to the Devon county pauper lunatic asylum, 184–1900', *Continuity and Change*, 12 (1997), pp. 373–401.
3. Although recent research has uncovered that migration was much larger and more frequent than historians have assumed, early modern migration did not cause the rapid growth of cities as known in European countries.
4. Scull, *The Most Solitary of Afflictions*.
5. Works on the city and the country in modern Japan are vast. The most inspiring still remains K. Yanagida, 'Toshi to Inaka' [The city and the country], in *Yanagida Kunio Zenshu* [Collected works of Yanagida Kunio], vol. 4 (Tokyo: Chikuma Shobô, 1998), pp. 177–324.
6. O. Saitô, *Edo to Osaka* [Edo and Osaka] (Tokyo: NTT Shuppan, 2002).
7. S. Ito, 'Jinkô Zôka, Toshika, Shugyô Kôzô' [Population growth, urbanization, and employment structure], in S. Nishikawa and Y. Yamamoto (eds.), *Sangyôka no jidai ge* [The age of industrialization, Part II] (Tokyo: Iwanami Shoten, 1990), pp. 227–69.
8. For a very brief account of OBH and Komine Shigeyuki, see Suzuki, 'Family, the state and the insane in Japan 1900–1945'.
9. See M. Kôichi, 'Jo' [Preface], in *Komine Kenkyūjo Kiyō* [Bulletin of Komine Research Institute], 1(1930), pp. 1–2.
10. One of them was Komine Shigesaburô, who was Shigeyuki's son and had studied psychiatry at Tohoku Imperial University, which was the stronghold of Freudian psychoanalysis in Japan under professor Marui Kiyoyasu. For an early history of Freudianism in Japan, see G. H. Blowers, S. Yang, and H. Chi, 'Freud's *Deshi*: The coming of psychoanalysis to Japan', *Journal of the History of the Behavioral Sciences*, 33 (1997), pp. 115–26.
11. The standard work for general history of psychiatry in Japan is Y. Okada, *Nihon Seishinka Iryôshi* [History of psychiatry in Japan] (Tokyo: Igakushoin, 2002). For medieval and early modern history, see W. Omata, *Seisin Byôin no Kigen* [The origins of the psychiatric hospital] (Tokyo: Ôta Shpppan, 1995).
12. Omata, *Seisin Byôin no Kigen*.
13. A. Hashimoto, 'The invention of a "Japanese Gheel": Psychiatric family care from a historical and transnational perspective', in T. Mueller and W. Ernst

(eds.), *Transnational Psychiatries: Social and Cultural Histories of Psychiatry in Comparative Perspective, c.1800–2000* (Cambridge: Cambridge Scholars, 2010), pp. 142–71.

14. Omata, *Seisin Byôin no Kigen*, pp. 145–71.
15. Ibid., pp. 174–92.
16. E. Iwafuchi, 'Kanse—Tenpôki no Yôjôsho Seisakuto Bakufu Igakukan' [Policy of the Yôjôsho Hospital and the Medical School of Bakufu during the Kansei and Tempô Periods'], *Ronshu Kinsei*, 22 (2000), pp. 40–61.
17. For the French situation, see J. Goldstein, *Console and Classify: The French Psychiatric Profession in the Nineteenth Century* (Cambridge: Cambridge University Press, 1987).
18. See T. Furushima, 'The village and agriculture during the Edo period', in J. W. Hall (ed.), *The Cambridge History of Japan*, vol. 4, *Early Modern Japan* (Cambridge: Cambridge University Press, 1991), pp. 478–518.
19. K. Yanagitani, *Kinsei no Joseisôzoku to Kaigo* [Women's inheritance and nursing in the early modern period] (Tokyo: Yoshikawa Kôbunkan, 2007).
20. G. Hiruta, 'Seishiniryô no Nihon' ['History of psychiatry in Japan'], in G. Hiruta and M. Matsushita (eds.), *Seishiniryô no Rekishi* [History of psychiatry] (Tokyo: Nakayama Shoten, 1999), pp. 35–64; K. Naruse (ed.), *Kinsei Shôgaisha Kankei Shiryôshû* [Sources for early modern disability studies] (Tokyo: Akashi Shoten, 1996), pp. 330, 346, 356, 358, 650.
21. Naruse, (ed.), *Kinsei Shôgaisha Kankei Shiryôshû*, pp. 436–37, 444–46.
22. M. Ujiie, *Edo no Yamai* [Diseases of Edo] (Tokyo: Kôdansha, 2009).
23. G. Hiruta, *Hayariyamai to Kitsunetsuki* [Epidemics and fox-possession] (Tokyo: Misuzu Shobô, 1985).
24. For detailed examination of these acts, see T. Akakura, 'Meiji 33 Nen Seishinbyôsha Kangohô no Seiritu' ['The making of the Mental Patients' Confinement Act'], *Rokkodai Ronshu*, 47:1 (2001), pp. 1–68; T. Akakura, 'Meiji 33 Nen Seisinbyôsha Kangohô no Mondaiten to Sinpô Seiritsu ni muketeno Katsudô' ['The problems of Mental Patients' Confinement Act of the 33rd year of Meiji and the preparation for a new legislation'], *Rokkôdai Ronshu*, 48:2 (2001), pp. 1–38; T. Akakura, 'Taishô Hachi Nen Seishin Byôinhô no Seiritsu', ['The Making of Mental Hospitals Act in the 8th year of Taishô'], *Kobe Hôgaku Zasshi*, 52:3 (2002), pp. 51–120. I have also discussed the impact of two laws in A. Suzuki, 'Family, the state and the insane in Japan, 1900–1945', in R. Porter and D. Wright (eds.), *Psychiatric Confinement in International Perspective* (Cambridge: Cambridge University Press, 2003), pp. 193–225.
25. Y. Okada, *Kure Shuzô: Sono Shôgai to Gyôseki* [Kure Shuzô: His life and works] (Kyoto: Shibunkaku, 1982).
26. For a critical assessment of Kure's works, see A. Hyôdô, *Seishinbyô no Kindai: Tsuku Shinshin kara Yamu Shinshin he* [Mental disease and Japanese modernity: From the possessed mind/body to diseased mind/body] (Tokyo: Seikyûsha, 2008).
27. The data were taken from *Eiseikyoku Nenpô* [Annual review of hygiene], an official statistics of medicine and public health. For detailed analysis of this material, see A. Suzuki, 'Family, the state and the insane in Japan, 1900–1945'.
28. Ibid.
29. K. Shuzô, *Waga Kuni ni okeru Seishinbyô ni kansuru Saikin no Shisetsu* [Recent psychiatric institution in Japan] (1907; reprint, Tokyo: Sôzôshuppan, 2003), pp. 121–28. The work is one of the earliest surveys of psychiatric institutions of various types in Japan conducted by Kure. The survey obviously covered only a fraction of the national picture of religious healing for the insane.

30. 1937/10/18–1938/9/1, male, thirty-eight years old (at the time of admission), public. Hereafter the case record in the archive of OBH will be referred to with the date of first admission and first discharge, sex, age, and private/public.
31. 1943/07/12–1944/02/05, female, aged thirty-one, private.
32. 1937/04/23–1937/11/22, male, aged thirty, public.
33. 1913/11/03–1913/11/22, female, aged twenty-eight, private.
34. For another similar case, see 1942/03/12–1942/05/05, male, aged forty-six, private.
35. A. Offer, 'Between the gift and the market: The economy of regard', *Economic History Review*, 50 (1997), pp. 450–76.

10 'Suitable Girls'

Recruitment of British Women for New Zealand Mental Hospital Nursing Post–World War II

Kate Prebble and Gabrielle Fortune

In June 1946, a young Englishwoman caught sight of an advertisement that changed her life course. The poster in the Labour Exchange in Manchester, England, sought women to work in New Zealand mental hospitals, and despite having no nursing experience, Margaret Storr applied to the New Zealand High Commission in London where applications to immigrate were processed. In exchange for two years' work as a trainee psychiatric nurse she was eligible for a free passage and immigration rights. Having endured bombing raids, rationing, and six years in a munitions factory, she was ready for a new life abroad. With approximately 200 other young single British women, Margaret and her friend Ivy Preston became part of New Zealand's targeted recruitment campaign for female mental hospital workers.[1] This forerunner to the assisted immigration scheme addressed a specific national employment need for female hospital workers and was more akin to the Canadian (and other colonies) 'bulk ordering' schemes that sourced labour from Britain and other European countries for specific industries in the post-war years. A workforce crisis in New Zealand was to be resolved by docile and compliant immigrants willing to live where directed and undertake whatever tasks were required.

Whereas most chapters in this volume on migration, ethnicity, and mental illness focus on patients, this chapter makes a contribution to on-going and new discussions about the relevance of migration to the study of medical recruitment, in this case, of psychiatric nurses. It illuminates the place of ethnicity and class as indicators of the suitability of migrant workers to work with the mentally ill in the mid-twentieth century. It also considers the disruption to two discourses prevailing in post-war New Zealand: the professionalisation of psychiatric nursing and the dominance of the ideology underpinning the return to domesticity of New Zealand women in the post–World War II period. The chapter will show that although the intention was to solve a workforce crisis and at the same time enhance psychiatric care with improved standards of nursing, the reality was that these aspirations were often stonewalled by the migrants' response to the dreadful conditions and isolated locations of New Zealand mental hospitals. The chapter will also document the 'women as workers' discourse, which contradicted that of 'women as wives and mothers'. Evaluating and hiring these psychiatric nursing trainees focused, not on their potential as homemakers, but exclusively on the possibility of their enduring employment in the public health system.

The chapter commences by putting the actions of the then director-general of mental hospitals Dr. Theodore Gray in historical context by briefly outlining the history of immigration and nursing in New Zealand, before tracing the history of mental hospital staffing in New Zealand and the negative connotations that dogged recruitment and retention. In the post-war scramble for immigrants among Commonwealth countries, Gray claimed a head start for New Zealand's mental hospitals by procuring priority transport for his recruits and deftly attracting suitable candidates. His motivations and compromises are explained and illustrated by reference to the selection criteria, which included assessments of class, ethnicity, personality, and educational achievements. In the next section, a clash of interests becomes evident when the experiences of nurses and trainees are examined, exposing the gap between Gray's ideals and the reality in New Zealand mental hospitals, particularly in relation to 'de-skilling'. The strategies that aimed at protecting the Department of Mental Hospitals' investment by countering the actions of recruits who defected to other employment, married, or became pregnant are documented. In the final section, the success or failure of the scheme is examined. Questions are raised about how well this 'bulk order' of untrained workers addressed the staffing needs of mental hospitals and whether the scheme contributed to the larger goal of raising the professional standard of mental nursing.

DOCUMENTS SEEN, VOICES HEARD

Archival documents, newspapers, and oral accounts by two British recruits who came to New Zealand and one local nurse who worked alongside them form the basis of this study. Although archival collections of official documents and contemporary correspondences with recruits proved worthwhile, searches of archival repositories failed to reveal any collections of letters or diaries of mental hospital recruits from the period. Oral histories were therefore sought as a means of capturing first-hand accounts and of giving voice to the women's experiences. Tracing surviving members of the cohort of recruits was difficult because of the high attrition rate among their number after arrival in the 1940s; the low numbers of recruits that qualified; possible return migration of trainees back to Britain; the advanced age of recruits in 2010; and the difficulty of tracing single women who changed their surnames on marriage. With this in mind, some comment on the value of the interviews—in this case only 2 out of a cohort of 200—is appropriate.

With the rise in popularity of oral history has come regular challenges. Eric Hobsbawm dismissed it in 1997 as 'a remarkably slippery medium for preserving facts'.[2] The problems associated with the reliability of oral history have been addressed by Penny Summerfield, Luisa Passerini, Alessandro Portelli, Alistair Thomson, and Graham Dawson among others.[3] In general these scholars have promoted a move away from regarding oral histories as reliable, factual accounts, and towards the concept of 'composure', pointing to the ways in which people construct 'memories using the public languages and meanings of our culture'.[4] It was found that 'composure' formed a significant element of the stories told by Margaret and Ivy, whose memories convinced them that they had taken up the offer of hospital work in New Zealand for altruistic reasons and whose accounts implied that they had persevered to the end of their contracts, although the research suggests otherwise. These recent interviews also converged with the archival material. For example, letters written by nurses in 1946 complaining of the lack of explanations given to recruits while still in Britain correlated with what Margaret and Ivy recounted. The memories of the third woman also correlated with the archival reports of tensions between the new recruits and their New Zealand colleagues. Although few in number, these interviews help illuminate aspects of the immigration scheme and give voice to women's experience of nursing in mental hospitals in post-war New Zealand. In line with Thomson and others, the interviews are seen as remembered versions of past experiences with which the participants appear to feel comfortable.[5]

IMMIGRATION AND NURSING IN NEW ZEALAND

Literature on nursing migration in the nineteenth century largely focuses on the trained nurses who ventured from Britain to the far reaches of the world to promote the Nightingale model of nursing education and practice.[6] A steady stream of nurses migrated to countries such as Canada, Australia, New Zealand, and Ceylon to take up senior appointments in general hospitals and to help professionalise nursing. The Nightingale ethos, including the belief that nurses should be imbued with womanly attributes of forbearance, obedience, and endurance, influenced nursing in New Zealand well into the twentieth century.[7] Although Nightingale nurses occasionally took over the administration of mental asylums, they concentrated mainly on the reform of general nursing and general hospitals. Little is written on the migration of mental asylum workers, although there is evidence that head attendants and matrons (usually married couples) of a number of New Zealand asylums had previous training or experience in British asylums.[8] Unlike the case of general nursing, however, there has been no suggestion that the migration of asylum workers was linked to a professionalisation agenda.

The history of the migration of health workers in the twentieth century is yet to be comprehensively explored, although attention has been given to the somewhat desperate recruitment of health workers by so-called 'developed' countries to address workforce shortages following World War II.[9] Recent literature has also focused on the mass recruitment of migrant health workers as a product of globalisation since the 1980s.[10] Recruitment schemes for nurses during the twentieth century, rather than being tools for gentrifying and professionalising nursing as in the nineteenth century, were largely aimed at filling workforce gaps caused by increased institutional demands, changing employment patterns for women, and high occupational attrition. Academic debate centres on the ethics of large scale poaching of trained nurses from poorer countries to meet demand in wealthier nations, and the often poor treatment of immigrant nurses.[11] 'Deskilling' resulted from the channelling of trained immigrants into low-status and low-paid health sector jobs;[12] and in psychiatric nursing, stigma and racism came into play as health authorities, unable to attract workers to this unpopular specialty, recruited staff from countries that had previously been deemed inappropriate as sources of nursing labour.[13] This 1940s case study of recruitment for New Zealand mental hospitals suggests that many of the problems identified in the later literature were present in this campaign. Despite health officials' aspirations to attract well-educated middle-class women who would contribute to the professionalisation of mental hospital nursing, they were forced to compromise because of the stigma of 'madness' and the reality of mental hospital conditions.

MENTAL HOSPITAL NURSING: THE PERPETUAL PROBLEM OF WORKFORCE SHORTAGES

'Mental nursing', as it was called until the mid-1940s, had never been an attractive career option for New Zealand women, as many New Zealanders considered it to be unsuitable and morally dangerous for young females.[14] Distance from social amenities, hard work, long hours aggravated by the stigmatisation of mental illness, and the expectation that female nurses resign on marriage made it difficult to attract and retain women. A steady rise in patient numbers contributed to arduous working conditions, with the patient population growing by 2,500, or more than one third[15] between 1939 and 1959. The percentage of chronically disabled patients with conditions such as senility, intellectual disability, and neurological impairment also increased. Between 1939 and 1949, for example, the numbers of patients aged over sixty years grew from 21 per cent to 28 per cent of the total mental hospital population.[16] As a consequence of the stigma of mental illness, assumptions about the unsuitability of the work for women, and the reality of working conditions, mental hospitals almost always experienced shortages of staff on the female wards.

With the advent of World War II, interest in traditionally female occupations, including nursing, fell. The shortfall of nurses in mental hospitals rose dramatically from 44 in 1939 to 220 in 1942.[17] From the late 1930s, the Department of Mental Hospitals instigated various strategies to address the staffing problem, and when these failed, the government introduced manpowering under wartime emergency regulations.[18] From January 1942, working-age civilians were required to register for manpowering and were directed into hospitals, food production, and other essential industries[19] under the National Service Emergency Regulations. Unfortunately for the Department of Mental Hospitals, the negative perceptions of mental nursing undermined the success of manpowering. Rather than attracting altruistic workers, the publication of working conditions confirmed in the public's mind the unsuitability of the work for women. The manpower committees, while acknowledging public prejudice, also admitted that the work was potentially damaging to young women and could 'amount to mental cruelty in the case of young girls on the threshold of life'.[20] So although many were manpowered to mental hospitals, it was relatively easy for women to successfully appeal.

Negative connotations notwithstanding, the desire to raise the standard of training and to support the advancement of the 'profession' in New Zealand continued apace. Registration of psychiatric nurses was introduced

Table 10.1 Shortages of Nursing Staff in New Zealand Mental Hospitals at Annual Intervals, 1936–46

Year end 31 March	Average number of resident patients	Authorised nursing staff establishment (recommended staff levels)		Shortfall of male and female staff	
		Male	Female	Male	Female
1936	7,494	475	580	1	11
1937	7,637	631	765	6	29
1938	7,706	632	777	5	53
1939	7,697	632	776	5	44
1940	7,785	644	779	12	82
1941	7,920	650	782	29	102
1942	7,955	664	780	83	220
1943	7,970	668	755	81	216
1944	8,051	665	763	83	205
1945	8,246	720	768	99	134
1946	8,290	734	770	72	215
1946*	8,345	765	785	90	304

Source: Adapted from 'Report of Staffing of New Zealand Mental Hospitals', H-MHD, 1, 8/116/0, Appendix A, p. 71, Archives New Zealand, Wellington Regional Office.
*30 June 1946

under the Nurses and Midwives Board in 1945. Initially, registration was only to apply to female nurses and, in tandem with that intention, the post-war targeted recruitment scheme applied only to women. Ideally, the new recruits from Britain would become registered psychiatric nurses and contribute to the professionalisation of the occupation. However, even at this crucial point in nursing reform, mental health administrators were compelled to compromise. Trade union pressure and sympathy for returning servicemen seeking employment meant extending the privilege of registration to male mental hospital attendants.[21]

By the end of the war in 1945, and with manpowering lifted, the staffing situation was desperate. In December, the nation's mental hospitals were 253 nurses short of the authorised establishment.[22] As mentioned, patient numbers had grown steadily and increasing numbers of chronically disabled and aged patients needed more care and simultaneously reduced availability of worker-patients to help.[23] The workload on the female wards became overwhelming as is demonstrated in table 10.1.

THE OVERSEAS RECRUITMENT SCHEME: DESPERATE MEASURES FOR DESPERATE TIMES

During the war, Dr. Theodore Gray had battled the New Zealand manpower committees, convinced that their strategies exaggerated the mental hospital staffing problems by undermining the status of mental nursing; pandering to young women's fears could only perpetuate stigmatisation of the work. It was not until he visited England in 1945 that a solution to the increasing staff shortages presented itself. Gray was able to advise government in Wellington that British women wanted to immigrate to New Zealand, and requested permission to recruit nurses. He was declined. At the time, the government was under pressure to open up immigration to ease critical labour shortages in industry and on farms. Immigration officers were already in London dealing with preliminary enquiries regarding the projected assisted passage scheme.[24] Gray lobbied government again six months later as a more acute staffing crisis loomed. With the assistance of Dr. Ronald Lewis (the Department of Mental Hospital's director of clinical services), in London on sabbatical, he argued for a targeted recruitment campaign. Gray's request was prioritised ahead of the commencement of the wider scheme, and in May 1946, the New Zealand cabinet granted approval to recruit '200 suitable girls from Britain for employment as psychiatric nurses'.[25]

A potential obstacle to recruitment of an adequate supply of single British women as mental hospital staff was British blocking of the emigration of health workers.[26] Britain was canvassing in Ireland (and in France, Italy, and Germany) to alleviate its own severe shortage of nurses and did not look kindly on poaching by Dominion governments.[27] A cornerstone of British government strategy, however, was supporting the empire and securing Britain as a world power in the post-war period by an injection of British nationals into the populations of the dominions and colonies. Consequently, the British Labour Government facilitated emigration, in spite of its own labour and finance shortage, while trying to control the wholesale exodus of its skilled work force.[28] Gray, who had been educated in Scotland, assured the New Zealand authorities that 'Jameson [Sir Wilson Jameson, the chief medical officer for the British ministry of health] is an old school friend of mine and I feel sure that he would use his influence to smooth matters'.[29] Gray's request that qualified or semi-qualified nurses be permitted to immigrate was agreed to, with an understanding that untrained women be the main targets.

RECRUITMENT AND SELECTION

The psychiatric nurse trainee scheme aroused much interest in Britain. In July 1946, R. M. Sunley, acting official secretary of the New Zealand High Commission in London, reported that 'some hundreds of enquiries have been received and others arriving. Interviews have commenced and we hope to send an initial party early September'.[30] Dr. Lewis and an official from the New Zealand High Commission interviewed the shortlisted candidates, initially in Glasgow, Bristol, and Manchester, and selected applicants had a medical examination and chest X-rays.[31] Despite explicitly advertising for inexperienced women, Sunley reported in July 1946 that many applicants were trained or semi-trained nurses, and predicted that 'it may still be necessary to accept some trained girls'.[32] He hardly seemed regretful on this score. His preference for well-educated applicants reflected the commitment to the new standards it was hoped to achieve with the new training and examination system and the establishment of psychiatric nurse registration in New Zealand. Hospital tutor-sisters also saw the immigration scheme as an opportunity to implement their ideas for promoting psychiatric nursing as a profession. Rita McEwan of Ngawhatu Hospital and Betty Dandy of Tokanui wrote to Gray, outlining their plans for preliminary schools for the new recruits, an idea never tried before in mental hospitals. As McEwan explained, 'The welfare and future of the psychiatric nurse has always been very close to my heart . . . and I know that there is a splendid future in this field, but unless we make progress we are going to slip back and I currently request that all steps be taken to bring the profession out in the front where it belongs'.[33] The consensus was that selecting educated women and providing them with a solid orientation would help raise the status of the profession.

Ultimately, a sizable number of state registered nurses, qualified mental nurses, and other experienced staff were included in the first party of twenty-six that left Britain in September 1946. Contrary to Sunley's expectations that their training would be beneficial, these nurses had difficulty settling into the work and proved to be an embarrassment for the mental hospital authorities. As early as mid 1946, the reality of mental hospital conditions in New Zealand was directing Lewis and Gray towards less educated, working-class women who would presumably tolerate the hospital conditions and the proximity to 'madness'. Margaret Storr and Ivy Preston were young, single, and working class, and they had proved themselves as hard workers in difficult wartime conditions. They were interviewed and accepted in July 1946, but waited five months for berths on a ship. Their selection exemplifies the compromises deemed necessary if the vacancies were to be filled and staff retained.

HARD-WORKING TYPES

A mix of idealism and pragmatism drove the selection criteria. Lewis's preference was for 'well educated girls' but he also accepted the 'hard working type'. At this point, parliamentarians in New Zealand expressed similar opinions about the attributes necessary for the nursing profession. They posited that nurses needed to be of superior education and intelligence, but also that those with primary education from working-class backgrounds made 'the finest nurses'.[34] Lewis's three-grade system for assessing British trainees reflected these views.[35] Knowing that conditions in New Zealand mental hospitals were tough, wards were overcrowded, resources were scarce, and there were few domestic workers and a shortage of cooks, Lewis considered there was ample room for the less academic but hard-working type. His decisions in this regard also reflected the Department of Mental Hospitals' ambivalence towards enforcing regulations associated with registration. Even before the advent of psychiatric nursing registration, the department had relinquished its hopes of a qualified female nursing workforce assisted by unqualified male attendants. The shortage of female workers and resistance from unionised male attendants made the ideal of having a female nurse on all wards unworkable. Consequently, the discourse of professionalisation of the mental nurse was undermined from the beginning and the arrival of less well-educated immigrant trainees would do nothing to advance that goal.

ENGLISHNESS VERSUS SCOTTISHNESS, ETHNICITY AND CLASS

Lewis's judgements about 'suitable types' extended to ethnicity and class. Consistent with New Zealand's long-standing immigration policy and under the provisions of the Immigration Restriction Act of 1908, trainee nurses had to be of British birth and of European race and colour. The restrictiveness of the act seems to have been exacerbated by Lewis's preference for the Scots over the English. Lewis recorded the place of origin of his candidates: more than half were Scottish, just less than half were English, and only one or two were from Wales or Northern Ireland. It is not clear from surviving archival material whether the scheme was as extensively publicised in Wales and Northern Ireland or even whether any interviews were conducted in those locations. The Irish government was actively blocking the British from recruiting nurses in the late 1940s by refusing to allow advertising; the same may have been true for this campaign. Scotland, on the other hand, was the target for concentrated levels of recruitment advertising by English colonies in the post-war years. Such advertising appears to have proved very effective in Perth and Inverness, causing New Zealand officials to report in 1950 that 'it seems that these districts have recently been thoroughly gleaned by the Australians'.[36]

Scotland had a history of achievements in medical training and psychiatry. However, as Gray had quickly relinquished the goal of attracting trained professionals by opting for women with no medical work experience whatsoever, it seems unlikely that Scotland's aptitudes in this speciality played any part in the favouring of Scottish women. There is some evidence that women recruited in this campaign had contacts in New Zealand that might have contributed to their desire to migrate; in several cases, women requested that they be posted to hospitals in close proximity to relatives. However, this was as true of English as of Scottish recruits. Both Lewis and Gray had Scottish family connections; personal preference may have influenced their decision making. Whatever the reasons, they were in step with the New Zealand immigration officials in London. In her statistical analysis of assisted immigration to New Zealand in the post-war period, L. B. Brown commented in 1957, 'It is apparent that there are fewer people from England and Wales than would be expected from the census and more than would be expected from Scotland'.[37]

Lewis's comprehensive notes provide insights into his interpretation of Scottishness and Englishness.[38] He was less complimentary about the English than the Scots, although his comments did not refer to all English women but to an attribute of 'Englishness', apparently associated with the manner and accents of the upper classes.[39] Lewis suspected that the 'superior type' of woman might find it difficult to adjust to a more basic way of life, or in his words, 'get down to it', warning against several individuals being sent to Hokitika, a remote settlement on the west coast of the South Island. His judgments were echoed by a district employment officer in Auckland in January 1947 who, having interviewed several disaffected recruits, concluded that 'the type of woman whom it is considered would be most suitable are those from the working classes of Britain, those to whom the domestic side of mental nursing would present an acceptable contrast and whose mental and social outlook would promote ready acceptance of living conditions superior to those they were accustomed to in England'.[40]

Decisions about ethnicity and class reveal that, in essence, the policy makers and Department of Hospitals had modified their expectations of recruiting better-educated women, giving preference to working-class 'solid' types with 'common sense' and that indefinable quality attributed to pioneers. This reflected an awareness of conditions in mental hospitals, and also a belief that the New Zealand culture and way of life required self-reliance and endurance. In a parliamentary debate, suitable immigrants were described by the Member for Wairarapa, Mr. Mackley, as 'like the old pioneers'. To which Mr. Macfarlane (Member for Christchurch Central) added, 'Yes, that is the kind of people we want'.[41]

APPEARANCE, INTELLIGENCE, AND PERSONALITY

Lewis defined personal suitability according to three criteria: appearance, intelligence, and personality. The tensions between the aspirations and actuality of mental hospital nursing are most apparent in his ambivalence in relation to appearance. Although he chose women whom he thought would work hard and was adverse to women whose accents suggested upper-class roots, Lewis did not want them to *look* as though they came from the working class. The department's ultimate goal of elevating the public perception of psychiatric nursing seems to have contributed to Lewis's desire for intelligence and good, 'middle class appearance', whereas the practical realities of mental nursing in New Zealand directed him to qualities of enthusiasm and a strong work ethic.

SINGLENESS

In spite of the dominance of an ideology that underpinned the return to domesticity by New Zealand women in the post–World War II period, the single status of recruits was central to their selection, and the possibility that they might marry after arrival went unremarked in surviving archival records. Historians have suggested that the prevailing ideology in New Zealand deterred women from the workforce.[42] Women were encouraged to contribute to the restoration of peacetime society through their support of returning soldiers. Inspired or constrained by the ideal of rebuilding family life, women left the workforce in large numbers once the war was over.[43] So immigration officials, assessing the suitability of applicants, focused on their potential as workers and career nurses. Between October 1946 and June 1947, 193 women were selected and transported in six groups to New Zealand.[44] Ranging in age from twenty to thirty-six years, they averaged twenty-four years. Most were single, but there were a handful of widows and two women who had divorced under 'satisfactory circumstances'.[45] Their singleness was of vital importance if they were to be distributed to hospitals around the country and if a worthwhile length of service was to be achieved. This alternative discourse of 'women as workers' is consistent with that discussed by labour historian Melanie Nolan who argues that the New Zealand government's post-war social policy, while supporting women to stay at home, simultaneously encouraged married women into the workforce.[46] Evaluating and hiring these psychiatric nursing trainees focused, not on any potential as homemakers, but on their capacity for continuing employment in the public health system.

A previous generation of female domestic servants from Britain had been required to sign contracts that prohibited marriage for one year after arrival.[47] Historian Katie Pickles suggests that in the context of 'surplus women' in Britain after World War I, female migration in the 1920s confirmed 'women's traditional place'.[48] At that time exporting single women for domestic service had a dual purpose: in the short term they would alleviate the shortage of house servants, but they would ultimately contribute to the strength of the empire by populating New Zealand with 'British stock' as they were obliged to remain in the country for five years, marriage only being prohibited in the first year. In July 1945, Sir Patrick Duff, the newly arrived British high commissioner to New Zealand, expressed similar sentiments about the efficacy of importing 'British stock' and shoring up the empire after World War II. He explained that 'the whole question [of migration] is rather a delicate topic. So far as Britain is concerned we have a great deal of [reconstruction] work to do and we shall need every pair of able hands. On the other hand, from the point of view of the peace of the world, it is a good thing to have the Dominions and British outposts strengthened by British stock'.[49] Rather than entertaining any aspirations of populating New Zealand for the sake of empire, the mental nursing immigration scheme appears to have been focused on filling vacancies in psychiatric hospitals and retaining staff for as long as possible. The scheme's instigators tried hard to curtail the drift of trainees into marriage and homemaking. Even when the career options proved untenable, the Department of Mental Hospitals persisted in holding the recruits to their employment commitments.

MIGRANTS' EXPECTATIONS VERSUS THE REALITY OF MENTAL HOSPITAL LIFE

Optimism prevailed among mental hospital and immigration officials awaiting the first shipments of workers. The first group of twenty-six sailed on the *Rangitata* on 11 September 1946, and although it was not appreciated then, they proved the most problematic. Subsequent groups followed on the *Moreton Bay*, *Rangitiki*, *Dominion Monarch*, and *Largs Bay*. By Christmas 1946, 119 women had set sail. All had signed contracts to work as trainee psychiatric nurses for at least two years and in spite of stated preferences were allocated to hospitals with the greatest need. Gray directed each hospital to cooperate with immigration officials to prepare welcomes, social activities, introductions to the community, and formal work orientations. Local newspapers were encouraged to feature stories about the new arrivals. Gray was 'most anxious that nothing should be left undone to make them feel welcome'[50] and demonstrated how important he thought the mental hospital recruitment scheme was in solving the employment crisis by personally welcoming new recruits in Wellington.[51]

On 24 November 1946, Margaret and Ivy set sail on the *Dominion Monarch* with eighteen other young women. Excited about leaving England, the would-be nurses enjoyed the voyage, the food, and the company of male passengers heading to Australia as construction workers. Unfazed by the prospect of working in a mental hospital, Margaret recalled that she 'thought it was nursing. I thought I could handle that'.[52] Arrival in New Zealand was a mixed experience for the two women, although they were happy to have been allocated to Avondale Hospital in a suburb of Auckland, the largest city. The British women were warmly welcomed by newspapers, by members of the public, and by young men who phoned the Nurses Home trying to make a date, much to the chagrin of the New Zealand nurses. Food in the Nurses Home caused further tension. As a contemporary recalled, 'the English girls were complaining about the breakfast—we had good breakfasts, we had bacon and eggs—this big New Zealand girl . . . she stood up and said, "If you don't like it, go back to where you came from"'.[53] In contrast, the Māori nurses were generous and friendly to the new recruits, facilitating socialising and sharing of food. In spite of Gray's directives to be welcoming, the medical and nursing hierarchy at Avondale did little to assist them to adjust. The matron had a reputation as a rigid administrator and tough disciplinarian, and the attrition rate at Avondale supports the suggestion that it was a severe environment for the recruits. By January 1948, of eighteen immigrant women placed at Avondale Hospital, only two remained.[54]

ADAPTING (OR NOT) TO LIFE AS A MENTAL HOSPITAL NURSE

Finding willing recruits was easy, but assisting them to adapt to New Zealand mental hospitals was more difficult. Despite the best efforts of most, the campaign highlighted problems that had plagued the department for years. Within a few weeks of the first group's arrival, three nurses had left Nelson Mental Hospital (in the north of the South Island) and four nurses were threatening the same at Tokanui Hospital in rural Waikato. The women (some city dwellers) were ill prepared for the isolation, hard work, and conditions. At Tokanui, for example, there was little or no local social life. Buses to Hamilton were irregular, and the hospital had no vehicle to transport nurses to town. The four Tokanui nurses demanded release from their contracts because of the effect on their health. One nurse complained, 'I feel my health is being undermined by the constant worry and strain, the smells and dirty jobs and cleaning we sometimes have to do thoroughly upsets my stomach and I neither eat or sleep well'. Another wrote, 'Some of the patients are repulsive, especially ones with filthy habits. The smell of faeces when cleaning them makes me feel sick. The noise of insane chatter gets on my nerves so much that I feel like screaming'.[55]

Trainees found the early weeks of their assignments particularly taxing. Margaret and Ivy were dismayed by the seeming lack of care by medical staff and were shocked that some female patients might have been committed to the hospital unnecessarily. As Ivy later reflected, 'A lot of people went through a cruel lifetime in there. What Margaret and I got really upset by, the patients weren't even allowed to talk to the doctors. They would just walk straight through the ward, lock one door, unlock another'.[56] Despite their concerns, the two friends recalled that they resolved to stick it out and complete their contracts, although it appears they were unable to abide by that decision. Others left the hospitals after only weeks of employment, having made various arrangements for the repayment of fares. One trainee attempted to simply board a ship and return to Britain, which led to severe restrictions on passports which are discussed later. If trainees could not be retained in mental hospitals, the immigration authorities resolved that they would at least be detained in the country in hope of filling other employment vacancies in the health sector.

DESKILLING: THE PLIGHT OF THE QUALIFIED AND EXPERIENCED NURSES

The complaints of qualified and/or experienced nurses were more far reaching than those of the unqualified. The trained women complained about 'deskilling': being required to do work well below the skill levels of their nursing training. Newly arrived qualified nurses did not mince words when voicing their objections. As one wrote, 'The job is not in the least like what we were given to expect in London, it is just charring and we are slightly glorified by a uniform'.[57] A common complaint involved being required to start as juniors and do cleaning and cooking.[58] Two new immigrants, qualified general and mental nurses working at Kingseat Hospital on the rural outskirts of Auckland, claimed that doctors carried out all the nursing tasks such as tube feeding and giving injections, leaving them with the domestic chores. They resigned within two weeks and, in a move that suggests proactive resistance and a desire to have something done about the situation, went to the newspapers to publicise their complaints.[59]

Deskilling has been recognised in recent studies of recruitment of foreign-trained nurses in the 1990s as a major component in dissatisfaction among newly arrived professionals.[60] In 1946, New Zealand health officials rapidly concluded that trained nurses simply would not comply with work schedules requiring them to do domestic chores, but rather than address the conditions that were the stumbling blocks to retaining trained staff, the department altered its recruitment processes. Subsequent recruits signed a form before leaving Britain stating they understood that there would be 'unpleasant aspects' to the work, including the care of 'faulty patients' who may need to be 'changed, washed and cleaned up like a young child', and nursing on 'disturbed wards' where 'patients' conduct is disordered, where a patient may become excitable and require controlling'. The form also warned recruits that the lack of domestic staff meant a fair amount of domestic work. Applicants were assured, however, that the patients would help with the work if the nurse 'made a genuine attempt to be kind and understanding'.[61] This implied reliance on work, fresh air, and a structured daily schedule as the main tools for managing 'madness' reflected the state of psychiatric care in New Zealand, which still relied heavily on nineteenth-century moral therapy practices despite the recent introduction of somatic treatments.[62]

To circumvent complaints of deskilling, nurses with prior experience who had already been selected, signed a second form agreeing to forgo seniority. In addition, the department decided in future not to employ women with previous nursing experience. The Director of Employment claimed to be 'very strongly of the opinion that future selection should be confined to girls of a suitable type who are inexperienced in nursing of any kind, who are willing to settle down to hard work and are not going to raise objection to domestic work, including cooking'.[63] In effect, this redrafting of the recruitment criteria amounted to a down-grading of the expectations of elevating the profession which Lewis and his contemporaries had entertained.

MANAGING DEFECTORS

Defectors were dealt with in different ways depending on their qualifications.[64] Registered nurses were offered work in general hospitals, whereas mental hospital and labour officials tried to persuade untrained women to stay at their jobs. If unsuccessful they offered them positions in other health-related services. A group of new recruits at Porirua Hospital near Wellington defected after one weekend claiming that the conditions were untenable. The Wellington employment authorities tried remonstrating with them, but they collected their luggage from the ship's crew and boarded an overnight train for Auckland. Arriving ahead of the New Year's holidays, the Auckland officials were compelled to arrange alternative employment and accommodation at short notice.[65] One registered nurse was immediately offered a position at Greenlane Hospital, a general hospital in Auckland, and the others were offered positions in general nurse training schools. Defectors who refused alternative employment had to repay their passage and the salary advanced while on-board ship. Concerned that some might renege on their two-year contracts, immigration officials decided to confiscate the women's passports on arrival[66] to prevent defectors returning to Britain. However, the willingness of the officials to try to accommodate complaints and arrange for new positions indicates that maintaining the women in the health workforce was as important as recouping costs.

Women who married after arrival and wished to cease work were advised that they would be in breach of contract, and they were refused new passports in their married names until the end of their contracts,[67] further evidence that the government was not entirely motivated to promote domesticity in post-war New Zealand. Their options were to continue employment or repay debts; marriage was not seen as a reasonable excuse for terminating employment. Married women who were pregnant were not necessarily released from their work contract either. Nurse L., who married a mental hospital attendant and stopped work when she became pregnant, chose not to resign. Her decision effectively delayed any pressure to repay debt and shifted the responsibility of her on-going employment to the Department of Mental Hospitals.[68] Single women who declared themselves pregnant were treated similarly to those who became ill or injured and were granted temporary release from their jobs and financial support until they could return to work. They were expected to complete their contracts, although more usually in alternative health-related services rather than in mental hospitals. Time off to prepare for the arrival of an infant was credited towards their contract.[69] Marriage and/or pregnancy did not automatically free women from their commitment to the department; the women were valued as workers rather than as wives and mothers. Domesticity was not the official goal.

It is worth noting that the mental illness of trainee candidates, although a reason for exclusion from the recruitment programme, was addressed sympathetically when manifested after the migrants arrived in New Zealand. One nurse, whose medical assessment in Britain had stated that she might 'break down under psychological strain', proved herself to be 'unfit for mental nursing' after a few weeks' work.[70] She was allowed to transfer to household duties at a local general hospital.[71] Another migrant, a registered nurse, became severely ill and questionably psychotic. The department managed her illness incrementally, first allowing her to move hospitals, then transferring her to the sickbay of a third mental hospital where she was eventually admitted as a voluntary patient and given electroconvulsive therapy. It is unclear whether she was able to return to work, although there is no suggestion in the archival record that she was prevented from doing so. A third woman was removed from duty because of alcohol problems, but allowed to return after a short period of time working at a local hostel.[72] The Department of Mental Hospital's response to these three migrants suggests that there was a willingness to retain and support nurses who suffered from mental illness even though mental fragility was seen as a weakness for a woman in this occupation.

SUCCESS OR FAILURE OF THE MENTAL
HOSPITAL RECRUITMENT CAMPAIGN

In the months immediately following the introduction of British immigrants, conditions on the mental hospital wards improved; New Zealand psychiatric nurses later recalled their relief at having assistance with their daily chores. Unfortunately, the relief was short-lived as many of the new nurses left the service and were not replaced by local women. Margaret and Ivy, despite their resolution to stick with their contracts, lasted as psychiatric nurses for only six months; they were offered alternative employment as nurse aides in a general hospital. Both women met their future husbands and married soon afterwards. There is no record of their work after marriage, but from the policy outlined in the archival record it can be assumed that they either kept working or repaid their debts.

Women continued to be recruited into psychiatric nursing under the general Assisted Immigration Scheme, but the rate of retention was poor. By 1953, approximately 400 women recruited from Britain since the end of the war, only 48 remained in hospital employment. Twenty-four had stayed beyond their two-year contract and only 10 had completed their psychiatric nursing qualifications.[73] Despite the professional compromises made by mental hospital officials, and their efforts to retain the single female workers, the 'bulk-ordering' recruitment scheme was largely unsuccessful in resolving the workforce crisis in psychiatric nursing in New Zealand during the post-war years.

CONCLUSION

In this chapter, the experiences of a cohort of mental hospital staff recruited in Britain in the immediate post-war period were examined in the context of New Zealand immigration policy. In the immediate post–World War II years, Commonwealth countries vied with one another to attract war-weary British subjects. New Zealand revitalised its pre-war plans to attract new residents of 'British birth', but before the main thrust of this assisted immigration scheme got under way, Theodore Gray, the director-general of mental hospitals, was lining up 'suitable girls' to relieve the acute shortage of staff in the nine public mental hospitals around the country. These women were to fit the general criteria set down by a government that traditionally sourced migrants from Britain and, in addition, were to have qualifications or attributes that would contribute to the advancement and professionalisation of psychiatric nursing in New Zealand, just as immigrating Nightingale nurses had contributed to general nursing in the nineteenth century. It rapidly became apparent that, rather than recruiting trained psychiatric nurses or workers from British mental hospitals, the women best suited to dealing with the outmoded hospitals and isolated locations of New Zealand mental institutions appeared to be unqualified women with no previous experience of working with the mentally ill.

Margaret Storr and Ivy Preston typify important aspects of the mental hospital recruitment scheme. They were selected in the spirit of compromise that favoured women with enthusiasm, personality, and a propensity for hard work over the 'superior (middle-class) type' with formal education who might have raised the status of psychiatric nursing. Pragmatism dictated that Margaret and Ivy were 'suitable girls' in the context of the New Zealand government's desperate search for nurses to work in under-resourced mental hospitals in the post-war period. The Department of Mental Hospitals had to reduce its expectations, explicitly telling British applicants about the 'unpleasant aspect' of the job and reinventing contracts to secure compliance with existing hospital conditions rather than improving the service. Therefore, the recruitment campaign did little to enhance the status of psychiatric nursing. Temporarily filling gaps with the semi-skilled workforce supervised by a sparse supply of trained nurses, the imported trainee nurses continued the long hours and domestic duties, thus ensuring that the status quo was not disturbed.

The Department of Mental Hospitals battled to retain the hard-won cohort of single women they had attracted from Britain. They valued the women primarily as workers rather than as future wives and mothers or indeed as health professionals, and their singleness was central to maintaining a flexible, even malleable, female presence on the wards. To hold on to this valuable workforce, obstacles were placed in the way of marriage and emigration. Despite the dominant rhetoric of domesticity in post-war New Zealand, there was a significant alternative discourse of 'women as workers' among government officials who arranged financial and practical support for those who became ill, injured, or pregnant in the hope of attracting them back to their jobs rather than losing them to marriage and/or motherhood. As the minimal retention rates suggest, for the most part this was unsuccessful.

ACKNOWLEDGMENTS

Access to archival material kindly granted by the Departments of Mental Health and Labour for this research requires the authors to maintain the confidentiality of all applicants for the trainee recruitment scheme. Therefore, pseudonyms have been used and other identifying features avoided.

NOTES

1. Margaret Storr and Ivy Preston are pseudonyms for two women who were interviewed by Kate Prebble in October and November 2009. Both women have requested that their identities be protected. For this reason, pseudonyms were selected and some identifying details have been altered.

2. E. Hobsbawm, *On History* (New York: New Press, c. 1997), quoted in P. Summerfield, 'Culture and composure: Creating narratives of the gendered self in oral history interviews', *Culture and Social History*, 1:1 (2004), p. 65.
3. A. Thomson, *Anzac Memories: Living with the Legend* (Melbourne: Oxford University Press, 1994), p. 8; see also G. Dawson, *Soldier Heroes: British Adventure, Empire and the Imagining of Masculinities* (London: Routledge, 1994); A. Portelli, *The Death of Luigi Trastulli and Other Stories: Form and Meaning in Oral History* (Albany, NY: State University of New York Press, 1991); A. Portelli, *The Battle of Valle Giulia: Oral History and the Art of Dialogue* (Madison: University of Wisconsin Press, 1997); S. Leydesdorff, L. Passerini, and P. Thompson (eds.), *Gender and Memory: International Yearbook of Oral History and Life Stories*, vol. 4 (Oxford: Oxford University Press, 1996); P. Summerfield, *Women Workers in the Second World War: Production and Patriarchy in Conflict* (London: Croom Helm, 1984); P. Summerfield, 'Culture and composure', pp. 65–93.
4. Thomson, *Anzac Memories*, p. 8.
5. Ibid., pp. 8–11.
6. For example, see C. Helmstadter, 'Reforming hospital nursing: The experiences of Maria Machin', *Nursing Inquiry*, 13:4 (2006), pp. 249–58; J. Godden and L. Osburn, *A Lady Displaced: Florence Nightingale's Envoy to Australia* (Sydney: Sydney University Press, 2006); J. Godden, 'The dream of nursing the Empire', in S. Nelson and A. M. Rafferty (eds.), *Notes on Nightingale: The Influence and Legacy of a Nursing Icon* (Ithaca, NY: Cornell University Press, 2010); M. Jones, 'Heroines of lonely outposts or tools of the empire? British nurses in Britain's model colony: Ceylon, 1878-1948', *Nursing Inquiry*, 11:3 (2004), pp. 148–60.
7. P. Sargison, '"Essentially a Woman's Work": A History of General Nursing in New Zealand, 1830–1930' (PhD dissertation, University of Otago, 2001); J. Rodgers, 'Nursing Education in New Zealand, 1883–1930: The Persistence of the Nightingale Ethos' (MA dissertation, Massey University, 1985).
8. W. Brunton, *Sitivation 125: A History of Seaview Hospital, Hokitika and West Coast Mental Health Services, 1872–1997* (Hokitika: Seaview Hospital 125th Jubilee Committee, 1997); M. Seagar, *Edward William Seagar, Pioneer of Mental Health* (Waikanae: Heritage, 1987).
9. S. Mullaly and D. Wright, 'La grande seduction? The immigration of foreign-trained physicians to Canada, c. 1954–76', *Journal of Canadian Studies*, 41:3 (2007), pp. 67–89; R. Hatchett, 'The History of Workforce Policy and Planning in British Nursing, 1939–1960' (PhD dissertation, London School of Hygiene and Tropical Medicine, University of London, 2005).
10. J. Connell (ed.), *The International Migration of Health Workers* (New York: Routledge, 2008).
11. J. Connell, 'Towards a global health care system?', in J. Connell (ed.), *The International Migration of Health Workers* (New York: Routledge, 2008); A. Calliste, 'Women of "exceptional merit": Immigration of Caribbean nurses to Canada', *Canadian Journal of Women and the Law*, 6:1 (1993), pp. 85–102; M. Shkimba and K. Flynn, '"In England we did nursing": The immigrant experiences of Caribbean and British nurses in Great Britain and Canada', in S. McGann and B. Mortimer (eds.), *New Directions in the History of Nursing* (London: Routledge, 2004).
12. T. O'Brien, 'Overseas nurses in the National Health Service: A process of deskilling', *Journal of Clinical Nursing*, 16:12 (2007), pp. 2229–36.
13. C. S. Chatterton, '"The weakest link in the chain of nursing"? Recruitment and Retention in Mental Health Nursing, 1948–68' (PhD dissertation, Institute for Health and Social Care Research, University of Salford, 2007), pp. 184–91.

14. K. Prebble and L. Bryder, 'Gender and class tensions between psychiatric nurses and the general nursing profession in mid-twentieth century New Zealand', *Contemporary Nurse*, 30:2 (2008), pp. 181–95.
15. National Health Statistics Centre, Mental Health Data 1973 (Wellington, 1973), p. 5.
16. *Appendix to the Journals of the House of Representatives of New Zealand (AJHR)*, (Auckland: Government Printer, 1939), H-7, p. 12; *AJHR*, 1950, H-31, p. 29.
17. Archives New Zealand (ANZ), Wellington, H-MHD, 1, 8/116/0, 'Report of staffing of New Zealand Mental Hospitals', 1946.
18. Strategies included advertising for staff in local newspapers, movie theatres, and shops, extending employment to local married women and permitting temporary appointments.
19. *AJHR* (1946), H-11A, pp. 30–31.
20. *Public Service Journal (PSJ)*, 30:6 (1943), p. 228.
21. Prebble and Bryder, 'Gender and class tensions', pp. 181–95.
22. *AJHR* (1946), H-7, p. 3
23. *AJHR* (1939), H-7, p. 12; *AJHR* (1950), H-31, p. 29.
24. The National Employment Service (NES) commenced operations in April 1946. It amalgamated with the Labour Department to become the Department of Labour and Employment in April 1947.
25. ANZ, H-MHD, 1, 8/116/821, letter by Arnold Nordmeyer, Minister in Charge of Mental Hospitals, to Theodore Gray, May 1946.
26. For their part, the Irish government was attempting to block recruitment in Ireland by the British government in this period also. See Chatterton, '"The weakest link"', pp. 184–91.
27. M. Daniels, 'Exile or opportunity? Irish nurses and Wirral midwives', *Irish Studies Review*, 5 (1993), pp. 4–8; N. Yeates 'Here to stay? Migrant health workers in Ireland', in John Connell (ed.), *The International Migration of Health Workers* (New York: Routledge, 2008).
28. Kathleen Paul, '"British Subjects" and "British Stock": Labour's postwar imperialism', *Journal of British Studies*, 34:2 (1995), pp. 223–276, particularly p. 265.
29. ANZ, H-MHD, 1, 8/116/8, part 1, letter by Gray to Nordmeyer, 26 June 1946.
30. ANZ, H-MHD, 1, 8/116/8, part 1, memo by R. M. Sunley to Gray, June 1946.
31. Medical examinations were arranged with the assistance of the British medical officers of health.
32. ANZ, H-MHD, 1, 8/116/8, part 1, memo by R. M. Sunley to the Minister of External Affairs, 31 July 1946.
33. ANZ, H-MHD, 1, 8/116/8, part 1, letter by Rita McEwan to Theodore Gray, 12 August 1946.
34. *New Zealand Parliamentary Debates (NZPD)*, (Wellington: Government Printer), 11 July 1946, p. 435.
35. ANZ, H-MHD-1, 8/116/8, part 1, Schedule of nurses sailing on the *Rangatikei*, December 1946.
36. ANZ, L1/22/1/37/2, part 2, Reports from High Commissioner, Monthly Report, 28 February 1950, quoted in A. McCarthy, *Personal Narratives of Irish and Scottish Migration, 1921–65: 'For spirit and adventure'* (Manchester: Manchester University Press, 2007), p. 21.
37. L. B. Brown, 'Applicants for assisted migration from the United Kingdom to New Zealand', *Population Studies*, 11:1 (July 1957), p. 87.
38. ANZ, H-MHD, 8/116/8, parts 1 and 2, notes on individual applicants recorded in a schedule for each group leaving for New Zealand.
39. Paul, '"British Subjects" and "British Stock", pp. 223–276, particularly p. 269, for a discussion of 'Britishness' in the context of assisted immigration

schemes from the United Kingdom to Australia and New Zealand. In our study, however, 'Englishness' or 'Scottishness' used by Lewis to describe candidates, denoted class differences that he considered might impact their ability to work in mental hospitals.

40. ANZ, NES 22/7/14, letter by C. F. Shapcott to Director of Employment, Wellington, 15 January 1947.

41. *NZPD*, 16 September 1947, p. 330.

42. Shortages of female workers in all industries worsened in the immediate post-war years. Between December 1943 and December 1945, the female workforce had declined by 20 per cent and continued to decline during 1946. D. Montgomerie, *The Women's War: New Zealand Women 1939–45* (Auckland: Auckland University Press, 2001), p. 171.

43. D. Montgomerie, 'Sweethearts, soldiers, happy families: Gender and the Second World War', in C. Daley and D. Montgomerie (eds.), *The Gendered Kiwi* (Auckland: Auckland University Press, 1999), pp. 163–90.

44. ANZ, L1, box 138, 22/1/14, Schedule of Shipping Drafts, 31 July 1947.

45. ANZ, H-MHD, 1, 8/116/8, part 2, Schedule No. 4—*Dominion Monarch*, 24 November 1946.

46. M. Nolan, *Breadwinning: New Zealand Women and the State* (Christchurch: Canterbury University Press, 2000), p. 200.

47. Support for single immigrants had been a recurring theme in government policy for many years. Previous schemes in the nineteenth century and earlier in the twentieth had included large batches of single women. K. Pickles, 'Pink cheeked and surplus: Single British women's inter-war migration to New Zealand', in L. Fraser and K. Pickles (eds.), *Shifting Centres: Women and Migration in New Zealand History* (Dunedin: University of Otago Press, 2002), pp. 63–80; C. Macdonald, *A Woman of Good Character: Single Women as Immigrant Settlers in Nineteenth-century New Zealand* (Wellington: Allen and Unwin/Department of Internal Affairs, Historical Branch, 1990).

48. Pickles, 'Pink cheeked', p. 63.

49. *New Zealand Herald (NZH)*, 25 July 1945, p. 9.

50. ANZ, H-MHD, 1, 8/116/8, letter by Gray to Medical Superintendents, 18 September 1946.

51. *The Dominion* (Wellington), 12 November 1946, p. 8.

52. Margaret Storr (pseudonym) interviewed by Kate Prebble, 22 October 2009, author's private collection.

53. Betty Prince (pseudonym) interviewed by Kate Prebble, 2 May 2008, author's private collection.

54. Two others who had been appointed as cooks were still employed in January 1948. ANZ, L,1, box 138, 22/1/14, letter by M. Ross, District Superintendant, Auckland Office, NES to Head Office, NES, 28 January 1948. Interestingly similar retention rates in British mental hospitals in 1948 are described by Chatterton, '"The weakest link"', p.196.

55. ANZ, H-MHD 1, 8/116/8, letter by Tokanui Hospital nurses to District Employment Officer, 4 December 1946.

56. Ivy Preston (pseudonym) interviewed by Kate Prebble, 6 November 2009, author's private collection.

57. ANZ, L,1, box 138, 22/1/14, letter by Nurse H., Ngawhatu Hospital to Department of Labour, 18 December 1946.

58. In 1946/1947, the New Zealand Nurses and Midwives Board had not yet established reciprocity with the UK for psychiatric nursing qualifications. The board did not recognise either the RMPA or GNC qualifications for the purposes of granting entry to the New Zealand Register of Psychiat-

ric Nurses: ANZ, H-MHD, 1, 8/116/8, part 2, letter by Lewis to Gray, 3 December 1946.

59. ANZ, H-MHD-1, 8/116/8, letter by Dr. G. Tothill, Medical Superintendent of Kingseat Hospital to Gray, 30 January and 18 February 1947; *NZH* (10 February 1947), p. 8.

60. Mireille Kingma, 'Nursing migration: Global treasure hunt or disaster-in-the-making?', *Nursing Inquiry*, 8:4 (2001), pp. 205–12; L. Hawthorne, 'The globalization of the nursing workforce: Barriers confronting overseas qualified nurses in Australia', *Nursing Inquiry*, 8:4 (2001), pp. 213–29.

61. ANZ, H-MHD-1, 8/116/8, part 2, appendix to letter from Lewis to Gray, 18 February 1947.

62. Kate Prebble, 'Ordinary Men and Uncommon Women: A History of Psychiatric Nursing in New Zealand Public Mental Hospitals, 1939–1972' (PhD dissertation, University of Auckland, 2007).

63. Ibid.

64. The number of defections by the end of July 1947 was forty-three: ANZ, L1, box 138, 22/1/14, details of defection, 31 July 1947.

65. ANZ, L1, box 138, 22/1/14. Letter by Director of Employment to Gray, 7 January 1947.

66. ANZ, L1, box 138, 22/1/14. Letter by Director of NES to District Employment Officers, 5 December 1946.

67. Essentially, marrying led to being blacklisted in passport offices around the country. ANZ, L1, box 138, 22/1/14, letters by Director of Employment to the Passport Officer in Auckland, Christchurch and Dunedin, 9 September 1947.

68. ANZ, L1, box 138, 22/1/14. Details of defections—denoted, 31 July 1947.

69. ANZ, L1, box 138, 22/1/14, letter by Director of Employment to District Offices, NES, 10 March 1948.

70. ANZ, H-MHD, 1, 8/116/8, part 1, letter by Lewis to Gray, September 1946.

71. ANZ, L1, box 138, 22/1/14. Details of defection, 31 July 1947.

72. Ibid.

73. ANZ, L1, box 138, 22/1/14, letter by Lewis to Director of Employment, 11 May 1953.

11 The Impact of Migration on the Mental Health of Refugee Women in Contemporary New Zealand

Lynne Briggs

INTRODUCTION

Ana

Ana is a twenty-eight-year-old Somali refugee who lived in a refugee camp for six years before coming to New Zealand in 2002 with her mother, her sister, and her sister's five children. Her general practitioner (GP), who had exhausted all other means of investigation of Ana's symptoms, was at a loss as to what to do next and made a referral to the mental health service. On arrival at the service, Ana made it clear that she did not believe she needed its assistance. Her story intimated that she had adjusted well to life in New Zealand. She lived in a rented house with her mother, her sister, and her sister's family; had a part-time position stacking supermarket shelves; and was doing well at night school.

Ana agreed reluctantly to a psychiatric assessment, during which she reported the following:

- On-going intermittent headaches, gastric complaints, and abdominal pain despite extensive negative investigations to ascertain the problem.
- Sleep disturbance.
- Symptoms of anxiety (but not sufficient to meet *DSM-IV*[1] criteria for generalised anxiety).
- Dysthymia (on-going low mood) rather than clinical depression.
- Traumatic memories (but did not meet criteria for post-traumatic stress disorder).
- Fainting spells.

After undergoing psychiatric assessment, Ana made it clear that she did not want to attend the service for any therapeutic intervention. Therefore, with all physical explanations for her symptoms exhausted, the service decided that the best treatment option was to offer a trial of clonazepam to help her sleep, to monitor her mood, and if possible, to refer her to a service to assist with finding appropriate full-time employment. This had positive results, and after awhile Ana reported feeling better, was sleeping at night, and no longer needed the clonazepam. She was therefore discharged from the service.

Twelve months later Ana re-presented to the service with the same problems as identified during her previous admission. Although it was noted that she was not sleeping again and there were difficulties with her employment, there was still no evidence of a psychiatric disorder. Once re-medicated with clonazepam, Ana reported her sleep improved again, and the employment issues were resolved a little.

At that stage, Ana began to tell her story. She had trained as a nurse in Somalia and had worked in a hospital for two years. When war broke out, she was forced to leave with her family. During the journey, Ana, her mother, her sister, and her sister's children were separated from her three brothers, brother-in-law, and father. While in a refugee camp, Ana had been raped repeatedly and the camp guards had subjected her to regular beatings. She had witnessed her mother and sister being tortured for daring to leave the camp to try to find food in the local village. On leaving the refugee camp for New Zealand, Ana had a vision of what she thought would be a better world for them all in a safe and happy place.

On arrival in New Zealand, Ana was informed that two of her brothers were alive, one was still missing, and her brother-in-law and father were probably dead. Ana and her mother made applications to sponsor her brothers to New Zealand, which at the time of writing are still grinding through the immigration process. Her mother and sister have been unable to settle in New Zealand because they are grieving for their husbands. They have been unable to get on with their lives and wait daily for news from immigration about the outcome of the applications made for Ana's brothers to join them.

Ana's nursing qualifications are not recognised in New Zealand so she has been unable to work as a nurse. She faces almost daily discrimination where she does work, despite having good social and interpersonal skills. Her English skills have improved remarkably since her initial admission period. An employment agency found her work and eventually assisted her into more appropriate employment with the elderly. Over time, Ana has made gradual but good progress and has begun to 'feel' again. Her English language skills have reached a level that will allow her to retrain as a nurse.

Ana has had a reasonably good outcome, but her case is only one of many stories about life for women refugees which incorporates what happens in refugee camps and during resettlement in New Zealand. They face on-going discrimination and lack of recognition of their qualifications, which prevents them from restarting their lives in the way they envisage when entering their new country.

Women seeking asylum face major problems because their claims are often not recognised as entering within the remit of international and national conventions and laws governing the granting of refugee status. Although these conventions supposedly offer protection to women, they are in fact often undermined by gendered practices that fail to offer protection to women because their persecution is not recognised as such.

Amina

Amina is a twenty-nine-year-old Algerian mother whose case demonstrates the difficulties encountered in attempting to gain refugee status.[2] She reports experiencing religious persecution and police brutality in Algeria to the extent that she fled with her two-year-old son, Mehdi, and four-year-old daughter, Nawel. In 2003, after crossing several international borders, Amina finally entered New Zealand where she immediately made an application for refugee status, but this was denied. Several subsequent appeals have been made through the New Zealand Immigration Service and all have been declined. Amina was eventually issued with a removal order, but as a last attempt an appeal was lodged to a higher authority.

While waiting for a final decision, Amina is living with no entitlement to any financial assistance or schooling for the children who have become quite 'Kiwi' in their thinking. They have little knowledge of life in Algeria. A decision has been expected from the Appeals Board for well over eighteen months. In reality, it may not go in Amina's favour. She manages financially somehow and has some interesting business ideas. She is an excellent English speaker. It appears that if given the opportunity, she could make a good life for herself and children in New Zealand.

This woman is very difficult to diagnosis clinically. Major depressive disorder, personality and post-traumatic stress disorder, and dissociative disorder have all been considered, but none have been confirmed. She frequently presents in a state of overwhelming distress and requests assistance. Several antidepressants have been tried, but none have helped her.

As with Ana, Amina also re-presented to the mental health service after having been discharged. On her second admission, she began to tell her story of rape and brutality at the hands of the occupying forces. She has spent considerable time in therapy with a variety of therapists, both within and outside the mental health service, but reports that nothing helps. She just wants her immigration status confirmed and believes all will be well if this happens.

Both Ana's and Amina's case studies are offered as an illustration of the challenge of meeting the mental health needs of refugee women. Although they are examples of clients presenting at mental health services, they are based on actual stories, with salient details changed to protect client identities. They are presented here to provide a deeper understanding of the complexity of issues clinicians face when working with women refugees attending specialist mental health services.

This chapter highlights the plight of refugee women migrants such as Ana and Amina in New Zealand and aims to provide a greater understanding of the impact of migration experiences on their mental health. It describes the differences between forced and voluntary migration[3] and gives a brief description of New Zealand's history of refugee resettlement, with a focus on humanitarian migration for women. It identifies and discusses key resettlement issues and their impact on mental health, leading to a discussion of demoralisation and the findings of a three-year study that used self-report scales to examine the degree of demoralisation and psychological distress among a sample of seventy refugee and migrant women living in Australasia.[4] Although results for this study combine New Zealand and Australian participants, sixty-one of the seventy women were from New Zealand, making the results more typical of refugee migrant women in New Zealand. The women in this study attended a mental health or a community agency, but the experiences of all women refugees are important as they are the link between life in the country of origin and life in the host country. In this way their experiences are passed on to their families which in turn can impact on the ability of the family to adjust to their present circumstances.

MIGRATION

An historically important activity, migration is defined as 'a permanent or semi-permanent change of residence'.[5] A number of factors at social and individual levels over a prolonged period of time influence the process of migration, including the pre-migration, migration, and post-migration phases, which have been found to impact on migrants' psychological well-being.[6] Whereas some individuals, such as refugees, have compelling reasons for migration, others seek economic or material improvement. Despite some similarities, there are marked differences between migrants who choose to migrate to another country and refugees and migrants coming from refugee-like backgrounds who must flee their home countries.[7]

Refugees are casualties of crises, brutal regimes, civil war, anarchy, and famine. They are at risk because of their ethnicity, political beliefs, or religion, and most likely have endured persecution, torture, rape, or abduction, or have witnessed killings. Many refugees arrive in their new country after perilous journeys and traumatic detention in refugee camps, having lost loved ones, homes, possessions, and jobs.[8] The United Nations High Commission for Refugees (UNHCR) designates the category 'refugee' to migrants who 'owing to a well-founded fear of being persecuted for reasons of race, religion, nationality, membership of a particular social group or political opinion, [are] outside the country of [their] nationality, and . . . unable, or owing to such fear . . . unwilling to avail [themselves] of the protection of that country'.[9] As such, refugees cannot return home, whereas other migrants can if they wish.[10]

The UNHCR promotes three durable solutions for people who are classified as refugees. The first preference is voluntary repatriation, a solution which assumes that the original causes of refugee flight have been ameliorated sufficiently to permit the refugees' safe return. If this is not possible, the UNHCR attempts to integrate the refugees locally, in what are known as 'countries of first asylum'. The third durable solution is third country resettlement. Although this is considered the most expensive solution and the one that can help the least number of people, it is the solution promoted for highly vulnerable individuals and groups.

THE PLIGHT OF WOMEN REFUGEES

The international literature on refugees generally focuses on political, economic, and social issues. There is little reference specifically to refugee women's experiences and the resultant mental health implications. These women suffer a variety of human rights violations, but although they are sometimes subjected to similar abuses as men, such as political repression, women are often invisible victims because the dominant image of the political actor in our world is male. Many violations are distinctly connected to being female, with women discriminated against and abused on the basis of their gender. They may experience sexual abuse in situations where their other human rights are violated, for example as political prisoners or members of persecuted ethnic groups.[11]

The UNHCR also points to differing forms of persecution that women experience in contrast to men. Although forcibly displaced men and boys also face protection problems, women and girls can be exposed to particular protection problems related to gender, cultural and socio-economic position, and legal status. Therefore, they are less likely than men and boys to be able to exercise their rights.[12] Women on their own in refugee camps with their children, whether they are single, widowed, abandoned, unaccompanied minors, lone heads of households, or separated from male family members in the chaos of flight or during voluntary repatriation, are at risk of sexual violence.[13]

The plight of refugee women continues in their resettlement country. Those without partners tend to be particularly vulnerable. They are more likely to suffer ill health, both physically and mentally, and to have continuing nightmares about their pre-migration experiences. They are less likely to receive help from government employees to make new friends, get social support, earn money, or drive cars than women with partners.[14]

Not all refugee women with partners are better off than those without partners however, because some women with husbands but without protection from traditional family networks are more likely to be abused by their husbands. Furthermore, women are more disadvantaged by resettlement than men because they often lose their traditional sources of income while their husbands acquire a monopoly over new income. In their traditional cultures, women may have formerly been responsible for providing food for the family, but men may take over this role in the new environment. The refugee experience for women can be very different from that for men because traditional gender roles can be affected. Factors impacting on changes to traditional gender roles include disruption of status and power hierarchies, geographical dispersal of kin and friendship networks, new residence patterns, loss of economic resources, differential access to new resources, shifts in work patterns, exposure to strangers with different lifestyles, and different expectations.[15]

In 2002, the UNHCR identified that approximately 75 per cent to 80 per cent of all refugees were female, with 300,000 girls serving as child soldiers around the world.[16] In its 2009 report, the UNHCR adjusted the total number of women refugees coming under their care as being closer to 50 per cent.[17] However, both reports point to the increased risk of many females being subjected to widespread sexual abuse, sexual slavery, and people trafficking. These women and girls are a largely invisible population, vulnerable to rape and sexual abuse by border guards, soldiers, citizens in their country of asylum, and other refugees. Despite needing protection from gender-related persecution, these refugees are outside the normal criteria for acceptance by most resettlement countries.

New Zealand, however, accepts women at risk and specifically reserves places for them in the annual refugee quota each year. This subcategory covers refugee women who are without the support of their traditional family protectors or community and are at risk in their country of refuge. These women would usually be outside the normal criteria for acceptance by resettlement countries and are in need of protection from gender-related persecution such as abduction, sexual abuse, and exploitation. This subcategory generally includes the principal applicant's nuclear and dependent family members.[18]

New Zealand Immigration and Refugee Resettlement

New Zealand has depended on migration for its economic development and growth, and its immigration objectives fall into two main categories. First, it serves specific national interests, such as providing needed staff resources for industrial and economic development. Second, is its humanistic dimension, such as family reunification and acceptance of refugees.[19] New Zealand's long history of refugee resettlement dates back to the nineteenth century. Since 1840, it has given refuge to people from Europe, South America, Asia, the Middle East, and Africa. Early refugees included Danes fleeing suppression of their language and culture under German occupation in the 1870s, Jews escaping persecution in Tsarist Russia in the 1880s and 1890s, and French Huguenots also fleeing religious persecution.[20] Today there are increasing numbers of refugees from North East and Central Asia, and African nations.[21]

New Zealand has a Humanitarian Response Programme through which it admits refugees, migrants, and their families for third-country resettlement under key international agreements. These are the 1951 United Nations Convention and the 1967 Protocol Relating to the Status of Refugees. New Zealand, by signing these agreements, has committed itself to working with the international community to help resolve refugee problems.[22] Thus, the Humanitarian Response Programme meets the UNHCR (1996) criteria for refugee status.[23] Each year, the programme offers resettlement to 750 to 800 UNHCR quota refugees, reserving 10 per cent of the quota for women 'at risk' of sexual violence.[24] As early as the late 1940s, New Zealand was willing to resettle single mothers with children displaced in the aftermath of World War II. Thus, New Zealand provides a preferential option for marginalised and vulnerable refugee women.

In 1959, New Zealand was the first country in the world to accept refugee families with handicapped members. In the 1970s, the number and ethnic diversity of migrants and refugees entering New Zealand increased. This trend accelerated following changes to legislation in 1987 and 1991 that removed a bias in favour of British and Western Europeans, which had largely dictated migrant flows into the country for over a century. Since 1991, New Zealand has consistently exceeded its immigration target of 20,000 migrants and 800 refugees per annum.[25] Although the New Zealand quota system has a set number for resettlements per year, family members of refugees migrating to New Zealand from refugee-like situations are officially termed 'migrants'. As such, when including migrants entering under family sponsorship policies, the number of resettlements is closer to 1,250 rather than 800.[26] Refugees and their families accepted into the country have status as New Zealand residents.

There is no agreed time limit within which resettlement should occur and no agreement on the extent to which refugees are expected to assimilate rather than integrate with their host society. Thus, the concept of refugee resettlement is open to a range of interpretations. Terms commonly used include 'acculturation', 'biculturalism', 'multiculturalism', 'marginalisation', 'assimilation', 'integration', 'segregation', and 'settlement'.[27]

New Zealand is one of the highest migrant-receiving countries in the world. The 2006 census data show refugees and migrants as an increasingly significant proportion of New Zealand's population. Some are made more welcome than others. For example, refugee intakes are larger when there are clear economic benefits for New Zealand, reflecting how history provides specific information that is rich in context for understanding how processes may be conditioned, created, or constrained by political or economic circumstances.[28] One in five New Zealanders is born in another country, compared with one in eight people in the United States of America and one in fifteen in Europe.[29]

New Zealand society is rapidly increasing in diversity. Refugees and migrants from a variety of cultural backgrounds now comprise a distinct, significant, and very visible component of the country's demographic profile. All of these refugees and migrants tend to have similar social and mental health issues but refugees tend to face the toughest challenges. They have often suffered imprisonment or torture. Most have endured months in refugee camps. Many cannot speak English, the mainstream language in New Zealand, and arrive with no belongings.[30]

MIGRATION, RESETTLEMENT, AND MENTAL HEALTH

Migration is a complex process and a stressful life event capable of putting an individual's mental health at risk. When considering the impact of the migration experience on an individual's mental wellbeing, the most important factors to note are the differing cultural understandings of mental health and the individual's pre-migration, migration, and post-migration experiences, especially in relation to adverse events and trauma.[31]

Social skills; concepts of the self; and psychological, social, and biological vulnerabilities may play a role in mental well-being at the pre-migration level. Once migration has occurred and the process of acculturation has begun, additional factors like negative/positive life events or bereavement issues related to loss of relationships, assets, and support may become relevant. Such events determine not only the migratory forces but also the type of response in the individual and others involved with the individual. The voluntary or forced nature of migration influences all of these factors, while the geographical distance traversed in the migratory process plays a key role in the genesis of stress related to migration. The longer the distance, the greater the environmental change that occurs. Distance plus motives for migration create a complex picture of migration.[32]

The key resettlement issues that all refugees face centre on the typical constellation of losses they have incurred through forced migration and relocation: loss of homes, employment, income, mobility, primary and social supports, life roles, choices, autonomy, security, cultural environment, and citizenship. This complexity in the migration process demands adjustment for both the newcomer and the receiving host countries.[33]

Newly arrived refugees have varying degrees of preparation for their new environment. The majority have limited English-language skills and face adaptation problems regardless of previous economic and social status. The commonly held belief that refugees are associated with poor health, greater risk of infectious diseases, and psychological or mental health problems adds to the challenges they face during resettlement and in becoming an integral part of the communities in which they live. Challenges include finding affordable and appropriate housing; learning a new language; getting credentials recognised and finding employment commensurate with current qualifications; learning local cultures and how to adapt family or personal ways of behaving; facing discrimination and barriers to services; understanding the New Zealand health system; and accessing needed services for psychological problems such as post-traumatic stress disorder (PTSD), anxiety, or depression.[34]

The impact of these challenges is considerable. It affects the overall health and well-being of the refugees and their families, as well as the health of resettlement communities in general.[35] Thus, refugees' backgrounds and experiences have important implications for the provision of health care in New Zealand. The complexity of the issues facing refugees requires increased efforts by host countries to ensure that resettlement and mental health service delivery are cognisant of refugees' needs, and that professional intercultural understandings of social, emotional, and economic distress are enhanced. Nowhere in the health system are refugees' needs more pronounced than in the realm of mental health.[36]

The post-migration period is accorded greater importance because the processes of acculturation and adjustment begin once the refugee is in the host country. 'Culture shock' and all of its stages must be considered for both the refugee adjusting to a new environment and the receiving host country adjusting to the new refugee. Some idea of the adjustment process can be gained from a five-stage 'U-curve of adjustment'[37] (see figure 11.1) beginning with excitement and eagerness to go to the new (and anticipated better) country and culture.

The second, 'honeymoon' stage occurs upon arrival in the new culture when everything in the new culture is considered favourably. In the third stage, reality and doubt set in. Everything in the new culture can feel terrible before adjustment begins. In stage four, the newcomer begins to feel comfortable and takes steps to become more familiar with the culture. In

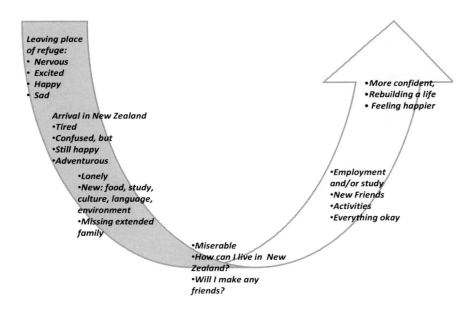

Chart 11.1   U-curve of adjustment.

stage five, the newcomer adapts to the culture and in some ways begins to embrace it as their own.

Issues of acculturation experienced on the way to adaptation may include changing roles within families, such as the role of the male in a family; living in nuclear families; the on-going pleas from families left behind for assistance with reunion; and children adapting well by adopting the host country culture, with parents becoming somewhat redundant as role reversal occurs with children. The latter change can cause generational conflict because Western values differ from traditional family values.[38]

These are just some of the everyday issues that refugee and migrant families deal with on a daily basis. These social and cultural issues can lead to elevated levels of psychological distress, which in turn increase an individual's sense of helplessness, hopelessness, and loss of purpose. Coupled with social isolation from extended family and friends, this can lead to existential distress, low mood, and demoralisation.

REFUGEES, MIGRANTS, AND DEMORALISATION

'Mental health' is a state of well-being in which the individual realises his or her own abilities, can cope with the normal stresses of life, can work productively and fruitfully, and is able to make a contribution to his or her own community. 'Mental illness', on the other hand, is seen as a syndrome that combines low levels of emotional, psychological, and social well-being, and includes a diagnosis of a recent mental illness, such as depression. Somewhere in between there is a condition in which individuals with a mental health problem do not necessarily meet the criteria for a 'mental illness' but have low levels of emotional, psychological, and social functioning.[39] Such feelings are common among refugees and can leave the individual feeling demoralised.[40] Although symptoms of depression and anxiety often accompany demoralisation and despair, demoralisation itself is more than just a combination of anxiety and depression. It is about people feeling unable to 'cope'. Often, such feelings are voiced as 'giving up' or 'depression', typically accompanied by the effects of hopelessness and helplessness. Viewed this way, 'demoralization is seen as a change in morale spanning a spectrum of mental attitudes from disheartenment (mild loss of confidence) through despondency (starting to give up) and despair (losing hope) to demoralization (having given up)'.[41] The middle of this spectrum is a comprehensible response to adversity, but the severe form is pathological. It is maladaptive, a source of considerable personal distress, and it has the potential to generate greater harm through further deterioration and suicidal behaviour. Given this degree of morbidity, it is suggested that demoralisation, as a syndrome, would meet the usual requirements for conceptualisation as a 'mental illness'.[42]

It is also argued that the critical feature distinguishing depression from demoralisation is the presence or absence of 'anhedonia' (a diminished ability to experience pleasure). A depressed person has lost the ability to experience pleasure generally, as well as motivation and drive, even when an appropriate direction of action is known. In contrast, a demoralised person, while unable to look forward with pleasant anticipation, may laugh and enjoy the present moment, but feel helpless, subjectively incompetent, and inhibited in action by not knowing what to do.[43] Lack of family cohesiveness and quality social support, and avoidance coping have been identified as factors uniquely associated with demoralisation.[44] All of these factors are issues for refugees and migrants. Therefore, it is important to consider the presence of hedonic tone (the ability to feel pleasure) and anhedonia (the absence of ability to feel pleasure) when working with refugee and migrant clients because it appears to have theoretical and clinical importance.[45]

DEMORALISATION STUDY WITH REFUGEE AND MIGRANT WOMEN

Between 2005 and 2008 a quantitative study was undertaken to explore the concept of demoralisation among 100 resettled refugees and migrants from refugee-like backgrounds residing in Australia and New Zealand, of whom seventy were women—sixty-one from New Zealand and nine from Australia. A set of standardised self-report scales (including the Demoralisation Scale developed by Kissane and Associates, the Beck Depression and Beck Hopelessness Inventories, and the Snaith-Hamilton Pleasure Scale) and a questionnaire were used to assess the degree of psychological distress among the sample. The questionnaire was specifically designed for the study to capture factors found in the literature that may impact on eventual resettlement outcomes.[46] The use of Western instruments required modification in the way the questions were asked, including finding proper and consistent substitutes for words, symptoms, and states of mind that are part of linguistic and cultural idiosyncrasies, to make them suitable for use with the largely non-Western participants. Interpreters trained in working with people from the participants' cultures enabled all participants to give informed consent, and understand and give responses to the self-rating scales.

Major findings included a comparison of the mean total scores for the women and the men. It showed that the women were moderately depressed (mean=22, SD=13.85), whereas the men were mildly depressed (mean=18.83, SD=11.94). Overall, the women felt slightly more hopelessness (mean=7.37, SD=5.31) than the men (mean=5.77, SD=5.02), had abnormal hedonic tone (mean=2.90, SD=3.66) compared to the men (mean=1.53, SD=2.67), and were generally more demoralised (mean=41.99, SD=20.05) than the men (mean=33.73 SD=17.02).

The fact that the majority of participants recruited were women mirrors the situation with the general population. Just as women in the general population tend to present to health services more frequently than men, so too refugee women tend to present more frequently than refugee men. However, refugee presentations are complex and usually somatic in nature, at least at the beginning, which makes accurate diagnosis difficult, as reflected in Ana and Amina's case studies in the introduction to this chapter. Both women presented twice to the mental health service before they began to talk about the realities of their pre-migration, during migration, and post-migration experiences.

Approximately 90 per cent of all refugees presenting to mental health services would initially do so with issues of 'unhappiness' and generally would be 'demoralised', as confirmed in this study. The majority of the participants (80 per cent) were assigned a *DSM-IV* diagnosis for mood disorder following a psychiatric assessment, either as a major depressive episode, adjustment disorder with low mood, dysthymia, or anxiety.[47] Almost all participants reported experiencing some post-traumatic stress symptoms, and 50 per cent reported somatic complaints. These problems were compounded by domestic violence, social isolation, and economic hardship.

The study findings, in conjunction with the case studies of Ana and Amina, advance our understanding of the compromised mental health of refugee women and its impact on their resettlement. They support the literature pertaining to the mental health of refugee and migrant populations, which makes many references to the association between acculturation, somatisation, anxiety, depression, and 'demoralisation'. Specifically, the findings and the case studies support the literature that discusses how somatic complaints, such as migraine headaches and stomach pain, often occur in the context of hopelessness and helplessness,[48] particularly among refugee and migrant clients from non-Western cultural backgrounds.[49]

CONCLUSION

There is no doubt that forced migration and resettlement impact refugees' mental health. This is particularly so for women. The common pre-migration, during migration, and post-migration experiences of gender-based violence and persecution evidenced in the literature, and described by Ana and Amina, point to the need for professionals working with refugee women to understand the many forms of this violence and persecution, its prevalence in refugee settings, and the mental health consequences for the women involved. Rapid solutions to such violence are needed at several levels: at a societal level, at a professional level, and through research. At the professional level, a current lack of understanding of these realities for refugee women, as well as other issues involving culture, gender, pharmacology, and appropriate therapy, means mental health treatment outcomes are uncertain. Thus, while refugee mental health is a challenging, fascinating, and essential component of modern mental health practice, clinically there are diagnostic inadequacies. There is a pressing need for services to ensure the mental health and well-being of refugee women and their families are met in a timely and appropriate way that will allow them to adjust more rapidly, to make full use of their skills and knowledge, and begin to rebuild their lives successfully in their new country.

NOTES

1. American Psychiatric Association, *Diagnostic and Statistical Manual of Mental Disorders*, 4th ed. *(DSM-IV*; Washington, D.C.: American Psychiatric Association, 1994).
2. A clear analysis of the specific position of female asylum seekers and the gendered aspects of refugee and asylum situations can be found in F. Freedman, 'Protecting women asylum seekers and refugees: From international norms to national protection?' *International Migration*, 48:1 (2010), pp. 175–98.
3. E. S. Lee, 'A theory of migration', *Demography*, 3:1 (1966), p. 49.
4. L. Briggs and S. Macleod, 'Demoralization or clinical depression? Enhancing understandings of psychological distress in resettled refugees and migrants', *World Cultural Psychiatric Research Review* (in press).
5. E. S. Lee, 'A theory of migration', p. 49.
6. Ibid.
7. K. E. Cortes, 'Are refugees different from economic immigrants? Some empirical evidence on the heterogeneity of immigrant groups in the United States', *Review of Economics and Statistics*, 86:2 (2004), pp. 465–80.
8. 'Refugees' in *Te Ara, the Encyclopedia of New Zealand* (updated 13 August 2009), available at: http://www.TeAra.govt.nz/en/refugees/1 (accessed 23 December 2010).
9. United Nations High Commission for Refugees, Convention and 1967 Protocols Relating to the Status of Refugees: Public Information Section (Geneva: UNHCR, August 1996), p. 16.
10. Cortes, 'Are refugees different from economic immigrants?', p. 465.
11. C. Bunch, 'Women's rights as human rights: Toward a re-vision of human rights', *Human Rights Quarterly*, 12:4 (1990), pp. 486–98.
12. United Nations High Commission for Refugees, *Handbook for the Protection of Women and Girls* (Geneva: UNHCR January 2008), p. 65. See also United Nations High Commission for Refugees, 'Proposed executive committee conclusion on women at risk, follow-up paper' (4 May 2006), available at: http://www.unhcr.org/excom/EXCOM/45082362c.pdf (accessed 20 April 2011).
13. Ibid., p. 68.
14. L. Manderson, M. Kelaher, M. Markovic, and K. McManus, 'A woman without a man is a woman at risk: Women at risk in Australian humanitarian programs', *Journal of Refugee Studies*, 11:3 (1998), pp. 90–101.
15. Many studies about the experiences of women refugees are found in D. Indra (ed.), *Engendering Forced Migration: Theory and Practice*, vol. 5, *Refugee and Forced Migration Studies* (New York: Berghahn, 1999).
16. United Nations High Commission for Refugees, 'Refugees', 1:126 (2002), p. 7.
17. United Nations High Commission for Refugees, *2008 Global Trends: Refugees, Asylum-seekers, Returnees, Internally Displaced and Stateless Persons* (Geneva: UNHCR, 2009), p. 6.
18. New Zealand Government, 'Country chapters NZL: Women-at-risk subcategory', (January 2002), p. 3. See also *Refugee Women—The New Zealand*

Refugee Quota Programme published in 1994 by the Department of Labour, New Zealand Immigration Service.

19. R. Pernice and J. Brook, 'Relationship of migrant status (refugee or immigrant) to mental health', *International Journal of Social Psychiatry*, 40:3 (1994), pp. 177–88.

20. A. Beaglehole, 'Refugees 1870s-1940s: Refugee groups', in *Te Ara, the Encyclopedia of New Zealand* (updated 4 March 2009), available at: http://www.TeAra.govt.nz/en/refugees/1 (accessed 20 December 2010).

21. Statistics New Zealand, *QuickStats about culture and identity, 2006 Census* (New Zealand: New Zealand Government, 2006), available at: http://www.stats.govt.nz/Census/2006CensusHomePage/QuickStats (accessed 22 October 2010).

22. A. Beaglehole, 'Refugees—New Zealand as a haven', in *Te Ara, the Encyclopedia of New Zealand* (updated 4 March 2009), available at: http://www.TeAra.govt.nz/en/refugees/1 (accessed 20 December 2010).

23. United Nations High Commissioner for Refugees, *Convention and 1967 Protocols Relating to the Status of Refugees: Public Information Section* (Geneva: UNHCR, August 1996).

24. G. Campbell, 'The intergenerational settlement of refugee children in New Zealand: A report on the findings of a survey conducted for the New Zealand Refugee and Migrant Service' (Wellington: New Zealand Refugee and Migrant Service, 2003), p. 2.

25. Ibid.

26. New Zealand Immigration Service, *Refugee Voices: A Journey Towards Resettlement* (Wellington: Department of Labour, 2004), p. 44.

27. New Zealand Immigration Service, 'Refugee resettlement research project—refugee voices', in *Te Ratonga Manene* (Wellington: Department of Labour, 2001), p. 2.

28. J. Liu, M. C. Wilson, J. McClure, and T. Higgins, 'Social identity and the perception of history: Cultural representations of Aotearoa/New Zealand', *European Journal of Social Psychology*, 29 (1999), pp. 1021–47.

29. Statistics New Zealand, *QuickStats about Culture and Identity, 2006 Census*.

30. A. Beaglehole, 'Refugees—New Zealand as a haven'.

31. D. Bhugra, 'Migration and mental health', *Acta Psychiatricia Scandinavica*, 109 (2004), pp. 243–58.

32. Ibid.

33. D. Bhugra, 'Migration and mental health'; D. Claassen, M. Ascoli, T. Berhe, and S. Priebe, 'Research on mental disorders and their care in immigrant populations: A review of publications from Germany, Italy and the UK', *European Psychiatry*, 20 (2005), pp. 540–49; M. Fazel, J. Wheeler, J. Danesh, 'Prevalence of serious mental disorder in 7000 refugees resettled in Western countries: A systematic review', *Lancet*, 365 (2005), pp. 1309–14.

34. For fuller accounts, see M. Nash, J. Wong, and A. Trlin, 'Civic and social integration: A new field of social work practice with immigrants, refugees and asylum seekers', *International Social Work*, 49 (2006), pp. 345–63.

35. M. Smith, 'Viewpoint: Health care for refugees', *Asia Pacific Family Medicine*, 2 (2003), pp. 71–73.

36. For fuller accounts, see Bhugra, 'Migration and mental health'; Claassen et al., 'Research on mental disorders'; Fazel et al., 'Prevalence of serious mental disorder in 7000 refugees'.

37. See J. S. Black and M. Mendenhall, 'The U-curve adjustment hypothesis revisited: A review and theoretical framework', *Journal of International*

Business Studies, 22:2 (1991), pp. 225–47 (model adapted to illustrate process of adjustment for refugees).

38. L. Briggs, 'Multi-cultural issues in New Zealand social work', in M. Connelly (ed.), *Social Work in New Zealand* (London: Oxford University Press, 2001).

39. World Health Organisation, *Promoting Mental Health: Concepts Emerging Evidence, Practice-Summary Report/A Report of the World Health Organisation* (Geneva: Department of Mental Health and Substance Abuse/Victoria Promotion Foundation/University of Melbourne, 2004), p. 12. See also L. Briggs and B. Cromie, 'Social work mental health in New Zealand', in M. Connolly and L. Harms (eds.), *Social Work: Contexts and Practice*, 2nd ed. (Melbourne: Oxford University Press, 2009), p. 223.

40. Bhugra, 'Migration and mental health', p. 244.

41. D. W. Kissane, D. M. Clarke, and A. F. Street, 'Demoralization syndrome: A relevant psychiatric diagnosis for palliative care', *Journal of Palliative Care*, 17 (2001), pp. 12-21.

42. Briggs and Macleod, 'Demoralization or clinical depression?' See also for diagnostic criteria Kissane, Clarke, and Street, 'Demoralization syndrome', pp. 12-21.

43. D. M. Clarke and D. W. Kissane, 'Demoralization: Its phenomenology and importance', *Australian and New Zealand Journal of Psychiatry*, 36 (2002), pp. 733-42.

44. D. W. Kissane, S. Wein, A. Love, Xiu Qing Lee, Pei Lee Kee, and D. M. Clarke, 'The demoralization scale: A report of its development and preliminary validation', *Journal of Palliative Care*, 20 (2004), pp. 269-76.

45. L. Briggs and S. Macleod, 'Demoralization—A useful conceptualization of non-specific psychological distress among refugees attending mental health services', *International Journal of Social Psychiatry*, 52 (2006), pp. 512-24.

46. For a full description of the methodology, the instruments used, and a preliminary analysis of the data, see L. Briggs, C. Talbot, and K. Melvin, 'Demoralization and migration experience', *International Review of Modern Sociology*, 33 (2007), pp. 193-209.

47. American Psychiatric Association, *Diagnostic and Statistical Manual of Mental Disorders* (*DSM-IV*).

48. J. M. de Figueiredo, 'Depression and demoralization: Phenomenological differences and research perspectives', *Comprehensive Psychiatry*, 34 (1993), pp. 308-11.

49. Briggs et al., 'Demoralization and migration experience'.

12 Afterword
Madness is Migration—Looking Back to Look Forward

Bronwyn Labrum

As was remarked on at the symposium upon which this volume is based, madness *is* migration—in space, time, socially, culturally, or in a more interior mode. Movement and mental health has been a staple of much of the existing historical literature on psychiatric hospitals and patients, although not always with a focus on migration. My own much earlier work on this topic in the New Zealand context illustrates this trajectory, especially in terms of work in social and cultural history. Influenced by the anti-social control concepts animating the work of historians of psychiatry such as Mark Finnane and the gendered analysis of feminist historians such as Elaine Showalter,[1] I examined the committal and treatment of female patients at the Auckland Lunatic Asylum from 1870 to 1911.[2] My findings supported Finnane's contention that families were an important set of actors in the decision to commit patients, and that for women it was often only when the family could spare them that they were reluctantly let go. In other ways I modified the more emphatic equation of women with madness. Although it was true that doctors viewed women as being captive to their biology, developing categories of madness related directly to their biology, such as puerperal (childbirth) and climacteric (menopause), married and single women were committed far less often than men, especially single men. In a detailed consideration of the committal certificates and case notes I concluded that the material circumstances of families and individuals, as well as the responses of families, neighbours, and police were critical. My study also considered the question of ethnicity in terms of indigenous patients, very few of whom utilised public hospitals and asylums in this period. It became clear that consideration of Māori was rather more related to Pākeha (non-Māori, European). Some patients who showed sympathy with Māori grievances over land or behaved in ways that seemed more Māori than Pākeha were more likely to be considered mad and in need of incarceration, illustrating that ethnicity related to white as well as non-white populations, a point which has only been taken up slowly in the wider literature. Once inside the asylum, I explored the way that female patients entered a woman's world in the asylum. Treatment was emphatically segregated by gender. Whereas the men could work on the farm and in the gardens and move around the huge asylum complex, the women were restricted to ladylike occupations and recreation, mostly indoors. Because of the increasing overcrowding during the late nineteenth century, the female wards became wretched places of confinement, and women only went outside to the 'airing courts' which still kept them walled in. Any treatment was rudimentary before large-scale dispensing of drugs or occupational therapy and relied on food, exercise, and 'suitable' occupations.

Although I focused on movement to and within the asylum and considered how the female patients shuttled back and forth to the asylum (often several times) depending on their family situations, the institution and its patients remained at the centre of my analysis. In contrast, the wide-ranging chapters in this stimulating collection enlarge this idea of movement. They show that the necessary journey into states of mind and behaviours that others perceive as problematic or dangerous have their parallels in the physical journeys of those who become patients, whether they are migrants spending six months sailing to New Zealand from the other side of the world or, in later centuries, refugees forced to abandon turbulent homelands. The migrations of the medical men and nursing staff that appear in these pages are also highlighted, pointing to the wide-ranging nature of psychiatric 'travels'. A further innovative aspect of this volume is the way that the medical ideas of staff also migrate in a transnational fashion. The influences are shown to be more than one way: 'webs' of engagement and influence, in Elspeth Knewstubb's chapter, range across colonies and back to metropoles, and not just from the English-speaking world.

Here the authors consider movement in a wide range of productive ways. Successive chapters canvass the psychiatric experiences of the Irish, thought to be madder than other groups, but here shown to have a similar pattern of experience to Scottish migrants in Canada, with their experiences becoming more similar over time at home and abroad. They also delineate the different cultural backgrounds of institutionalised patients and thereby further the project of disaggregating 'the British'. They focus on patient records, whether through linking them to asylums in their home countries, or through close attention to the production of knowledge about patients and colonial society as an extension of focusing on indicators of difference and diversity. Other chapters trace the development and diffusion of medical men and medical ideas through their various texts, and recover the historical record of those often overlooked, but essential, female staff who had most contact with those deemed mad, through more recent experiences via oral histories. The international scope of the volume is accentuated by chapters on non-British world regimes, such as Fiji and Japan, teasing out the different cultures of colonialism in the former and the migrations within societies of the latter. Finally, the moving and evocative recounting of New Zealand refugee experience brings this largely historical volume right up to the present and demonstrates how ideas of migration, ethnicity, and mental health continue to intermix in volatile and often long-standing ways. As all the authors show so well, ethnicity also evokes a journey into a different state of 'otherness', whether marked by voice and speech, conduct, appearance, prior education, training, or traumatic experiences of war and other terrors.

The authors are more than equal to the huge task of engaging with these critical historical and contemporary questions, and it is so pleasing to see postgraduate students stand alongside leaders in the field. The exploration of migration, ethnicity, and mental health over a century and a half in this book has extended our knowledge in some key areas. The first concerns the definition of the key concepts of 'migration', 'ethnicity', and 'mental health'. Our thinking about these concepts can remain remarkably stubborn and resistant to considering change over time or the daily lived experiences. In these pages, abstract concepts become fleshed out in all their variety and complexity. 'Migration' is not just about here to there, country to country, either in the present or in the past. It is also about return journeys and circulation. It is about moving from rural to urban areas. It is about willing and forced travels. It is about social and cultural shifts and different 'states of mind'. Although movement to institutions is emphasised, there is more to be made of returns home (wherever that is) and movement *between* institutions, geographical areas, and countries which was (and is) a frequent occurrence. The possibly different experience in the United States has already been raised as a theme for further research in the introduction to this volume. Last, in possibly a counter-intuitive step, it would be fascinating to consider more closely when and why migration was *not* an issue. As Angela McCarthy so carefully reminds us, not all migration led to madness and institutionalisation, and from her case study, incarceration usually occurred after a reasonably lengthy period of re-settlement; it was not an immediate consequence of mobility or migration.

'Ethnicity', particularly for British peoples, is finely parsed in several chapters. Its marked and unmarked forms are clearest perhaps in the records and 'archival flows' of nineteenth-century institutions, to use Jacquie Leckie's phrase, where appearance, speech, and unrespectable or overly religious behaviour are symptomatic of 'difference'. Yet the twentieth-century yearning for respectability in nursing staff and continuing desire for cultural homogeneity through the twentieth century are topics that have not yet been addressed.

In the second key area where our knowledge is extended in this volume, new theoretical frameworks complement existing modes of inquiry. We have fine examples of orthodox statistical analyses in this volume, using the wide-ranging sources of public institutions and other public records. We also have statistical analyses prompted by what is not in the record: counting the way bodies are referred to and how that thinking is reliant on contemporary mores around ethnicity and difference. Webs of empire are set alongside the hegemony of Scottish psychiatric training or the European innovations of kindness and care. Colonialism and colonisation emerge as a variegated set of practices and processes, with some ethnic groups appearing in records, such as the Chinese, but not always the indigenous members of a society. New ways in which scholars are thinking about colonisation has influenced depictions of the colonisers as well as the colonised. Oral histories and other forms of interviewing in the present complement methods of archival and textual analysis.

Listening to all the papers presented at the symposium and reading the ones revised for this volume, I am also struck by what has not changed in research terms; where knowledge continues in similar tracks to the existing scholarship and even, to a degree, echoes earlier work such as my own. Part of the reason for this is the way that the large, rambling, seemingly all-encompassing Victorian asylums still stand at the centre of our thinking. They were some of the largest public buildings of their day, they generated some of the bulkiest runs of public records, and their traces continue in the archives, in museum collections, and as abandoned or reused buildings in the landscape today. We can, however, use this historical and contemporary dominance to tell new stories and reinterpret old ones, based on the premise that fresh thinking relies on innovative or, at the very least, reconceptualised sources.

As Catharine Coleborne aptly puts it in her chapter, institutional patient records remain 'that most worked-over of archival materials'. While a wide range of source material is analysed in this volume, including case books and admission registers, official reports and statistics, medical literature, and for the later twentieth century onwards, oral interviews, it demands to be extended still further. The institution and the medical men who ran them—and they mostly *were* male—continue to occupy the limelight. Despite the increasingly sophisticated theoretical and methodological tools of current scholars, evident in this collection, the aim of the new social and cultural history from the 1980s onwards, to get at patient experience more directly and also to put the asylum in its community and society contexts, is yet to be fully realised.[3] Although some fear that we have once again lost sight of the institution in the effort to recapture patient experiences, nineteenth-century psychiatry has a wider history.

We can go further and capitalise on this plethora of sources, as a number of studies of other historical periods and topics usefully suggest. Utilising images, objects, and other non-textual media not only expands the range of sources, but they can also lead to the re-conceptualisation of research questions.[4] There are a steady stream of studies of psychiatry and imagery of various kinds, whether paintings or more recent technologies such as photography, the cinema, and television.[5] More studies are needed of images and the visual culture of mental health, what can be referred to quite literally as the 'practices of looking'[6] of both patients and staff. This would extend the focus in this volume on how the mad appeared, and were visualised by themselves and others, through an emphasis on the social construction of psychiatric vision and visuality. For example, the practice of photographing patients from the late nineteenth century to just after World War I provides an abundant set of sources. These can be set along-side the classic images of hysteria and mania at the Surrey County Lunatic Asylum by British psychiatrist and photographer Hugh Welch Diamond that are frequently published.[7] I reproduced some of these images, as well as portraits of staff and the buildings, in my earlier study and in subse-quent research on clothing in a range of social institutions.[8] Collections of patients' own cultural representations—now often seen as 'outsider art' and fiction—are another under-utilised source, which provide pathways into patients' practices of looking and how they responded to their condi-tion and circumstances.[9] The few existing studies might be extended to consider migrants in particular. Are they imaged—or do they visualise themselves—in similar or perhaps in different ways?

As well as the social construction of vision and visuality, similar ques-tions could be posed for the other senses: hearing, smell, touch, and so forth. The identification of ethnic difference through voice, accent, and how patients sounded, so evocatively described in this collection, might be extended. Such research would sit neatly alongside present considerations of the sound-scape of the asylum: the constant noise and clamour of patients, the use of sound as well as sight to diagnose patients, or such events as the musical entertainments provided for patients.[10] The innovative emphasis on bodies in this volume could be broadened to a consideration of a range of different kinds of bodily contact and embodiment, both medical and non-medical, through smell and touch.[11]

It is then just a small step to consider objects and the material culture of migration, ethnicity, and mental health.[12] In the classic era of the asylum, patients' clothing, about which I have written elsewhere, was drab and stan-dardised and tried to minimise difference. It also erased prior experiences and identities.[13] As well as the vast array of medical equipment surviving in collections and on psychiatric campus sites, there are other items associ-ated with the patients and staff that focus on the themes of this volume. What, if anything, did those deemed mad bring with them, either to the asylum or in transit from other countries? How did these things represent, or more specifically, how did they materialise their experiences of migra-tion, ethnicity, and mental health? An exhibition in New York displayed the suitcases left behind in an attic of the Willard Psychiatric Centre in Fin-gers Lakes, which closed in 1995. Many of them were untouched since they were packed decades ago before their owners entered the institution. The suitcases 'bear witness to the rich, complex lives their owners lived prior to being committed to the institution'. The clothing and other objects inside the cases speak to aspirations, accomplishments, and community connec-tions, as well as loss and isolation.[14]

The social construction of vision and visuality and a consideration of materiality encompass the representation of buildings and other aspects of psychiatric built environments. These questions, with all their conceptual and methodological complexities, are beginning to be explored. Pondering the construction, intentions, and actual uses of the spaces within the buildings of psychiatric care, which are often now having a second or third life as local and community museums, offers additional stimulating questions for consideration. As I found when I visited one such complex with a volunteer-run museum on site in Goulburn, New South Wales, Australia, it was one thing to research these buildings and sites through written sources and quite another to walk in and among the now-empty buildings, literally decaying through neglect. I confronted long patient wards up precarious staircases with bare iron bedsteads arranged along each wall, and looked through the peephole into an isolation cell for straight-jacketed patients.[15] As a 'family' of institutions or built welfare regimes—alongside industrial schools, welfare homes, schools, lodges, and so forth—how were they differentiated from each other, and how did patients and inmates move in and between them?[16]

The very availability of extant buildings and other objects require us to develop and to evaluate the exhibition of the cultures of psychiatry as well as the experiences of mental health over time and space. My investigation of the display of items of clothing from Australasian asylums concluded that very few garments were shown, especially when compared with medical technology, crockery, and building remnants. Straightjackets remain the symbol and stereotype of the horrors of Victorian psychiatry; patients are secondary figures; and the displays reflect the purposes and priorities of those who constructed them (who were frequently former staff members). Visitors in the present are allowed to put madness and psychiatry firmly in the distant past, negating its links and continuities with the present. Visitors are also allowed to forget (or not know) what more recent scholarship shows: that some patients wanted to go to asylums and their families readily agreed, that others moved in and out when they needed to, and that these institutions were significant features of the local and national communities.[17] These exhibitions tell us about the past, or more accurately, how the past is represented in the present. Because any historical interpretation is really a story of what we think now and what preoccupies us in the present, rather than providing a pathway to the 'reality' of an earlier time, this is an important task. New research focuses on collectors, collections, their display, and the reactions to exhibitions of the history of insanity. This work 'broadens the study of the history of psychiatry by investigating the significance and importance of the role of twentieth-century psychiatric communities in the preservation, interpretation and representation of the history of mental health through the practice of collecting'.[18] Given the number of large Victorian psychiatric complexes that are now museums and whose objects, displays, and memories are kept alive by volunteers and ex-staff members, such examinations lead us into considerations of public history and memories in the community at large.[19]

Consideration of mental health over the twentieth and twenty-first centuries pushes out the horizons still further, as the chapter on contemporary refugees in this volume shows. Similarly, when it comes to migration and ethnicity, the other key concepts in this collection, it seems we may still be captured by our existing limited sources, although these include oral histories and interviews. Other kinds of reminiscences and public representations are abundant. If you enter appropriate search terms into Internet search engines, there is a plethora of serious research available, as well as numerous contributions from the critical to the informal. The self-representations and recollections of those in mental health-care systems past and present offer a richness that is missing from surviving case book documentation from the nineteenth century, for example, or that remains unavailable behind privacy legislation to protect those still alive. Given the mobility of twenty-first century individuals and populations, and the vast changes in regulation and legislation around mental health amidst de-institutionalisation, it is important to look at all available sources and to track opinions and interpretations through multiple sites.

The demarcation of 'mad' from 'sane', or 'normal' from 'strange', which depended so much on family and friends in the nineteenth-century institutional context, is presented in this book in richly nuanced accounts from the sources, which often report friends' and family's words verbatim. But we can and should move beyond the great waves of migration. Was this also the case over what may be termed the 'long' twentieth century, which reaches almost unbroken into our own? How exactly 'madness' turned into 'mental health' and why and how the boundaries of normality were redrawn is perhaps the subject of another volume. Although late twentieth century de-institutionalisation suggests this process was irrevocably altered, and that there were fewer places to 'migrate' to, more exploration is vital.[20] This is also the case for the examination of patient and lay ideas. Given the proliferation of literature of all kinds from the early twentieth century onwards and even more so now with sources such as the Internet and World Wide Web, the unofficial views of migration, ethnicity, and mental health are ripe for evaluation.

One of the great strengths of this volume is the way it prompts further questions and opens up new areas for interrogation. As the chapters so emphatically show, in so many ways madness *is* migration. We can acknowledge this, not just in our conclusions, but also in the way we conduct our discoveries and in what we base them on. We need to move our historical research practices onto new tracks in order to capture the mobile, unstable, and inherently complex nature of migration, ethnicity, and mental health over time and across space, both in the past and also in contemporary representations and materialisations.

NOTES

1. M. Finnane, 'Asylums, families and the state', *History Workshop Journal*, 20:1 (1985), pp. 134–48; S. Garton, *Medicine and Madness: A Social History of Insanity in New South Wales* (Kensington: New South Wales

University Press, 1988); E. Showalter, *The Female Malady: Women, Madness, and English Culture, 1830–1980* (London: Virago, 1987).

2. B. Labrum, 'The boundaries of femininity: Madness and gender in New Zealand, 1870-1910', in W. Chan, D. E. Chunn, and R. Menzies (eds.), *Women, Madness and the Law: A Feminist Reader* (London: Cavendish, 2005), pp. 59–77, which is a revised version of 'Looking beyond the asylum: Gender and the process of committal in Auckland, 1870–1910', *New Zealand Journal of History*, 26:2 (1992), pp. 125–44; B. Labrum, 'A woman's world in a male universe: Treatment and rehabilitation at the Auckland Lunatic Asylum, 1870–1910', in L. Bryder and D. Dow (eds.), *New Countries and Old Medicine: Proceedings of An International Conference on the History of Medicine and Health* (Auckland: Auckland Medical Historical Society, 1995), pp. 196–203.

3. As well as those cited in n. 1 from the 1980s, see more recently C. Coleborne, *Madness in the Family: Insanity and Institutions in the Australasian Colonial World, 1860–1914* (Basingstoke: Macmillan, 2010).

4. A. Clark, 'Editor's introduction' [to special issue on material culture], *Journal of British Studies*, 48 (2009), pp. 279–82. The volume encompasses material arrangements for the dead, country houses, claret, and port, diamonds, Kashmiri shawls and modernist architecture. K. Harvey (ed.), *History and Material Culture: A Student's Guide to Approaching Alternative Sources* (London and New York: Routledge, 2009). For a more general introduction to material culture studies from a sociological and anthropological point of view, see I. Woodward, *Understanding Material Culture* (London: Sage, 2007).

5. See the classic study by S. L. Gilman, *Seeing the Insane* (New York: Wiley, 1982); S. Harper, *Madness, Power and the Media: Class, Gender and Race in Popular Representations of Mental Distress* (New York: Palgrave Macmillan, 2009); S. Cross, *Mediating Madness: Mental Distress and Cultural Representation* (New York: Palgrave Macmillan, 2010).

6. M. Sturken and L. Cartwright, *Practices of Looking: An Introduction to Visual Culture*, 2nd ed. (New York: Oxford University Press, 2008).

7. The Royal Society of Medicine holds his original prints. More information is available at: http://www.rsm.ac.uk/librar/diam_coll.php (accessed 28 October 2011). See also B. Brookes, 'Women and madness: A case-study of the Seacliff Asylum, 1890–1920', in B. Brookes, C. Macdonald, and M. Tennant (eds.), *Women and History 2* (Wellington: Bridget Williams, 1992), pp. 129–47; B. Brookes, 'Pictures of people, pictures of places: Photography and the asylum', in C. Coleborne and D. MacKinnon (eds.), *Exhibiting Madness in Museums: Remembering Psychiatry Through Collections and Display* (New York: Routledge, 2011), pp. 30–47.

8. B. Labrum, 'The social significance of institutional dress in New Zealand', in M. Maynard (ed.), *The Berg Encyclopaedia of World Dress and Fashion*, vol. 7, *Australia, New Zealand, and the Pacific Islands* (Berg: Oxford, 2010), pp. 332–37.

9. B. Robson, 'Preserving psychiatry through art: Historical perspectives on the Cunningham Dax collection of psychiatric art', in C. Coleborne and D. MacKinnon (eds.), *'Madness' in Australia: Histories, Heritage, and the Asylum* (St. Lucia: University of Queensland Press/API Network, 2003), pp. 195–206; 'Madness and modernity: Mental illness and the visual arts in Vienna 1900', exhibition at the Wellcome Institute, London, 1 April 2009–28 June 2010, and the book of the same name, G. Blackshaw and L. Topp (eds.) (London: Lund Humphries, 2009). Classic works of fictions include J. Frame, *Faces in the Water* (New York: George Braziller, 1961; reprint, London: Virago, 2009).

10. D. MacKinnon, '"Hearing madness": The soundscape of the asylum', in Coleborne and MacKinnon (eds.), *'Madness' in Australia*, pp. 73–82; D. MacKinnon, '"A captive audience": Musical concerts in Queensland Mental Institutions c. 1870-c. 1930', *Context: a Journal of Music Research*, 19 (2000), pp. 43–56.
11. See also M. M. Smith, *Sensing the Past: Seeing, Hearing, Smelling, Tasting, and Touching in History* (Berkeley: University of California Press, 2007).
12. B. Labrum, 'Material histories in Australia and New Zealand: Interweaving distinct material and social domains', *History Compass*, 8:8 (August 2010), pp. 805–16; B. Labrum, '"Always distinguishable from outsiders": Materialising cultures of clothing from psychiatric institutions', in Coleborne and MacKinnon (eds.), *Exhibiting Madness in Museums*, pp. 65–83.
13. Labrum, 'The social significance of institutional dress'.
14. For more about the exhibition, see http://www.suitcaseexhibit.org/flashSite. html (accessed 28 October 2011) and the accompanying book, D. Penny and P. Stastny, *The Lives They Left Behind: Suitcases From a State Hospital Attic* (New York: Bellevue Literary Press, 2008).
15. Labrum, 'Material histories in Australia and New Zealand'; Labrum, '"Always distinguishable from outsiders"'.
16. See the ESRC funded project, 'At home in the institution? Asylum, school and lodging house interiors in London and SE England, 1845–1914', principal researcher Dr. J. Hamlett, located at the Department of History and Centre for the History of Bodies and Material Culture, Royal Holloway College, University of London. For further ideas, see the podcasts of the papers delivered at the conference 'Inhabiting institutions in Britain, 1700–1950', Royal Holloway College, University of London, 14–15 September 2010, available at: http://backdoorbroadcasting.net/2010/09/inhabiting-institutions-in-britain-1700–1950 (accessed 28 October 2011).
17. Labrum, '"Always distinguishable from outsiders", pp. 78–80.
18. See the range of chapters in Coleborne and MacKinnon (eds.), *Exhibiting Madness in Museums*.
19. For discussions that range over past and present uses and memories of psychiatric institutions, see D. Kordes, 'The Arts of Care in an Asylum and a Community 1925–2004: Kenmore Hospital, New South Wales and Canberra, the Australian Capital Territory' (PhD dissertation, Australian National University, 2009); and T. B. Askin, 'Oregon's Forgotten Public Social Welfare Institutions: The Oregon State Hospital and the Multnomah County Poor Farm as Case Studies in the Challenge of Preserving Stigmatised Places' (Master of Science, Historical Preservation Programme, 2010). For more on public history and memories, see P. Ashton and H. Kean (eds.), *People and Their Pasts: Public History Today* (Basingstoke: Palgrave Macmillan, 2009).
20. See, for example, C. Coleborne and D. MacKinnon, (eds.), 'Deinstitutionalisation in Australia and New Zealand', special issue of *Health and History*, 5:2 (2003).

Contributors

Lynne Briggs is an associate professor of social work in the School of Human Services and Social Work, Griffith University, Gold Coast Campus, Queensland, Australia. In her previous position with the Department of Social Work and Community Development with the University of Otago she was responsible for teaching the Mental Health and Specialist Practice, Supervision, Advanced Counselling and Interpersonal Practice papers on the masters programme. Lynne has also had many years of clinical practice in mental health at a senior level and until recently was the clinical head of the District Health Board's Refugee and Migrant Mental Health Service in Christchurch, New Zealand.

Catharine Coleborne is an associate professor of history at the University of Waikato in New Zealand. She is the author of *'Madness' in the Family: Insanity and Institutions in the Australasian Colonial World 1860s–1914* (Palgrave Macmillan, 2010) and has published extensively on the nineteenth-century histories of institutional confinement in Australia and New Zealand. She is a member of the editorial board of the *Social History of Medicine* and is currently the joint editor of *Health and History*.

Maree Dawson completed a BA in history at the University of Auckland, New Zealand, and became interested in histories of mental illness while writing her BA Honours thesis on treatments of shellshock in New Zealand and Australia during the interwar period, at the University of Waikato. She is currently working on her PhD thesis at the University of Waikato, which is titled 'Insanity and Heredity in the Auckland Mental Hospital, 1867–1900'.

Gabrielle Fortune is a research fellow in the History Department at the University of Auckland, New Zealand. Her PhD thesis was titled '"Mr Jones' Wives": World War II War Brides of New Zealand Servicemen' (2005). Her MA (1997) dealt with the social history of Irish immigrants in Auckland from 1840 to 1870s. Gabrielle's current research interests and publications include war brides, war veterans, and the appropriation of images and icons of war and war service.

Elspeth Knewstubb graduated from the University of Otago, New Zealand, in 2008 with LLB (Honours) and BA (Honours) majoring in history. She completed her MA in history at the University of Otago in 2011 with distinction, studying Ashburn Hall, New Zealand's only private lunatic asylum.

Bronwyn Labrum teaches in the School of Visual and Material Culture, College of Creative Arts, Massey University, Wellington, New Zealand. She is the author of *Women's History: Researching and Writing Women's History in New Zealand* (Bridget Williams, 1993) and co-editor of *Fragments: New Zealand Social and Cultural History* (Auckland University Press, 2000) and *Looking Flash: Clothing in Aotearoa New Zealand* (Auckland University Press, 2007). She is a leading historian of New Zealand welfare and contributed a chapter on this to *The New Oxford History of New Zealand* (Oxford University Press, 2009). Her research in the history of women and asylums in New Zealand has been a foundation for the field nationally and internationally. She has also published widely both nationally and internationally in the history of women, twentieth-century welfare, and material culture and museums, contributing to a number of the key collections and reference works in these areas.

Jacqueline Leckie is an associate professor in social anthropology in the Department of Anthropology and Archaeology, at the University of Otago. Her teaching and publications relate to development, gender, ethnicity, migration, mental health, and work, within the Asia Pacific region—with extensive fieldwork in New Zealand, Fiji, and Gujarat, India. Her books include *Indian Settlers: The Story of a New Zealand South Asian Community* (Otago University Press, 2007); *To Labour with the State* (University of Otago Press, 1997); editing *Development in an Insecure and Gendered World* (Ashgate, 2009) and co-editing *Localizing Asia in Aotearoa; Recentring Asia: Histories, Encounters, Identities; and Labour in the South Pacific* (co-edited with C. Moore and D. Munro).

Elizabeth Malcolm is Gerry Higgins Professor of Irish Studies at the University of Melbourne, Australia. She has published extensively on a variety of Irish social history topics, including mental health, violence, police, drink, gender, and migration. She is the author of *Swift's Hospital: A History of St Patrick's Hospital, Dublin, 1746–1989* (Gill and Macmillan, 1989) and *The Irish Policeman, 1822–1922: A Life* (Four Courts Press, 2006); and with Greta Jones she edited *Medicine, Disease and the State in Ireland, 1650–1940* (Cork University Press, 1999).

Angela McCarthy is Professor of Scottish and Irish history at the University of Otago, New Zealand, and associate director of its Centre for Irish and Scottish Studies. She is the author and editor of several books on Irish and Scottish migration and of a pioneering article on migration, ethnicity, and madness published in *Social History of Medicine* (2008).

Kate Prebble is a senior lecturer in the School of Nursing, University of Auckland, New Zealand. Her research interests are the history of nursing, history of psychiatric services, and contemporary issues in mental health. Kate completed a PhD in 2007. The title of her thesis is 'Ordinary Men and Uncommon Women: A History of Psychiatric Nursing in New Zealand Public Mental Hospitals, 1939–1972'. Since graduation, she has continued to publish in the history of nursing and psychiatry.

Akihito Suzuki is a professor of history at Keio University in Tokyo, Japan. He has published many works on the history of psychiatry in Britain and Japan, including *Madness at Home* (University of California Press, 2006). He is currently finishing a monograph on mental illness in modernist Tokyo.

Tom Themeles is a research analyst, having completed his Bachelors of Science (Hons) and Arts (Hons) at McMaster University and a Master of Arts at Wilfrid Laurier University, specialising in the History of Canadian Psychiatry. He also holds a Bachelor of Education at Brock University. His research interests include psychiatry, environmental science, labour studies, health issues, statistical analysis, government policies, and education.

David Wright is Canada Research Chair at the Institute for Health and Social Policy and a professor of history, McGill University, Montreal, Canada. He is the author and co-editor of seven books on the history of psychiatry including *Downs: The History of a Disability* (Oxford University Press, 2011).

Index